K

Invisible Giant

Invisible Giant

Cargill and its Transnational Strategies

BREWSTER KNEEN

Fernwood Publishing
HALIFAX, NOVA SCOTIA

Pluto Press
LONDON • EAST HAVEN, CONNECTICUT

First Published 1995 by Pluto Press
345 Archway Road, London N6 5AA
and 140 Commerce Street, East Haven, Connecticut 06512, USA

First published 1995 in Canada by Fernwood Publishing
PO Box 9409, Station A, Halifax, Nova Scotia, B3K 5S3

British Library Cataloguing in Publication Data
A catalogue record for this book is available from the British Library
ISBN 0 7453 0963 1 (hardback)

Library of Congress Cataloging in Publication Data
Kneen, Brewster.
  Invisible giant: Cargill and its transnational strategies/
Brewster Kneen.
    p. cm.
  Includes bibliographical references and index.
  ISBN 0–7453–0963–1. — ISBN 0–7453–0964–X (pbk.)
  1. Cargill, Inc. 2. International business enterprises.
3. Agricultural industries. I. Title.
HD9014.C42C375 1995
338.8'873'0971—dc20
                                                  95–8620
                                                    CIP

Canadian Cataloguing in Publication Data
Kneen, Brewster.
  Invisible giant
  Includes bibliographical references and index.
  ISBN 1–895686–56–3
  1. Cargill, Inc. I. Title.
HD9039.C37K63 1995   338.7'63   C95–950165–7

Printed in the EC by WSOY, Finland

Contents

Preface

Patience is characteristic of the Cargill culture. As a private transnational corporation with very deep pockets, Cargill can not only afford to take a long view, it can make it a key strategic concept. For example, the company made a decision in 1983 to enter the seed business in India, took no visible action until 1988 and did not actually start selling its seed in India until 1992 — which is not to say that it was doing nothing for all that time.

I too am patient; otherwise the research for this book would not have been possible, nor would the book have been written. Perhaps it is this common trait that both enables and compels me to focus on Cargill and, in spite of its high degree of invisibility, analyze its strategies and expressions. While it is a challenge to research Cargill, and while much of who it is and what it is doing remains invisible, the company itself is certainly not mysterious. I do not think it is even devious, and (if they would have me) I think it would be both fun and challenging to work for Cargill. Provided, of course, I could find it in myself to accept its ideological assumptions.

Dartmouth College historian Wayne G. Broehl Jr. was commissioned by Cargill to write an official history of Cargill from 1895 to 1960. The resulting book,* the only official history of the company that I am aware of, provides the kind of visibility for the corporation that Cargill obviously wanted. With over 1000 pages it is highly visible on the bookshelf. It also contains many good stories (in voluminous detail) of Cargill encounters with financiers, government agencies and competitors, as well as stories about the internal dynamics and personalities of the company. In fact, there is so much detail that one can easily lose sight of the whole. I do not think this is accidental, because the appearance of telling all has the effect of making the whole invisible.

Duncan MacMillan has also written a colorful and very personal two-volume illustrated family history,† and I have drawn from these two books for the brief historical sketch of Cargill found in Chapter 5 and for other bits of historical information.

While there is also voluminous detail in this book, it is organized and presented in a vastly different fashion than either of the books just mentioned. What I have attempted to construct, with patience and attention to detail, is an outsider's guide to understanding how Cargill works and where it is going.

There are holes in my information — on Cargill's activities in Africa and China, for example — due to lack of contacts, any mention of these regions in printed resources, and the lack of time and money to go and get the information myself.

* *Cargill – Trading the World's Grain*, University Press of New England, New Hampshire, USA, 1992.
† W. Duncan MacMillan, with Patricia Condon Johnson, *MacGhillemhaoil – an account of my family from earliest times*, privately printed at Wayzata, Minnesota, 1990 (two volumes, illustrated).

On the other hand, I have been able to construct fairly detailed accounts of Cargill's strategies and activities in many of its lines of business and in certain regions of the world.

Cargill consistently utilizes certain basic strategies, and once these are grasped, it is possible to understand, if not predict, the moves it makes. This is crucial, of course, to those who feel that Cargill's development agenda for the world is not one they want to adopt or support.

Many people have asked how one researches a company that is so secretive and invisible. My first answer is: go and talk to people. In researching this book over the past two years, I have talked with many Cargill employees, competitors, academics and government personnel in many countries, and I have acquired as much of Cargill's own literature as I could find. I have also regularly read trade journals and monitored many other business magazines. Friends and librarians who believe that information is for sharing have also been helpful in sending clippings.

The whole project is very much like assembling a jigsaw puzzle. While there are still many pieces missing, you can get the picture, and my hope is that others will use this as a starting point to collectively create a fuller picture.

There are many numbers and statistics in this book. I have endeavored to make them as unobtrusive, consistent and helpful as possible. I have used figures primarily to indicate relative sizes, growth and magnitude. I have not tried to reduce all numbers to either a metric or a US measurement, but have tried for consistency where it is simply a matter of relative weights, sizes or amounts. US currency figures are used except where conversion from foreign figures would be in error due to changing exchange rates. Figures, however, are only one indicator; when the issue is power, the magnitude of the numbers themselves may be less important than the leverage they provide.

Finally, I undertook to write this book because I think Cargill is one of the most powerful and effective corporations in the world, and deserves to be known and understood for that reason. Cargill has and will continue to shape the agricultural policy of as many countries and geographies as it can, while the public's role in this policy is confined to that of passive consumer. It is my conviction, however, that public policy should be made by the public. There are fundamental choices to be made about how we and future generations are going to live and how we are going to feed ourselves. I do not think those choices should be left to Cargill or any other transnational corporation (TNC), regardless of the quality of its employees. I just don't think it is a good idea to put control over our food in the hands of a very small number of men whose job it is to serve corporate as opposed to public interests.

I want to thank all those who, over the past two years, have contributed to this work; guides and interpreters (Marion, Albert, Mika, Vanaja, Vandana and Michael in particular), hosts and financial contributors (especially the Third World Network), suppliers of clippings and artifacts, and particularly those who are steadfastly building alternatives to Cargill's global vision. Finally, special thanks to reader/editors Rod and Cathleen, and to Cathleen for putting up with my single-mindedness and egging me on.

CHAPTER 1

The Corporation: Visible and Invisible

In the world of capitalist business, the use of power has one primary objective: the accumulation of capital, and with it, more power. Cargill Incorporated is a shining example of a corporation successfully using power to accumulate capital, all the while shaping the global future of agriculture and the eating practices of people around the world.

Public confusion about the purposes of a corporation is not an accident. Corporations, like most people, like to be regarded as honorable, with public conscience and integrity; drug companies present themselves as being concerned about your health, food companies present themselves as being concerned with your nutrition and pleasure, and automobile companies advertise comfort and freedom.

This makes it is all too easy to overlook the fact that a corporation is a legal persona that exists to make a profit and thereby accumulate wealth while limiting the liability of the real people behind the corporation who make and implement decisions. It's called 'risk management', a term that Cargill applies primarily to its use of the futures market.

The fact that a corporation is considered a person under capitalist law, however, does not mean that we have to grant it the respect due to real persons. The corporation is, after all, simply a means to an end. For this reason I refer to the corporation as a neuter, a non-person, an *it*.

Person or not, this entity must nonetheless be held to account for its actions while at the same time we should avoid the temptation to demonize it by emphasizing its malevolent products and evil deeds. While pollution, union busting, manipulation of the futures market, or the adulteration of commodities are all scandalous issues that need to be acted upon, we cannot do so at the expense of the larger issues of which they are the symptoms.

When the (US) Council on Economic Priorities placed Cargill at the top of its 1992 list of environmental offenders in the US food industry, 'the experience brought home the need to communicate better the company's environmental record,' according to the company's employee magazine, *Cargill News*.[1] Cargill has placed more emphasis on communications, but it also continues to make significant environmental protection and enhancement investments. For example, Cargill used a major effluent spill in a Florida fertilizer plant it had recently purchased

1

to turn an expensive fine into a good PR investment when it advertised what it had done to clean up the mess and make sure nothing like that would ever happen again. In other words, Cargill used the negative publicity to generate public interest in its good deeds as a corporate citizen, thereby diverting public attention away from the fundamental issue of the power and control.

Again, we could, with good reason, focus on the legal battle Cargill and other chicken processors are engaged in with their contract poultry growers in Florida and Georgia. The growers' struggle for fair treatment at the hands of the giant integrated poultry companies is a deserving one, but it shouldn't cause us to lose sight of Cargill's role in the industrialization and centralization of beef and poultry production around the world.

Among the very many Cargill mementos and brochures I have collected and that others have sent to me – including a Culligan Water Softener salt bag from Missouri, a Cargill hybrid sunflower seed bag from India, and a Cargill feed bag from Taiwan – one stands out as best conveying the corporate culture that Cargill tries to instill in its employees and that it tries to convey to the public. This large format brochure published by Cargill Canada, with an outline of Canada and the Cargill toilet-seat logo embossed on its cover with 'CARGILL LIMITED' beneath it in simple gold lettering, is impressive in its grandeur and simplicity, as intended.* It conveys more than an image. It approaches the form of an icon, an expression of a kind of mysticism designed to give the corporate persona an authority and transcendence worthy of employee devotion and public admiration. It is also designed to ward off the evil spirits of state control and public criticism. Like many Cargill materials, there is no date on it, but it can be identified as vintage 1991 by its contents.

> Every organization has an idea of what it is. But it is the successful organization that also asks what it hopes to become. At Cargill, what we are, and what we want to be, are reflected in the values and beliefs that motivate and inspire our people and our business activities. These fundamental tenets of our organization ... comprise the Cargill corporate culture, and shape the goals, strategies and policies of our company.

There is here an intriguing conflation of the legally constituted corporate persona and the personality (or personalities) of the real people who constitute the corporation at any particular time. The effort to attribute to a commercial corporation the qualities of a feudal lord dedicated to the loftiest ideals of service to his people is impressive, if not altogether convincing. The brochure continues:

> We believe that consistent excellence, derived from integrity and effort, is the very core of our corporate culture ... The integrity of our focus upon increasing world food production from soil and sun is the essence of our strength

---

* The logo was apparently chosen in 1960 by then-president Erv Kelm as 'a traditional shield with a modern shape with a mercator or global symbol to indicate the company's worldwide operations.' (ST: 8 November 94) See page 209 for list of abbreviations of reference sources.

... We grow because growth is essential to the good health and vitality of our business, the food industry and our country.

Cargill follows classical strategies of accumulation. Bruno Latour has described the cyclical process by which scientific knowledge is accumulated, for example, as one in which each foray into the unknown builds on the previous expedition and brings back, possibly, a little more knowledge.

At every run of this accumulation cycle, more elements are gathered in the centre; at every run the asymmetry between the foreigners and the natives grows, ending today in something that looks indeed like a Great Divide, or at least like a disproportionate relation between those equipped with the satellites who localise the 'locals' on their computer maps without even leaving their air-conditioned [headquarters], and the hapless natives who do not even see the satellites passing over their heads.[2]

Although he has started with the question of how scientific knowledge is built up, Latour goes on to ask:

Will we call 'knowledge' what is accumulated at the centre? ... Maybe we should speak of 'money' or more abstractly of 'profit' since this is what the cycle adds up to ... We could of course talk of 'capital', that is, of something (money, knowledge, credit, power) that has no other function but to be instantly reinvested into yet another cycle of accumulation. This would not be a bad word.[3]

Latour's model of accumulation suits Cargill admirably well. Cargill is in the food business to make money. It is not in business to feed the hungry, though as the end-consumers of its products, people do have a role to play. If this is kept in mind, it is possible to make sense of Cargill's strategies and activities, its pragmatism and rationality. Given its purpose, Cargill does its job very, very well.

The ability to move capital instantaneously around the globe and apply its pressure when and where it can be most effective, including on national treasuries, has been a characteristic of modern TNCs since the 1970s. It is this immediacy, combined with sheer size and the ability to be more patient than most governments can politically afford, that has brought about the overshadowing of nation states by transnational corporations, Cargill paramount among them. As Barnet and Cavanaugh have put it, this has caused a shift in power from 'territorially bound governments to companies that can roam the world',[4] companies that can 'occupy public space' and marginalize governments just as they marginalize people. More wealthy than many national governments, these corporations play a determinative, though frequently invisible, role in even the most powerful and most wealthy states.

Corporations operating beyond national boundaries are nothing new, but until the late 1950s or so they were just that. Then for a time they were referred to as 'multinationals', a term that implies they are composed of, or represent the interests of, many nations; Nestlé and Unilever, Cargill and Mitsubishi, however, neither consist of nor represent many nations. While these collective personalities have to be incorporated under the laws of some land of convenience or tradition, they owe loyalty to no state or nation. They cannot function in the interests of any particular country precisely because they have to serve the interests of the corporate persona and its owners first. They live everywhere and nowhere in a world of markets.

Considerable attention was devoted to the study and analysis of the corporate sector in the 1970s. The role of corporations in the Third World and in the North was studied and analyzed and criticized on many grounds. Yet in the 1980s the corporations virtually disappeared from the public radar, their place taken by states and governments. Specific activities of the corporations, or the consequences of their activities, like oil spills, have appeared on the screen from time to time, but the corporations as such have become almost invisible.

Several years ago a Dutch colleague offered the explanation that the corporations did not like all the negative publicity they received in the 1970s, so they came up with a collective strategy of redirecting the public eye to governments as the villains. This well organized and, I am sure, well financed, campaign was very successful. The corporations were able to become the heroes of economic activity and the providers of jobs and all things good in life, able to fade from public criticism and quietly pursue their fundamental business of making money and gaining control. Cargill continues to epitomize this.

I do not want to suggest a conspiracy, although there is no doubt in my mind that the major TNCs have long collaborated in the formation of their collective strategy and its implementation. A conspiracy is not required when there is a common ideology and parallel interests among an elite. These interests are reflected in the multitudinous industry lobbying associations and the alliances formed to advocate particular public policies, including international trade policies, even while the pretense of competition is maintained on other fronts.

Since the early 1980s the corporate sector has also been generous in its financing and directing of the right-wing think-tanks and PR firms that have cranked out their neo-liberal ideology and propaganda. These agents have done their damage. The media and all public discussion have been distorted; their anti-government, pro-business message has been delivered to even the smallest villages and weekly newspapers.

The disinclination to look at the corporation was buttressed by the Social Darwinist individualism of the 1980s. When the pursuit of personal gain and individual advantage becomes the moral code, then anything that stands in the way of this becomes immoral and must be wiped away – or wiped out.

A prime example of this is the 1994 battle over the future of the Canadian Wheat Board (CWB) generated by the private grain trade. Cargill and Continental Grain Co. easily conceal themselves behind the opportunist farmers of the Western Canadian Wheat Growers Association and the Western Canadian Barley Growers Association, while paying their organizations' bills and egging them on with the battle cry of 'freedom of choice' to sell their grain where and when they want.

The CWB is the single-desk seller of all western Canadian wheat and barley for export. The CWB pools the prices it gets for all grain sales during the year and pays every farmer the same price for the same grade, regardless of where the farmer lives or when the grain was delivered to the elevator by the farmer. In other words, the basic principle is equitable treatment for every farmer. To be able to do this, the CWB has to have a monopoly on all exports, though the private trade can act as agents of the CWB, buying grain from the Board if it is profitable for the trader, and otherwise handling grain on behalf of the board for a fee.

The alternative that is being called for is the American model of every farmer for himself [sic]. While the freedom jingle may play well to an individualist right-wing mob, it is an illusion and delusion to think there would be any equity in the relations between individual farmers playing the market and the buyers that might be accessible to them. In the case of Canada this would be something like 120,000 grain farmers trying to sell into a market controlled by two to five giant companies. Regulation of the market and the monopoly of the CWB may well be done away with in the political climate of the 1990s; that will just strengthen the oligopoly of the grain buyers at the expense of every farmer.

The diversion of the public's attention to the state is only one half of the explanation for the corporate disappearance from the public radar. The other half is the deliberate policy of the corporation to present itself only at specific times and in places of its own choosing to suit its own purposes.

Cargill is a master at this. As a result, very, very few people are aware of Cargill's global activities, and even fewer could describe them, including (judging by the many I have talked with) most of Cargill's own employees. This is no accident. A picture of the whole would be disturbing to many people and would reveal the power of the corporation. Experience suggests it is better to remain largely invisible. So in Korea, Cargill advertisements in the farm press are large blank spaces with a wordless Cargill logo in one corner – and nothing else. At a Cargill subsidiary in Nebraska, the only Cargill identification is in small letters on the truck doors – otherwise the name is Walnut Grove. As Kerry Hawkins, president of Cargill Ltd (Canada) put it, 'Our experience is if you're too big, people don't want to do business with you.'[5]

In Memphis, Tennessee, the casual visitor to the Hohenberg office would be hard pressed to know that one of the major worldwide cotton trading companies is a Cargill subsidiary, and in many towns and cities the Cargill office is not where one might expect it, but rather in a nondescript office building outside the main business district where there is no indication of Cargill's presence except on the list of tenants in the lobby. More than once, when calling on Cargill executives, I have been asked, 'How did you find this office?'

Again, one comes across a yard full of gleaming tanker trucks bearing the name Transportation Services - another Cargill subsidiary, ascertainable if one specifically asks in the office. This is all one form of invisibility.

The cloak of invisibility, however, takes other forms; being private, for example. Cargill Inc. has always been a privately owned corporation (it has never offered shares for public purchase) and, like a private person, under corporate law it is not required to reveal its personal affairs. No quarterly statements, no annual reports, no disclosures for a bond issue (though Cargill did do that – once). Cargill does not even have to be forthcoming to those who give it credit ratings for the sake of suppliers and bankers.

On the other hand, when Cargill chooses to attract public attention, or at least, for its own purposes, to inform the corporate elite, it can ensure that an interview or article appears in the magazine or paper of its choosing. Thus an adulatory, apparently detailed but actually very unrevealing article appeared in *Fortune* magazine in mid-1992.[6] To be of value to Cargill, the article appeared at a critical juncture of the corporation's evolution when the confidence of the business community was essential. Two years later, when *Fortune* ran a feature article on the major losers in derivatives trading, the name of Cargill appeared in the index but the company was not mentioned in the article.[7] As the fifth-largest loser in the global derivatives market in the spring of 1994, Cargill certainly deserved recognition, but apparently the writer could not get enough information to include it in his story (see Chapter 4).

Invisibility should not, however, be confused with poor visibility. (An ad for Cargill Flour Millers that frequently appears in one trade journal depicts a mighty Cargill tanker truck rounding a bend in a highway at night in the rain with its headlights cutting the darkness. The caption: 'Neither rain nor sleet nor gloom of night can keep Cargill from delivering at the appointed hour.') Cargill devotes just as much effort to improving its ability to see what is ahead and what is going on around it as it does to being invisible. It does this by utilizing the most advanced intelligence and communications technologies available as well as a global network of informers. Of course the company would not refer to its staff as informers, but Cargill, like other TNCs, does maintain offices that are primarily information-gathering facilities, and certainly a function of its trading and financial staff is information gathering. According to its ads, Cargill even has its own meteorologists 'who get their information straight from the satellites ... and crop forecasters who spend the bulk of their time on the road, checking crops.'[8]

In 1990 Cargill installed a private telephone, data and fax system to link its international locations by transoceanic fiber-optic cable to switching hubs in Minneapolis and Geneva. It had already started in the fall of 1989 to aggressively advertise its financial services to the grain industry and its use of the futures market, particularly the Chicago Board of Trade. The ads emphasized that Cargill had probably the most sophisticated crop intelligence gathering network in the world, from infra-red satellite photographs of grain-growing areas to corporate staff in every grain producing and trading centre.

The privacy of its intelligence system provides Cargill with the good visibility necessary to maximize its gains in trading and to make strategic decisions about the future, from investing in a feed plant in Poland to purchasing futures contracts in Brazilian coffee.

Prior to the days of satellite imaging, one required a fertile imagination to see the world in terms of water and 'geographies' rather than as states or continents. My own favourite picture of the world is a composite satellite photo-map of the world that displays topography, highlights water, and is devoid of superimposed political jurisdictions. No counties, no provinces, no states, no nations, no World Bank, no UN. This image of the world is Cargill's starting point, even though it studiously cultivates relations with political jurisdictions at every level, from mayors to presidents and prime ministers.

Cargill maintains its satellite perspective on the world so steadfastly that one could almost naively describe Cargill as a global, ecological citizen with bioregional practices. It claims everywhere to do business in the best interests of whomever it is addressing – 'think globally, act locally', as the slogan goes.

But what does Cargill actually see from its satellite perspective? A relatively simple picture of the major growing areas of the world, and the water routes that can or might connect them to the major markets of the world.

Thus in Brazil, Cargill sees not rain forests and denuded mountains, but the great plain of the Mato Grosso and its potential for soybean production, if only the water routes to the sea can be made navigible. What it sees on the Indian sub-continent are two global resource areas: Punjab, for grain, and the plains of the south central area for corn and oilseeds.* The problem with Punjab is lack of access to 'global water' (see Chapter 16). And so on around the world.

I am sure that this 'ecological' sensibility is one of the reasons for Cargill's continuing success. Instead of allowing its activities and interests to be defined by existing political orders and structures, such as states, governments and even trade agreements, Cargill has started with populations, geographies, regions and water.

Cargill's development as a global commodity merchandiser has been built on the extensive and innovative use of water to provide the lowest-cost form of transport available. Water has always been the cheapest means for bulk transport of high volume bulk goods like coal, grain and oil. Next comes rail, with trucking a poor third. Of course, in any particular situation or location, the actual cost of utilizing these different means of transport will depend on the amount of public subsidy involved and the resulting 'distortions' in true costing (see Chapter 6).

Once its strategy is in place, Cargill works out the tactics required to deal with the appropriate political jurisdictions. In fact, Cargill appears to devote far more energy to establishing favorable national or regional business climates wherever it chooses to do business than it devotes to international trade agreements,

---

* In mid-1993 the government of India reversed its food policy and removed the restraints to the export of staple commodities such as wheat and rice that had been in place since the country's independence. 'It cited the possibilities for developing internationally competitive crop production in fertile areas of the country, such as the northern state of Punjab.' (M&B:4 May 93)

contrary though this may appear to the recent media fixation on trade negotiations and policies. Cargill has been developing its own internal global trading
arrangements for about as long as long as the World Bank and International
Monetary Fund have been around.

The language of Cargill's sophisticated literature for public consumption, such
as corporate brochures and trade journal ads, expresses its view of geopolitical
and economic reality. It carefully avoids using words such as 'nation', 'state',
'country' and 'government' and uses in their place words such as 'worldwide',
'geographies', 'areas', 'communities' and 'locations'.

On the other side, Cargill's language is also devoid of the the cheap clichés
and buzz-words that plague right-wing propaganda and policy documents,
words like 'stakeholder', 'agri-food', 'World Class', or even 'competitive'.

Coupled with Cargill's emphasis on geographies and locations is the use of
military terminology in discussion of strategy. 'Beachhead' is the key term and
strategic concept:

> Cargill speaks of beachheads ... Historic product-line beachheads for the
> company have been hybrid seeds (primarily corn), commodity export marketing,
> and animal feed milling. The strategy has been: create the beachhead with
> inputs of capital, technology and a management nucleus; get the cash flow
> positive; re-invest the cash flow and expand the beachhead.[9]

Cargill may not devote much space to discussion of global trade issues, but it
does devote a lot of energy and space to discussion of production policies, particularly in the US and Europe. Cargill is most interested in having the market
flooded with cheap raw materials for trading and processing. As long as the company
has the volume to play with, it has lots of ways around any international trade
limitations or requirements. In the 1990s it has aggressively advanced the
argument for unrestricted food production on the basis of the moral imperative
of feeding the growing world population and its middle class. Sheer quantity is
required for the first, but higher-value food products, such as meat, are required
for the latter. Cargill will happily supply both, if farmers are 'unshackled' and
permitted to produce. One of its constant themes is 'our' responsibility to feed
the growing world population. Being transnational, the 'our' may refer to the
US, Canada or any number of other 'geographies'.

Whitney MacMillan's retirement in 1995, after 18 years as president and then
chairman of Cargill Inc. will bring to an end 85 years of MacMillan family leadership
in the company. During his tenure at the helm MacMillan has clearly articulated the Cargill vision and rephrased it many times in the idiom of the day as
the company has developed from grain trader to transnational superpower. He
offers an ambitious vision of a powerful global force:

> We will be the best in improving the standard of living for the 5 billion people
> in the world ... by buying, storing, processing, transporting, and distributing
> basic raw materials, primarily agricultural materials. We will do this by

promoting, innovating, and creating competition and efficiencies in this distribution chain. Cargill will pay the producer better prices and sell to the
consumer for a little less.[10]

Three years earlier MacMillan had included in the same speech the statement
that 'This vision will increase purchasing power and/or capital formation for the
world population.'[11] He never did explain just how this capital formation would
be 'for the world population' and not just the Cargill population.

When Ernest Micek was chosen as president in 1994 he put a slightly different
emphasis on this point. Cargill, he said, is well-positioned for increasing globalization as many large customers look for one-stop suppliers that can suit their
needs around the world.[12] In 1994 Cargill's trade journal ads took on a Micek
character, proclaiming Cargill's ubiquitous invisibility as a supplier to food
manufacturers such as Campbell Soup. With a two-page-long arrow pointing
to the 'wheat flour' in fine print on a can's label, the gradually decreasing print
size on the arrow says, 'It's small, relatively anonymous and absolutely no
indication of how big our interest is in your success. Your brand – our flour.'

CHAPTER 2

A Statistical Portrait

Cargill is a private US company, established in 1865. It employs some 70,700 people worldwide in 800 locations in 60 countries in more than 50 lines of business. Its global operations are directed via satellite and dedicated fiber-optic cable systems from its headquarters in Minnetonka, Minnesota, a suburb of Minneapolis.

'In early years, Cargill was primarily a regional grain merchandiser.' Today Cargill is:

* the largest private company in the US
* the 11th largest company, public or private, in the US in terms of sales[13]
* the largest grain trader in the world (Continental Grain number 2, Bunge number 3)[14]
* the largest producer of malting barley in the world (Ladish Malting)
* the largest oilseed processor in the world[15] (ADM is number 2 and Bunge is number 3)[16]
* the third largest beef packer (Excel) and the fourth largest pork slaughterer in the US
* the fourth largest cattle feeder in the US (Caprock Industries)
* the sixth largest turkey producer in the US
* the largest beef packer in Canada
* the third largest flour miller in the US (19 mills)
* the second largest phosphate fertilizer producer in the world.

Cargill is also a major power in:

* salt (Leslie/Cargill - 10 per cent of the global market)
* peanuts (Stevens Industries)
* cotton (Hohenberg Bros, Ralli Bros and Coney)
* coffee
* truck transport
* river/canal shipping (towboats and barges)
* molasses
* livestock feed (Nutrena) with 60 feed mills in the US and 120 worldwide
* steel (North Star Steel - fifth largest steel company in the US)

10

- hybrid seeds
- rice milling
- rubber
- citrus – Brazil, Pakistan, Florida and Japan
- chicken – USA, UK, Thailand, and elsewhere
- fresh fruits and vegetables (Richland Sales; California and Chile)

and much more ...

A Financial Statement

'Just a bunch of people trying to make a living - a family company.'
Barbara Isman, vice president, Cargill Canada

Cargill stated its global revenues for 1992–3 (year end 31 May 93) as $47.37 billion, providing estimated operating profits of $1.4 billion and net profits of $358 million. The company states its total capital as $6.14 billion (with long-term debt 29 per cent of that) and its total assets as $15.86 billion.

Top contributor to Cargill's overall earnings in 1992–3 was its North American corn milling division. The food sector overall is said to generate nearly two-thirds of Cargill's profits. The second largest contributor to corporate profitability was the Financial Markets Division. Established in the late 1970s and employing some 500 people around the world, the FMD contributed $100 million of the company's $358 million total earnings in 1993.[17]

For 1993–4, Cargill Inc. had estimated operating profits of $1.5 billion and net profits of $571 million, in spite of a $100 million loss incurred early in 1994 by its Financial Markets Division in the trading of derivatives (contracts based on mortgage-backed securities).[18]

While the growth of Cargill's net worth was slow but steady up to 1940, when it had climbed to $9.3 billion, it then entered a period of more rapid ascent, with net worth rising to $70 billion by 1960. (Extreme care has to be exercised with all figures; 'total assets' stated here is not the same as 'net worth' cited below, and Cargill provides no explanation as to what such designations actually mean. The figures are useful for comparison and as indicators, however.) Cargill's net earnings did not show the same rapid increase, but this is to be expected since so much of the company's earnings are reinvested. The record from 1940 to 1960 shows earnings in the range of $2 billion to $5 billion, though it had its ups and downs, the bottom being stated as slightly more than $0.5 billion and the high being over $9 billion.[19]

The gross figures for the years 1970 to 1994 reveal the dramatic growth of the corporation. The take-off occurred in the 1970s during a period of great volatility in the grain trade, beginning with the overwhelming Soviet purchases in 1972–3 (see Chapter 3).

Table 2.1 Cargill's growth 1971–94

	1994	1993	1992	1991	1990	1989	1988	1986	1982	1971[20]
Sales ($billion)	$47.2	$47.4	$46.7	$49.1	$41.9	$43.6	$38.1	$32.3	$29.0	$2.0
Profits ($million)	$571	$358	$450	$351	$372	$305	$277	—	—	—

Since 1992, when the company's employee stock ownership plan (ESOP) was put in place, financial information on Cargill has been more widely available. Cargill has to provide information to the ESOP trustee which, in turn, reports some of it to employees and hence the public. Needless to say, this is still highly 'managed' information.

In 1992, *Fortune* magazine published a rare company-authorized look at Cargill's affairs.

Cargill earned just $351 million in 1991, a paltry return of less than 1 per cent on sales ... Not to worry, says chief financial officer Robert Lumpkins: Commodities companies make money by rapidly turning over their inventories – 15 times per year in Cargill's case. Also, the company's conservative accounting practices – including accelerated depreciation of assets – make the bottom line unnaturally thin. This year, predicts Lumpkins, Cargill will generate about $1.1 billion in cash flow, most of which will be reinvested or used for acquisitions.[21]

'The essence of Cargill's philosophy is patience,' is the way author Ronald Henkoff summed up what he saw of Cargill.[22]

In 1994 a Minneapolis newspaper published figures, obviously provided by Cargill, on the changes in Cargill's business activities from 1970 to 1990. They showed merchandising (trading in bulk commodities) dropping from 37.3 per cent of Cargill's business, as a percentage of net worth, to 17.6 per cent. Non-merchandising (processing of oil seeds, corn and flour milling; agricultural products, such as poultry, feed and seed; industrial products such as steel, fertilizers and salt; and financial services) increased from 62.7 per cent to 82.4 per cent. The only non-merchandising activity to show a decline was transportation, from 6.3 per cent to 2.3 per cent.[23] No explanation was given for decline, nor do I have one.

Dun & Bradstreet gave Cargill Inc. the strongest credit rating it offers in its 1994 Business Report on Cargill. Perhaps it has done this every other year as well, despite the fact that D&B told me that 'the co-operation we get from them is not exactly 100 per cent.'[24] Cargill does provide them with the company audit, but 'for summarization only.' This pretty well sums up the challenge when trying to report on or analyze Cargill Inc. (or most other private companies).

CHAPTER 3

Mechanisms of Accumulation I: The Visible – Oilseeds and Corn

'Our performance goal is to double the size of Cargill's business every five to seven years,' concludes a slim, elegant, timeless (that is, undated) brochure with a slate-gray cover bearing only a wordless Cargill logo in deeper gray. This goal might be achieved by means of trading, processing and transporting visible, tangible commodities and products, or by utilizing various intangible 'financial instruments.' However they are achieved, the results will be accounted in the same digital code.

Corn wet milling – the beginning of a highly visible process that deconstructs real hybrid corn into component parts for everything from animal feed to soft drink sweeteners and ethanol – is the most profitable of Cargill's lines of businesses. The Financial Markets Division (FMD), which trades in invisible, imaginary commodities, such as futures and derivatives of all sorts, and produces neither goods nor service, is Cargill's second most profitable line of business. It will be examined in the next chapter.

In examining corn milling and financial markets, we must remember that the success of these activities depends significantly on all of the other activities in which Cargill engages. One division may not ostensibly contribute much to 'the bottom line', but it may be essential to the healthy functioning of the whole organism, or two lines of business may relate symbiotically, such as oilseed processing and corn wet milling, which are treated together in this chapter. The primary North and South American oilseed crop, soybeans, has much in common with corn in terms of crop growing regions, handling and processing technology, and the utilization of end products.

Cargill's practice of 'building on its core competencies' does not simply imply expansion in a given line of business. It may mean moving laterally, as it were, from oilseed processing to corn wet milling, or from flour milling to corn dry milling. It may mean moving downstream from oilseed crushing (the primary process) into refining and even product manufacturing, or from flour milling into pasta manufacturing, as it has done in Venezuela. In other words, Cargill's growth may be seen as the product of a child's play with Lego - building in many different contiguous directions.

Oilseeds

The major attraction of oilseed processing is the potential market for both edible and industrial oils. Around the world there are extreme differences in levels of edible oil 'disappearance' (not necessarily consumption), the highest being in Malaysia, where annual disappearance is 70 kg per capita. The US is second with 44 kg per person annually while the European Community comes in at 40 kg per person. At the other end of the disappearance spectrum are China, at 8.5 kg per person annually, and India at 7.4 kg per person.[25]

The uses of edible oils, of course, vary tremendously according to diet and 'development' (which does not explain Malaysia), from cultures that use oil primarily in pan or stir frying to North Americans who deep fry foods in oil and consume many processed foods heavily dependent on oils in their manufacture. This variation in custom and diet is an irresistible challenge to companies, like Cargill, experienced in changing other people's eating habits through the imperialism of food aid and sophisticated promotion (see Chapter 8). Certainly the very low usage rate in the two most populous geographies of the world, India and China, must be a mouth-watering market challenge to Cargill.

For many decades after its establishment, Cargill remained, as one of its brochures put it, 'a regional grain merchandiser.' This description hid the fact that the company was already evolving into a trader in commodity abstractions such as contracts, futures, and now, derivatives. More substantially, however, Cargill has always understood that the key to long-term success in trading is the capacity to store and deliver commodities. The ability to hold staple crops and other commodities off the market while awaiting, or bargaining for, a better price is an obvious way to increase one's profit with only a small risk involved. The ability to originate (gather from the farm level), store and deliver provides both leverage and another source of profit.

It was nearly 80 years before Cargill moved 'downstream' beyond these activities into a significantly different line of business, commodity processing. The purchase, in 1943, of three soybean processing plants, two in Iowa and one in Illinois, was the starting point. There is little available record of the company's steady growth in oilseed processing since that first acquisition, but a French oilseeds trader commented in 1991 about Cargill's interest in palm oil that: 'Cargill won't want to get involved in small, complicated markets.'[26] By 1991 the company was operating more than 40 oilseed processing plants around the world and by 1993 it was the second largest oilseeds processor in the United States with 25 per cent of total capacity (ADM was first with 28 per cent, Bunge third with 16 per cent and Central Soya fourth with 10 per cent).[27]

Along the way it acquired six mills in the US, purchased from Ralston Purina in 1985; two oilseed processing mills and three rice processing mills in Malawi, where Cargill has been active since 1981; and two palm oil refineries in Malaysia in 1991.*

The company's global oilseed processing capabilities continue to expand around the world. In 1992, Cargill was supervising the building and operation of a cottonseed processing plant in Shandong Province, China, apparently the outcome of a joint-venture agreement in existence with the government of China since the mid-1980s.[28] It also acquired, from Continental Grain Co., four more oilseed crushing plants: one in Alabama; one in Argentina; and two in Australia. (Cargill also picked up three feed mills in Australia from Continental Grain in the deal.)[29]

Around the same time it also purchased Huilerie Felix Marchand SA, a 145-year-old oil refiner in western France which processes 70,000 tonnes a year of sunflower, rape, soya, peanut, grape, corn and palm oil, marketing it under its own Amphora label as well as private brand labels.[30]

By 1992 Cargill was claiming that Germany was the only major oilseed-producing country in the world in which it did not yet have an oilseed processing facility.† (The company was apprently including Canada, where it does not have oilseed processing facilities, as part of the US.) To remedy that, Cargill began construction that year of an $80 million oilseed and malt processing plant in the port of Salzgitter, near the old border between East and West Germany. The plant is to have a rapeseed crushing capacity of about 350,000 tonnes a year and a refining capacity for one-third of that output. The facility will also produce 75,000 tonnes of malt a year, and Cargill intends the plant to be the lowest-cost malt producer in Europe.

Cargill continues to improve its oilseed facilities and in 1994 announced the expansion of two of its Iowa soybean plants by 25,000 bushels (635 tonnes) per day.[31]

Moving Downstream

Vegetable (edible) oil production is a two-stage process. The first stage is the separation of the oil from the seed fiber, either by crushing, which itself can take several forms, or extraction by means of solvents that are then removed from the extracted oil. The second stage, refining, removes impurities from the oil and produces the desired product or products. The most easily recognized product is the refined cooking or salad oil that is almost universally used in home cooking. 'Oilseed processing' may refer to crushing or extraction only or to

---

* The Malawi mills were actually acquired by the National Seed Company of Malawi, which Cargill manages and in which it owns a 55 per cent interest, in a joint venture with National Oil Industries (NOIL) of Malawi. The NOIL plants in Blantyre and Mzuzu crush and bottle locally grown cotton and sunflower seeds for the local market, with the Blantyre plant producing about 30 per cent of the total Malawi output. (M&B: 7 July 92)

† Cargill has had trading operations in Germany since 1955 and in 1987 it opened a seed development and sales operation there. (CN: February 93, June–July 94)

crushing and refining. Further processing ('value-added' in today's jargon) ranges from margarine manufacturing to specialty oils for use in food manufacturing.

With oilseed processing (crushing and refining) facilities in almost every oilseed producing region of the world, Cargill is now continuing to move further downstream into the manufacturing of edible oil products. For example, it bought most of the assets of the vegetable shortening business of Fresh Start Foods Ltd as part of the company's 'continuing effort to move up the value chain of refined oils.'[32]

In a similar move, Cargill reached an agreement with Kraft in 1993 to lease, with an option to purchase, the Kraft Food Ingredients vegetable oil refinery and packaging plant in Memphis, Tennessee, one of the largest in the US. This gives Cargill the ability to produce different types of oils, such as shortenings and oils for the foodservice sector. Cargill has had a major corn processing complex on the south side of Memphis since 1976. With this addition, Cargill has 18 oilseed processing plants and ten vegetable oil refineries in the US.[33]

Among the major industrial users of edible oils are the fried chicken franchises, the french fried potato market and the snack foods manufacturers. Cargill reports that when it started doing business with PepsiCo's Frito-Lay division in 1987, it supplied Frito-Lay with a mere eight million pounds of oil per year. By 1993 Cargill was shipping 179 million pounds of vegetable oil to Frito-Lay's snack food plants annually.[34]

Continuing its push into new products for its established lines of business, Cargill formed an alliance with SVO Specialty Products, a subsidiary of Lubrizol Corp., to expand vegetable oil markets for SVO's high oleic sunflower oil, Trisun, in January 1994.[35] It also reached an agreement with United Oilseeds of the UK to promote production of oilseed rape for conversion to biodiesel. With farmers' and government help, the two companies hope to be able to build a biodiesel plant to utilize the crop.[36]

Cargill's peanut subsidiary, Stevens Industries in Georgia, also reached an agreement with Calgene of California to process Calgene's specialty canola oils (see Chapter 15). The first such oil to be approved for commercial production is a canola oil containing laurate, 'a key raw material used in the manufacture of soap, detergent, oleochemical and personal care products' according to Calgene's press release.[37] The oil is produced by a strain of canola into which has been introduced a patented gene from the California Bay tree.

Processing raw commodities into simple oils and then moving to produce more refined and esoteric products is a reasonable progression, but Cargill's recent alliance with Hoffmann–La Roche Ltd of Switzerland to manufacture and market natural-source vitamin E worldwide seems to me to be analogous to the move from selling real commodities to trading futures (see next chapter). Cargill is to operate the new plant, which is to be built in the US midwest, and Hoffman-La Roche will maintain quality control and handle marketing. Cargill and Archer Daniels Midland are the two major US manufacturers of the raw material for natural-source vitamin E, 'deodorizer distillate', a product of oilseed processing.

The vitamin E market in the US is estimated at $600 million in sales, growing 25 per cent per year.[38]

Canada

As we have mentioned, when Cargill claimed that Germany was the only major oilseed producing country in which it did not already have a processing plant, it was overlooking Canada, where it still does not have an oilseed plant, in spite of the fact that Canada has become a major oilseed producer in recent years with canola. Perhaps Cargill has simply been pursuing one of its basic strategies: sit back and let others take the risk, then step in when the dust has settled and long-term plans can be executed.

According to retired Cargill vice president Dick Dawson, Cargill wanted to get into the originating business back in 1972, and rapeseed was the only grain not under control of the Canadian Wheat Board. It made its first investment in Western Canada by building a rapeseed processing terminal at North Battleford, Saskatchewan. Cargill intended to build a crushing mill as well, but they never got around to it since the terminal was sufficient to give them fair access to the rapeseed trade. The location was chosen because it was equidistant, for rail transport purposes, between the West Coast and Thunder Bay, the two export positions on water.

The terminal was a success, according to Dawson, and two years later, when Cargill Ltd had a spare $20 million as a result of selling grain to the Russians during what is referred to in the trade as The Great Grain Robbery of 1971–3, they bought National Grain, giving Cargill a major presence in the Canadian west. (The Great Grain Robbery, or what some, looking at corporate results, might refer to as the Great Grain Rip-off, refers to the prolonged episode during which the Soviet Union bought up nearly all the grain available around the world, through a series of deals with private traders that caught national governments off guard and drove up grain prices very substantially as grain stocks were reduced to nothing.)

In the early 1980s Cargill bought land at Melfort, Saskatchewan, with the intention of building a crushing mill. It did not build the mill because when the Saskatchewan Wheat Pool got wind of their plans, they, together with Manitoba Pool Elevators, quickly built a mill at Harrowby, Manitoba, with help from the Federal Government courtesy of then Agriculture Minister Eugene Whelan.* When Whelan refused to help Cargill with a requested $2 million grant, Cargill scrapped its plans, figuring it would be the victim of unfair competition if its plant was not subsidized to the same extent as its competitors';[39] a government investigation of the Cargill books, however, indicated the company was prosperous

---

* Whelan also assisted United Cooperatives of Ontario with construction of what is now the ADM oilseed plant in Windsor, Ontario.

enough to build the rapeseed crushing plant on its own.[40] It worked out fine for Cargill in the end. Dawson says Whelan saved them the $25 million cost of a new mill, given the vast crushing overcapacity resulting from government subsidies to build plants.

Nevertheless, and letting neither pride nor principle stand in its way, in late 1994 Cargill Ltd announced that it intended to build a canola processing plant and refinery in western Canada with a daily processing capacity of 1500–2000 tonnes, for an annual crush of 500,000 tonnes. This would be two to three times the size of any existing plant in western Canada and bigger than either of the two big plants in Ontario that crush both soybeans and canola. The six or so western plants are all in the 600–725 tonnes/24-hour day capacity range while the CanAmera (Central Soya) and ADM plants in Ontario process about 1200 tonnes per day of soybeans and/or 600–1200 tonnes of canola.

Cargill also cagily announced it would build without specifying the location. This was unmistakably a deliberate, well-timed invitation to the provincial governments of Saskatchewan, Alberta and Manitoba to court Cargill with promises of favors and finance. This gave 'The Big Green Crusher', as one industry wag described Cargill, the opportunity to locate its plant according to the dowry promised – at public expense, of course. It will be interesting to see which province wins. Cargill has been generously supported in the past by Alberta and Saskatchewan, so maybe it is Manitoba's turn to add Cargill to its welfare rolls. On the other hand, Cargill already has well-established and highly favorable operating relationships with the government of Saskatchewan.

Corn Milling

In addition to moving downstream into the processing of oilseeds, Cargill moved down another tributary into feed milling and manufacture and then into livestock feeding (Caprock Industries) and slaughter. It also moved into corn wet milling (a form of processing) which has turned out to be the biggest moneymaker of all for Cargill. This does not necessarily mean that it has the highest profit margins – that the public will never know – but the size and scope of the company's involvement in corn wet milling combined with its profit margin causes it to contribute more than any other line of business to corporate 'earnings'.

Cargill entered the corn wet milling business (24 years after starting to crush soybeans) with the purchase in 1967 of a modest corn milling plant near Cedar Rapids, Iowa, that could grind 9000 bushels (230 tonnes) of corn daily. Over the years the plant has been considerably enlarged.

The first corn wet milling plant Cargill actually built was at Dayton, Ohio, in 1973. The plant opened with a daily capacity of 35,000 bushels (approx. 900 tonnes), but within two years that had been increased to 75,000 bushels (1900 tonnes per day). Cargill also began to produce high fructose corn syrup (HFCS) at that time.

In 1976 Cargill built a second corn wet milling plant, this one on President's Island in the Mississippi River at Memphis (see Chapter 6). Being on the river meant that Cargill could supply the plant with corn by barge from upstream elevators very cheaply, while the products leave the processing complex by pipeline, truck and railcar.

Corn was once something people ate directly, fed to animals, or dried so that it could be either ground for tortillas and cornbread or stored for long periods before being used for either animal or human consumption. Now corn is one of the basic agricultural raw materials out of which almost anything, it seems, can be made.

Until the 1970s, corn wet mills produced primarily corn starches and dextrose and glucose, but processes have gradually become more complex and the products more differentiated.

The first stage in the deconstruction of corn by the wet milling process is steeping (soaking) the corn to soften the kernel so that its major component parts – germ, starch, gluten and hull – can be separated. The starch becomes a slurry that can then be converted by means of enzymes into conventional corn syrups, high fructose corn syrup (HFCS), glucose, dextrose, crystalline fructose, corn gluten feed and ethyl alcohol (ethanol). Of course it cannot produce all of these things at once, but any of these products can be produced depending on what is desired. The starch from one bushel of corn can be converted to 33 pounds of HFCS or 2.5 gallons (4 litres) of ethanol, the most valuable alternative products.[41]

In 1992 the United States corn crop was 9.479 billion bushels (241 million tonnes). 1.5 to 1.7 billion bushels of this were exported. Disposition of the crop was roughly as follows:[42]

Table 3.1: US Corn Crop disposition, 1992

US animal feed	62%	
Seed	4%	
Exports	20%	
Food & Industrial	14% – consisting of:	
	fuel alcohol 34%	
	beverages 29%	
	industrial starch 10%	
	baked goods 3%	
	pharmaceuticals 2%	
	other 22%	
	or,	
	Fuel alcohol	445 million bushels
	HFCS	420 million bushels
	Corn syrup & dextrose	220 million bushels
	Starch	245 million bushels
	Beverage alcohol	83 million bushels

There is nothing aesthetically pleasing about a corn processing complex, but one has to see one to appreciate its scale and complexity. It's something like a petroleum oil refinery. Driving out to the President's Island plant in Memphis, Tennessee, one passes long strings of railroad tank cars with the Cargill logo on them, used for corn syrup (HFCS) delivery around the country. One also passes a trucking company called Transport Services Co. which displays no hint of being a Cargill subsidiary but which nevertheless is. The company operates a fleet of 57 gleaming stainless steel tanker trucks to deliver corn sweeteners to Cargill's industrial customers, such as Coca-Cola and Pepsi. The trucks now also carry vegetable oils from the recently acquired Kraft refinery on the north side of the city – 'Cargill North' as they refer to it (see Chapter 6).

Two years after opening its Memphis plant Cargill opened a corn wet milling plant at Bergen op Zoom in the Netherlands, providing another destination for US corn grown east of the Mississippi River. Cargill is pleased with this plant because of its highly sophisticated water treatment systems utilizing anaerobic sludge, odor-eating bacteria and biogas generation. It is also the only Cargill corn milling plant in the world that also uses wheat flour as a feedstock, in this case to produce gluten for European bakers who require it to improve the baking qualities of low-protein soft European wheats.[43] This means that even though Cargill, along with other companies, lost the European market for hard bread wheats from the northern high plains of the US and Canada due to the European policy of self-sufficiency, it came back in through the back door as a supplier of an essential ingredient for European bread. Cargill also has corn wet milling plants in Tilbury, England, in Turkey and in Uberlandia, Brazil.

In 1985 Cargill embarked on its biggest corn processing venture up to that time, the building of a corn wet milling complex at Eddyville, Iowa. The primary product of this plant was HFCS, the sweetener now used in about half of all soft drinks produced in the US. Five years later Cargill added a $45 million citric acid plant to transform corn-derived liquid dextrose into citric acid. By the end of 1992 the plant was producing 80 million pounds (36,000 tonnes) of citric acid per year and supplying 20 per cent of the US market. Another addition to the plant made it possible to also produce 15 million pounds annually of sodium citrate, the sodium salt of citric acid.

Both citric acid and sodium citrate are used in carbonated beverages, and sodium citrate is also used to suppress the bitter aftertaste of the saccharin used to sweeten many low calorie beverages. Both products are also used as biodegradable alternatives to phosphate in detergents. These products are more examples of an almost invisible company producing essential products that are virtually invisible to the people who use or consume them.

Meanwhile, on the other side of the world, in December 1992, the government of India approved Cargill's application for the construction of a molasses-based 20,000 tonnes per year citric acid plant to be owned solely by Cargill (that is, with no Indian partner). Total citric acid capacity in India is currently 6500 tonnes per year, with another 3000 tonnes imported. The only manufacturer in India is Dyeing of Bombay. Cargill said it plans to export up to half of the plant's output. The project, to cost $25 million, is only in its primary stages and may take several years to come on-stream. (It takes 4 tonnes of molasses to make a tonne of citric acid, and molasses costs as little as $8 per tonne, while citric acid is worth about $1200 per tonne.)[44] The governments of the two states where the project could be located, Maharashtra and Uttar Pradesh, have both offered dowry to their suitor, in this case allotments of the key raw material, molasses, from the government monopolies.

Back in Iowa, the next addition to the Eddyville complex was a $30 million ethanol refinery designed to produce 28.5 million gallons (about 115 million litres) of ethanol per year out of roughly 11 million bushels of corn.[45] Cargill's interest in ethanol goes back to the 1970s and 1980s, but the technology for ethanol was undeveloped then and it cost more to produce ethanol than it was worth as a fuel component. The industry was dependent on government subsidies. Although the economics of production may not have changed significantly, the politics have; new US legislation has mandated the use, starting in 1995, of ethanol as a blend in gasoline in order to make the latter burn more cleanly. Tax incentives have been used to encourage the production of ethanol and Cargill's rival, Archer Daniels Midland, has been the noisiest lobbyist both for its use and for the tax incentives and/or subsidies required to make it attractive.

The latest addition to the product line of Cargill's Eddyville plant was liquid carbon dioxide. In 1993 a 250 ton per day CO_2 plant was built along with a 50 ton per day dry ice plant to capture the carbon dioxide that had previously been vented off. Subsequently Cargill extended its corn sweetener line at the Eddyville plant with the addition of a $10 million dry sweetener facility to produce dry dextrose, corn syrup solids and dry maltose.[46]

Today Cargill's $225 million Eddyville corn wet milling complex consumes 220,000 bushels (5588 tonnes) of corn per day – more than two million tonnes per year – to produce corn syrup (dextrose), more than half of which it uses directly in the production of HFCS for the soft drink industry and the other products mentioned above. Pipelines also carry dextrose from the Cargill complex to two other nearby plants: Japanese-owned chemical giant Ajinomoto that makes MSG, and Heartland Lysine Inc. a joint project of Ajinomoto and Orsan, a French company, that makes lysine (an amino acid used in animal feeds).[47]

According to the Des Moines *Register*, the Iowa Department of Transportation decided to build a four-lane expressway between Des Moines and Ottumwa to accomodate the 10,000 trucks entering or leaving the Eddyville plants each month. 'Iowa development agencies have supported Cargill, Heartland and Ajinomoto with grants, loans and road construction projects not available to smaller businesses,' commented the *Register*.

While it was busy expanding its Eddyville operation, Cargill announced that it would build its fifth corn wet milling complex, at a cost of $200 million, at Blair, Nebraska. The plant is to process 120,000 bushels of corn per day into fuel ethanol, sweeteners, corn germ, carbon dioxide, corn gluten feed and corn gluten meal.[48] Together with the Eddyville plant, this new plant should bring Cargill's ethanol annual production to 100 million gallons (more than 400 million litres) by 1995. This will still not come close to ADM's annual production of 800 million gallons out of the total of 1.1 billion gallons of ethanol sold in 1992.[49]

A Cargill handout distributed in Nebraska suggests that the Blair plant, when fully operational, might process over 1 billion bushels (25.4 million tonnes) of corn annually. This would appear to be something of an exaggeration, since the total grain corn crop annually seems to vary between 7.5 and 9.5 billion bushels (190 and 240 million tonnes). In the next paragraph the handout is a little more realistic, saying that Cargill would be buying and processing approximately one of every 30 bushels of corn grown by the American farmer.[50] The one out of thirty, or about 40 million bushels (1 million tonnes) per year, is probably correct, but one billion really sounds impressive, especially when aimed at farmers. The sheet concluded, 'Cargill ... crop maker and market maker! What seed supplier does more to support American agriculture?'

Innovations

Never one to rest on its laurels, or last year's profits, Cargill is always looking for new uses for agricultural raw materials.

In the late 1980s a lot of excitement was generated by the corn industry over the advent of a 'biodegradable' plastic that could be used for all kinds of purposes including garbage bags. The novelty was the addition of corn starch to the normal plastic. When exposed to the weather, the corn starch would dissolve and the plastic would crumble. But that was all it did. There was, in fact, just as much plastic left, but it was in little bits. The perpetrators of this fraud, having acted probably more out of greed and ignorance than ill-will or deceit, quickly withdrew the product, and the corn growers' organizations hastily reasserted their ecological committment by lobbying hard instead for the use of corn-derived ethanol as an environmental good.

Not having jumped on the corn-starch bandwagon, in mid-1993 Cargill announced that it would undertake large-scale production of a genuinely biodegradable plastic. The company is building an $8 million plant at Savage, Minnesota, to manufacture ten million pounds a year of a corn-derived polymer that will degrade into water and dirt if composted.*

This is a trial project for a much larger – 250 million pound (120,000 tonne) – plant that Cargill intends to add to its Blair complex by mid-1996. The polymer, which the company refers to as EcoPLA, is made from lactic acid, a by-product of fermented sugars found in milk, sugar beets, corn and other

---

* Savage is the location on the Missouri River just south of St Paul/Minneapolis where Port Cargill is located, with its fertilizer terminal, grain elevator, corn milling and oilseeds plants, a liquid molasses plant (for use in feed supplements) and a salt terminal.

grains. The rice-like pellets to be produced in the new plant will be sold to packaging companies for about $2 a pound. Conventional petroleum-based plastics currently sell for about 60 cents a pound.[51]

Cargill's progression in the corn industry up to this point is fairly linear. It started with developing and selling hybrid seed and trading the basic product. The next phase was moving downstream into primary processing — wet milling — and then adding related processing activites, from cattle feeding to corn wet milling. When it decided to enter the processing sector, it minimized its exposure by purchasing an existing mill, a pattern that Cargill has followed in virtually every new sector it has entered. Only when it had gained some hands-on experience with the actual process did Cargill make a real commitment and build from scratch.

Dry Milling

In the same way, Cargill has recently committed itself to a new line of enterprise, corn dry milling. Having gained some practical experience by milling dry corn in a small mixed-product mill in Saginaw, Texas, which it closed in 1993, it then decided to invest seriously in corn dry milling.

Of course dry milling itself is not a new experience for Cargill since it has long been a major wheat flour miller in many countries, including the US. For a while, it was even cited as the largest flour miller in the world.[52] This was in 1982 after it bought Seaboard Allied Milling Corp., the seventh largest flour miller in the US, from Seaboard Corporation for $45 million. Harry Bresky, the majority owner of Seaboard, had decided that with industry consolidation and shrinking returns, it was better to withdraw to his overseas milling operations and his shipping interests than fight the obvious trend.[53]

In 1989, Cargill's flour milling division 'established a beachhead in the California campaign' with the opening of the mill in San Bernadino, the first flour mill Cargill had ever built from scratch.[54] Two years later Cargill expanded again with the purchase of two older mills, one in Utah and the other in Los Angeles, from Pillsbury. Then 'Northern California was penetrated in March, 1992' with the opening of Cargill's new mill in Stockton.[55] In three years Cargill had become the biggest flour miller in California, its three mills producing a total of 3.2 million pounds (1450 tonnes) of flour per day, more than a third of California's total production.

Cargill is currently the third largest flour miller in the US behind ConAgra and ADM Milling with 18 flour mills in the US with a combined capacity of 21 million pounds (9640 tonnes) per day. Its largest mill, in Albany, New York, has a capacity of 2.2 million pounds (1000 tonnes) per 24 hours. In 1993, the company closed the 96-year-old flour mill in Buffalo where it got its start in flour milling in 1981.

A union official in one of Cargill's flour mills pointed out the advantage of flexibility that Cargill has, being commodity based, as opposed to a brand-name business like General Mills. Cargill can be flexible, milling grain for storage or moving supplies from another mill if it is faced with a strike, while General Mills has to keep its cereals on the shelves at all times. This gives Cargill more leverage with a union than General Mills can afford. The same union organizer also told me that when Cargill bought four unionized flour mills from Grand Metropolitan, it fired 51 per cent of the workers, abolished the union, then hired back 20-30 per cent of the workers it had laid off. ADM, which also bought four mills at the same time, kept the union and the workers.

Cargill's non-union strategy takes many forms, including putting all employees in a facility on salary, as indicated by the president of Cargill's flour milling division: 'The staffing of Cargill's new mill under construction at San Bernardino is an example of ... the company's commitment to what some might think is a revolutionary way of thinking. Our employees, plant and office, are all salaried.'[56]

Cargill moved laterally from flour milling into the technically similar business of rice milling in 1992 with the purchase of the assets of Comet Rice Mill in Greenville, Mississippi, from Prudential Insurance Co.[57] The Comet mill is the biggest in Mississippi and is located on the river in the heart of the delta. The plant, according to Cargill, 'is ideally situated for receiving rice from some of the most productive rice-growing areas of the country – in Arkansas, Louisiana and Mississippi.' Its barge-loading capacity gives it a distinct advantage in rice exports, since most of the 30 or so rice mills in the US are landlocked. Cargill intends to raise the mill's capacity to 125 million pounds (56,000 tonnes) over the next few years. Rice is the world's third largest grain crop after wheat and corn, and rice consumption in the US has grown steadily in recent years, though exports have been dropping[58] (see Chapter 14).

The structural process through which Cargill moved into full-scale corn dry milling illustrates the increasingly complex relationships the modern transnational corporation is prepared to engage in in order to achieve the final organizational position it desires. Cargill's first step was to create Illinois Cereal Mills Ltd as a joint venture with corn dry miller Illinois Cereal Mills Inc. (The 'Ltd' indicates that the new company is a British enterprise. 'Inc' is a North American convention.) The second step, taken in 1994, was to join with Kellogg Co. to transform Seaforth Corn Mills, of Liverpool, England, into a joint venture between Illinois Cereal Mills Ltd and Kellogg Co., which had previously been the sole owner of Seaforth, the largest corn dry miller in Europe. The third step was for Cargill to acquire 100 per cent of Illinois Cereal Mills Inc., which had previously been an employee-owned company.[59]

The result is that Cargill now owns one of the two largest corn dry millers in the world, Illinois Cereal Mills, with plants in Illinois and Indiana that have a combined grinding capacity of 86,000 bushels (2188 tonnes) per 24-hour day. Illinois Cereal Mills also owned eleven country elevators in those two states, supplying General Mills, Pillsbury and Kellogg with ingredients for cereal, corn chips and corn curls and producing a special instant corn flour for tortillas, as well as starch 'adjuncts' for the brewing industry, complementing Cargill's global malting operation, Ladish.[60]

Earlier, in 1989, Illinois Cereal Mills Inc. had tried to purchase another corn miller, Lincoln Grain, from now-defunct Elders Grain of Australia, but the deal was blocked by the US Federal Trade Commission on the grounds that it would have substantially reduced competition in the production and sale of industrial dry corn mill products in the US.[61] Why Cargill's subsequent acquisition of Illinois Cereal Mills does not reduce competition is a question that Cargill's lawyers could probably answer.

The final step, perhaps, was Cargill's internal restructuring in an effort to thoroughly digest its big meal. Cargill's Dry Milling Division now consists of flour milling, malt production, rice milling, and Cargill's pasta and flour milling operations in Venezuela. Illinois Cereal Mills, as a member of this division, is to manage Cargill's worldwide corn milling activities.

This seems to reflect other recent changes in Cargill's structure, which include doing away with its industrial sector, moving fertilizer into its agricultural sector and salt into the food sector.*

Further 'refinement' of the manufacturing and marketing of synthetic products was indicated in the 1993 report to its employees that its subsidiary, Protein Products in Cedar Rapids, Iowa, was a supplier to General Mills of bacon-flavor bits (textured vegetable protein made from soya flour, water and food coloring). As Cargill describes it, the commodity business is different from the food business, and they now see 'a natural strategic alliance evolving between Cargill and General Mills,' with Cargill supplying flour, citric acid, cocoa, salt, refined oils and poultry products to General Mills.[62]

While Cargill makes no bones about wanting full control of the businesses in which it is involved, it obviously sees merit and acceptability in strategic alliances and joint ventures such as the one with Kellogg and the other with General Mills.

---

* At the same time, Cargill Steel was created to bring Cargill's various worldwide steel enterprises together under one management structure: steel making, scrap steel recycling, steel service centres, wire products manufacturing and ferrous metals trading.

CHAPTER 4

Mechanisms of Accumulation II: Invisible Commodities

'We define ourselves increasingly as a food company ...'
Chairman Whitney MacMillan, 1990.

It used to be that companies were known by the products they bought, sold or manufactured. This is still true of Cargill, but along with the growth of its real commodity production, handling and processing activities there is a rapidly growing segment or layer of the company's business that is not only invisible to the vast majority of people around the world but which is increasingly abstract or even nonexistent. This aspect of Cargill's financial activity has become the second highest contributor to the company's overall economic performance.

Cargill shuns the word 'speculative' – at least in public – while insisting that its financial management is conservative. As if to prove the point, the term 'risk management' is used to describe the invisible transactions of its Financial Markets Division.

The basic mechanism of risk management in commodities trading, from the farmer on up, is hedging, which Cargill defines as 'the process of transferring price risk from someone who does not want such risk to someone willing to accept it.'[63] 'Every time it buys a commodity, it hedges by selling a contract to offer a like amount at some future time. When it sells the commodity, it buys the futures contract back. It is a highly conservative and safe approach from which Cargill never strays.'[64] (This may have been true when it was said of Cargill in 1978, but apparently the company's standards have slipped as the commodities in which it trades have become increasingly abstract. We will return to this shortly.)

Thus when Cargill buys a carload of real barley at price x, it sells a contract to deliver a like amount of barley at the same, or slightly higher, price at a specified future date. That is, the contract for future delivery of the commodity barley itself becomes a commodity that can be bought and sold. Whatever the fate of the real barley, Cargill knows that it can actually sell that amount of barley at a known price in the future. (As discussed in Chapter 1, Cargill has long known the value of always having access to real grain in storage.) If, meanwhile, it can get a higher price for the real barley, it will sell it, perhaps at the same time

26

redeeming (buying back) the futures contract that it had purchased earlier or purchasing more barley to maintain its position. (The commodity barley and the commodity contract-for-delivery-of-barley become equivalent – or equivalently abstract.)

Conversely, if Cargill decides to sell oats that it has in storage to Saudi Arabia because the price is right or the US Government is offering a subsidy, then at the same time it will buy a contract to take delivery of a similar amount of oats somewhere in the world at a future date for a price the same as or lower than that of the sale just made, if possible. This way it keeps itself covered and avoids undue risk at the cost of passing up undue speculative profits. The extent to which it actually follows its own advice is another issue, along with what speculative financial activities are taking place elsewhere in the corporate labyrinth.

The company is avid in promoting its expertise in risk management to farmers, telling them that:

> When it comes to marketing your crop, you can count on Cargill's experience to help you get the best return ... We offer flexible grain marketing alternatives to reduce price risk and boost profits. If you prefer, we can store your crop to help reduce your on-farm investment, and position your grain for sale.[65]

One should not misunderstand such an expression of concern for the financial welfare of farmers. It is Cargill's task to make money coming and going, that is, buying as well as selling. It positions itself in the middle while presenting itself as the farmer's business associate, if not friend. The profit opportunities resulting from such a strategy would seem to be boundless, if prudently taken in small increments.

Historically, within the capitalist sector of economic activity, trading has moved from the face-to-face buy–sell relations that most people experience in their day-to-day shopping (from village market to superstore) to trading real commodities by contract on specifications and then to trading in contracts for not-yet-existent commodities (futures). The latest level of abstraction is the 'derivative', which is one form of what are now referred to as 'financial instruments' or 'financial devices'. 'Derivatives are financial instruments whose value is tied to something else – called an "underlying" by the trade – such as equity or an indicator like interest rates.'[66]

Fortune magazine provides a very good illustration of a derivative, in this case an option, by using a story by Aristotle about a man who was gifted at reading the stars: 'Thales foresaw an abundant olive crop and used some of what little money he had to reserve exclusive use of all the local olive presses. Essentially, Thales was buying options, with the underlying being the rental rate for the presses.' When the crop was harvested, thanks to his monopoly, Thales could charge handsome fees for the use of the presses, paying out the much lower rental to the owners of the presses as negotiated earlier in the season. His only additional expense was the cost of the option itself. The contracts that are traded as derivatives are all similar to Thales' option on the use of the olive presses: 'A change in the value of the "underlying" benefits one party to the detriment of the other. The increased value of Thales' olive press option, for example, was squeezed out of the press owners, who missed the chance to charge more when demand increased, and local farmers, who had to deal with Thales' monopoly rather then competing owners of the presses.'[67]

A derivative, apparently, can be derived from anything: interest rate movements, currency exchange rates, stock market indices or mortgages. Kevin Phillips, in his book *Arrogant Capital*, describes derivatives as 'hybrid financial instruments or arrangements with a particular speculative twist.'[68]

Hybrid is an apt term in this context, since Cargill's most rewarding line of business is based on a slightly different form of hybrid, corn itself. There are hundreds and hundreds of varieties of hybrid corn on the market for farmers to choose from, but there is little real genetic difference between them. Each is more esoteric in its supposed differentiation than the one it replaced, just like the financial derivative. The simile can be taken further: a brokerage like Goldman Sachs, or a company like Cargill, can create their own hybrids. Cargill is, at one location, developing new hybrid lines of corn while, at another location, developing equally esoteric hybrids of derivatives quite possibly based on its global trade in corn. The commodity trade in corn itself also involves dealing in currency exchange rates, interest rates, and the shifting prices of the products to which corn contributes. All of this, of course, has little to do with food, despite Cargill's presentation of itself as a food company.

As wheat prices rose in the latter half of 1994, there was a reasonable inclination to attribute the rising prices to the severe drought in Australia. Experienced voices, such as the trade journal *Milling & Baking News*, however, began to wonder whether the 'perplexing price moves' might be related more to 'the needs of the fund business' than to the needs of the food business, referring to the trading activities of derivative-based mutual funds. *M&B*'s concern focused on derivatives that are meant 'to allow investors to take financial positions in commodity markets without the physical exposure,' that is, without ever actually owning any real, physical commodities. 'After all,' *M&B* editorialized, 'everything about traditional markets, including one of the first derivatives, grain futures, is meant to maintain a relationship between these markets and "physical exposure" through the delivery system.'[69]

Trading

The evolution from buying and selling real grain to trading in futures and finally derivatives is both subtle and continuous, and the largely invisible character of futures and other financial instruments means there are few discernable landmarks in the development of financial markets. It is therefore not surprising that there is no available record as to when Cargill really began its worldwide trading activities,

activities which were, by their very nature, because of the time and distance involved, speculative.

Some accounts say that Cargill opened an office in New York for offshore trading in 1922 and an office in Argentina in 1929, while other accounts report that it established its first trading office outside of the US in 1954 in Panama. Cargill did establish a Panama office in 1954 and initiated a global offensive in grain trading, aided by the passage that year of Public Law 480, the US 'Food for Peace' legislation that continues to subsidize the sale of US commodities abroad to the benefit of US agribusiness, particularly the transnational traders (see Chapter 8). It is not possible for me to believe that it was all mere coincidence.

The Panama office did not last the year (except as a tax-avoidance facility), as it very soon became obvious that communications facilities there were inadequate to support international trading activities. A new trading company was established in Winnipeg, but this too proved to be the wrong location and the business was moved to Montreal and renamed Kerrgill Company Ltd.[70] The name was coined from Kerr-Gifford and Cargill, indicating the genesis of the business, but was soon changed to Tradax Canada Ltd to reflect the non-specific geography of the new company's activities. That is, 'Canada' indicated its base of operations while 'Tradax' inferred some sort of trading.

In 1956, while it was still located in Montreal, Tradax acquired Andrew Weir (Far East) Ltd, an importer and supplier of foodstuffs that had been set up just after the war and which had been acting as agent for Tradax. This provided a receiver for the commodities shipped out of Cargill's Kerr-Gifford facilities in Oregon, which Cargill had purchased in 1953. The purchase of Kerr-Gifford provided Cargill with terminal facilities in the Vancouver area as well as the north-western US.

A decade later, in 1966, the Tradax office was moved to Geneva, Switzerland, where it supposedly remains, although the name no longer appears in Cargill publications. *Business Week* reported in 1979 that Tradax was located in Panama but that this was merely a 'letter box' tax shelter. If Tradax has vanished, or been absorbed, or been 'disappeared' to serve some devious purpose, there are lots of other departments, divisions and subsidiaries to take its place: the Financial Markets Division (FMD), Cargill Investor Services Inc. (CIS), Cargill Financial Services Corp. and names like Cargill Global Funding PLC and Cargill Financial Markets PLC which appear only in investor research reports like Dan Bosworth, Bloomberg or Standard and Poors.

It may be that only a small handful of people actually know the true structure of Cargill's financial activities and businesses, but it is not necessary to understand the structural intricacies to understand their functioning. The goal, of course, is to accumulate capital, and the more mechanisms one can invent and control for doing so, the greater the chances of success. By shifting expenses and profits from place to place, while also trading in both real nonexistent commodities such as futures and derivatives, Cargill, or any other transnational, can mystify even the best government auditors. What is given as Cargill's sales or profits for any one aspect of its business, or any national unit, like Cargill Ltd of Winnipeg, are what Cargill chooses to allocate to those categories for its own purposes. If there is a tax advantage in showing a loss somewhere, that can easily be arranged. By the same token, profits can be siphoned off through Tradax or some other division in one location or another sight unseen, or made to appear to suit corporate plans. What to one accountant may appear as a 'dividend' could just as easily appear to another as a 'management fee' or an inflated price for goods or services, particularly if the accountant in question worked for the corporation being analyzed or simply shared the same ideological orientation.

Taxation Management

Cargill's taxation management (more accurately minimization or avoidance), is a frequently-recurring issue in W.G. Broehl's history of Cargill, and he makes it quite clear that the company's structure and organization have, over the years, been strongly influenced by the pursuit of minimum tax liability. This is illustrated by the remarks of Cargill executive W.B. Saunders before the US Congress in 1976 regarding Cargill's use of foreign subsidiaries:

> Taxes are a critical cost element in our business. Unlike firms involved in manufacturing operations, commodity traders possess no unique advantages like patents, trademarks, brand franchises, technology or product superiority which enable them to absorb high tax costs. We buy/sell the same commodities, dealing with the same sellers and the same buyers. To compete on equal terms we had to seek tax costs no greater than those to established foreign-owned companies.[71]

The complex of transactions related to a simple buy–sell contract of a real commodity is nothing compared to what can be generated by trading in abstractions such as futures and, now, derivatives. As more and more emphasis is placed by the company on the activities of its financial departments, its trading activities in conventional arenas like the Chicago Board of Trade (CBOT) and the Merchantile Exchange are increasingly overshadowed by unseen electronic communications that buy and sell currencies, bonds, contracts of all sorts, and bet on interest rate movements around the world 24 hours a day. It is hardly surprising that the company had to reorganize its affairs and bring all financial trading and related activity under the umbrella of the Financial Markets Division.

The Financial Markets Division

'This business is built on the recognition that money is the ultimate commodity,' said David Rogers, president of the Financial Markets Division.[72]

The origins of the Financial Markets Division (FMD) go back to 1973 when Cargill Leasing was established to take advantage of changes in US tax laws that made it advantageous for companies to lease a wide range of equipment rather than purchase it. This advantage exists even if the owning and leasing arrangements are carried out between subsidiaries within the same company. From these beginnings, the financial trading and financial services division has become 'one of the company's most rapidly growing businesses.'[73]

> Money is indeed a commodity – a commodity that can be traded, processed and managed, subject to the same rules and risks found in other commodity markets ... Financial assets are repackaged and redistributed to add value to the products.[74]

FMD has five departments: Capital Markets, which seeks to identify securities worldwide that are 'mispriced relative to their fundamental value' and to establish trading positions that will capitalize on those mispricings; Asset Management, which provides investment and money management services for insitutional investors and high-net-worth individuals; Emerging Markets, which invests in and trades financial instruments in developing countries (this department got its start trading in Latin American debt in 1988); Merchant Banking, which identifies and invests in 'undervalued assets' which are usually restructured and resold to investors; and Leasing, which owns and leases machinery, trucks, railcars, computers and real estate and other assets – including more than 1500 trucks and 1650 trailers, aircraft (leased to United Airlines and others), locomotives and poultry processing equipment.[75]

As was reported in *Corporate Report Minnesota*:

> Cargill has 128 years of collective wisdom on how to manage risk. The proof: long-term debt at the end of fiscal 1993 amounted to just 29% of Cargill's $6.144 billion in total capital. A rock-solid balance sheet allows the FMD to borrow more cheaply than banks and to make trades banks cannot.[76]

The company trades with Wall Street firms, rather than compete against them, because it considers it cheaper to 'rent distribution' from them than to build its own network of salespeople. In terms of sourcing and intelligence gathering, on the other hand, 'few companies of any type can match Cargill's international presence, with more than 800 offices in 60 countries.' Intelligence gathering is a function of any active trading office, of course, but some of Cargill's offices around the world that are identified as trading offices are simply intelligence-gathering locations.

The Emerging Markets Department is, as the name implies, a line of business taking advantage of the particular opportunities found in the unstable economies of the Third World. Of course, Cargill never uses the term Third World, preferring instead the generic term 'geographies'. The Emerging Markets Department attributes its growth 'to its ability to identify trends, find solutions to market barriers, creatively develop trading positions and capitalize on inefficient markets.'[77]

'Like other Cargill businesses, FMD acts opportunistically,' reports the same issue of *Cargill News*, and the Department foresees many future opportunities in the continued growth of 'emerging geographies,' which were identified in a 1994 survey of 1000 global companies, by rank, as: China, India, Indonesia, Mexico, Thailand, Brazil, Malaysia, Argentina, Hong Kong and Taiwan.[78] Cargill has the advantage, when entering a new country, of being viewed not 'as an American investment bank,' according to *Cargill News*, but 'as an international company,' the inference being that the presence of such a company brings some benefits for the host country rather than just the opportunity for it to extract wealth.

Cargill now considers trading in the financial instruments called 'derivatives' one of its 'core competencies' and at the end of fiscal 1993, $3.8 billion of Cargill's $15.9 billion in total assets were in financial instruments.

Identifying and utilizing its 'core competences' explains another common Cargill practice: taking what works in one place and applying it in another. Cargill's Nutrena feed division, for example, will source and price feed components much the way the FMD will source and price financial instruments to turn out a marketable and profitable product.

The first real 'product' of Cargill's FMD, which provided nearly one third of Cargill's $358 million in earnings in 1993, is the Minnetonka Fund, which invests money for dozens of wealthy clients who can put down the $5 million minimum investment it takes to get into the pool. The Minnetonka Fund is described by Cargill as 'a hedge fund where, in about 90 per cent of transactions, each investment in an undervalued security is balanced by the sale of a previous investment that has gone up in value. By buying relatively low and selling relatively high for each transaction, the fund tends to perform well independent of the ups and downs of the market.'[79]

The fund reportedly (though not reported by the company itself, as discussed in Chapter 1) lost about $100 million of its $420 million value when interest rates rose in March 1994, derailing a strategy based on derivitives of mortgage-backed securities. Mari Kooi, president of Cargill Asset Management, a unit of Cargill's FMD, assured investors that Cargill would provide the Minnetonka fund with the necessary money to keep it operating through the end of the year, which turned out to be the company's most profitable year ever (net profit of $571 million), in spite of the loss.

Derivatives have been given prominent coverage in the financial and business press since major losses were reported in the spring of 1994 after the US Federal Reserve Bank raised interest rates abruptly as a move to cool what it perceived as inflationary pressures. While immense losses had been experienced by a few other companies, it took a $157 million loss by Procter & Gamble to make the news. Then it was reported that others, including Cargill, had also made substantial losses in their speculative trading in derivatives.

Cargill's response to its speculative loss was in keeping with its public ideology. When its so-called risk management strategy failed, it apparently swallowed hard and adjusted accordingly. Procter & Gamble, on the other hand, after brooding for a while, sued Bankers Trust New York Corp., the company that had sold the derivatives to them, for $130 million plus punitive damages. Procter & Gamble claimed that Bankers Trust had deceived it by not explaining the nature of the risks inherent in a derivative. But P&G, by admitting that it did not know what it was doing, has exposed itself to being sued by its own shareholders for mismanagement.

The losses incurred by P&G, Cargill and others, however, are only minor bruises compared to the lumps taken by other TNCs, money managers and speculators, and national treasuries. George Soros, for example, is regarded 'with awe,' according to *Forbes* magazine, 'as the man who "broke" the British pound, forcing the UK out of the European exchange rate mechanism in 1992,' making $1 billion for himself in the process. Two years later Soros lost $600 million betting against the Japanese yen.[80] What Soros wrung out of the British Treasury for his personal gain of course added to the British national debt. At a time when social programs are being harshly attacked as the cause of national indebtedness, it is odd how such speculative practices are overlooked. TNCs such as Cargill are expert (through consultants and PR firms) at directing public attention away from derivatives speculators.

Cargill Investor Services (CIS), founded in 1972 and one of Cargill's more invisible lines of business, was designed to capitalize on the communications and trading facilities developed for the corporation's own internal use by charging a commission on investment services provided by CIS to outside clients. The first CIS office outside the US was opened in Geneva in 1980, and there are now offices in Geneva, Hong Kong, Kansas City, London, Minneapolis, New York, Paris, Sydney, Taipei and Tokyo. 'For our customers who trade in global markets, CIS offers capabilities that are accessible 24 hours a day to handle electronic markets, EFPs, cash forex [foreign exchange] and all international trades,' advised a Cargill advertisement. 'There are few firms who have the global reach of CIS, our policy of no proprietary trading [trading on Cargill's own account], our parent's financial strength, our breadth of market coverage.'[81]

> CIS strives to manage change by achieving a careful balance between discipline and innovation ... We service a diverse group, including multinational corporations, money center banks, energy suppliers, agribusiness companies, fund and portfolio managers, investment banking firms, professional traders and mid-sized hedgers. Yet, what attracts contemporary users of futures and options markets to CIS is the need to simplify and consolidate the complex fragments of their trading activity across markets, products and geographies.[82]

CIS takes advantage, for profit, of the new markets emerging around the globe that bring with them 'the volatility and opportunity that result from the presence of political and economic uncertainty.'[83]

The activities pursued by Cargill's financial operations are in no way unique, and while billed as capital formation or risk management, when put into the larger picture of global finance in the 1990s, these activities contribute to national indebtedness and the polarization of wealth and deprivation.

The rise of global financial markets makes it increasingly difficult for national governments to formulate economic policy, much less to enforce it ... The exchange of one currency for another, according to estimates of the Bank of International Settlements, is now about $640 billion a day.[84]

By the mid-1990s, the bond market – and the overall financial sector – had become a powerful usurper of control over economic policy previously exercised by ... elected officeholders ... By the 1990s, through a 24-hour-a-day cascade of electronic hedging and speculating, the financial sector had swollen to an annual volume of trading thirty or forty times greater than the dollar turnover of the 'real economy'.[85]

Phillips adds a note to the above which is a useful caveat to my use of the terms 'trading' or 'trader' herein: 'There is no longer an easy definition of "trading." The extent to which it now occurs in so many exotic forms explains why "trading" involves a dollar turnover 30 to 40 times the size of the so-called real economy.'[86] In fact, from Cargill's very beginning there has been an element of this amplification of trading activity through speculative 'risk management.' It has taken on a whole new character, however, with the advent of electronic communications and the 24-hour global market.

It is difficult to comprehend the ramifications of this electronic speculative – what Phillips refers to as 'spectronic' – trading. In fact, I dare say that no-one really does. Considering Cargill alone, one has to wonder what the ratio is between the real economy of the goods and commodities traded and processed and the nonexistent financial transactions in Cargill's year-end results. Phillips reports figures that I heard several years ago in the offices of the Canadian Wheat Board about the amount of money that now moves electronically around the globe non-stop: 'McKinsey and Company has estimated that of the $800 billion or so traded every day in the world's currency markets in the early 1990s, only $20 billion to $25 billion was exchanged in support of global trade in goods and services.'[87] The real economy that defines the day-to-day options of the vast majority of people pales against the shadowy achievements of finance. Phillips refers to the speculative overburden as 'financialization' which has 'only a vague definition' yet causes firms that were once committed to long-term thinking facing 'money managers and speculators little concerned about existence beyond the life of a futures contract.'[88] The outcome of this mentality has been a decline in real wages, the erosion of communities and the decay of infrastructure while executive compensation packages have 'roared off into the stratosphere.'

To its credit, it appears that Cargill is still committed to the real economy, to providing real goods and services, and even to providing real wages, however limited. Whether it will remain so is another question, given the at least apparent profitability of hedges, futures, and derivatives – even if you drop $100 million once in a while!*

---

* One way to compensate for such unforeseen expenses is to use the leverage of size to reduce the cost of services. In 1992, for example, Cargill consolidated its worldwide business travel and corporate card programs under American Express Travel Management Services, with expected savings of $1.2 million in the first year. Since travel agencies collect a 10 per cent commission on each ticket they book, a high-volume business like Cargill can use its leverage to negotiate a refund of some of that 10 per cent. Thus part of Cargill's $130 million worldwide annual expenditure in air fares and related expenses will now come back to the company in the form of 'revenue sharing'. (CN: February 93, ST: 27 April 94)

CHAPTER 5

Origins, Organization and Ownership

Origins

The official histories give 1865 as the founding year for Cargill Inc., but Duncan MacMillan, in his family history, writes that it was in 1867 that W.W. Cargill started in business for himself in Iowa and two years later when he and his brother Sam formed W.W. Cargill and Brother. They built grain elevators along the railways in Minnesota and Wisconsin and after the financial panic of 1873 the brothers took advantage of the opportunity to buy up properties cheaply, a practice that became fundamental Cargill strategy. They entered into partnerships with others, a pragmatic practice that the company contines to exploit, to trade in commodities other than grain, such as wool and hogs, and they traded in chickens 'by the carload.'

Cargill and partners were soon also buying land, and, as Duncan MacMillan tells it, by the end of 1879 the Cargill & Van partnership farm had become a small village, with 1000 sheep, 300 hogs, horses and small stock. W.W. Cargill also began experimenting with seed breeding. This was half a century before the invention of modern hybrid corn.

By 1881 the Cargill brothers, Will, Sam and Jim, were in business as Cargill Brothers and the partnerships with outsiders were ended. They began a period of rapid expansion to the north up the Red River Valley, and to the northwest. In 1884 the Cargills moved their office to Minneapolis, which was fast becoming the grain milling centre of the country.

LaCross, Wisconsin, was home for the Cargill family for a time, and just across the road lived Duncan McMillan and his family. The McMillan clan had made their initial fortune in logging and lumber milling. In 1895 Edna, eldest daughter of W.W. Cargill, married John MacMillan, son of Duncan McMillan (the spelling of the family name changed at that point).

The last years of the nineteenth century and the first decade of the twentieth were tumultuous and nearly disastrous for the Cargill businesses. Will Cargill, son of W.W., had become involved in some ambitious land development schemes in Montana that siphoned funds through his hands without the full realization of the families, leaving the entire dynasty on the verge of bankruptcy. The truth came to light in 1909 when Will Cargill died rather suddenly. In classic manner, the creditors descended, hoping to recover at least some of what they had invested or loaned. Most of the assets, however, were not liquid, leaving creditors with the choice of sticking it out or forcing the liquidation of the Cargill companies. Fortunately for the Cargills, John McMillan Sr., who was already deeply involved in the businesses, had just extended his personal credit resources and was able to convince the creditors that it would be better in the long run for them to stay with the company, under his leadership, than to force its collapse.

The history of the company since then has been one of relentless, though at times jerky, growth. Mistakes have been made, but Cargill as a company has developed great skill at knowing when to make a strategic retreat and when to stand fast.

In the late 1930s when the grain fields turned into the Dust Bowl, the company bought up all the corn futures on the Chicago Board of Trade (CBOT) and was charged by Secretary of Agriculture Henry Wallace with trying to corner the market. Cargill pleaded innocent, of course, but was nevertheless suspended from the CBOT. The affair dragged on for three years until 1940, 'when Cargill was allowed to plead not guilty, in return for the denial of the trading privileges on the CBOT of Cargill Grain Co. of Illinois and of John H. MacMillan. Everyone knew that MacMillan did not trade personally and that the Cargill Grain Co. of Illinois was being liquidated.'[89] In other words, a deal was made and business was carried on as usual.

Cargill Inc. fared well during World War II, enjoying government contracts for shipbuilding and grain storage and delivery, and serving the needs of agriculture. 'The Chase National Bank ... complimented the Company in the spring of 1945 on its strong financial position: "The working capital has been more than doubled since May of 1941 – a real accomplishment from which you should derive much satisfaction".'[90]

W.G. Broehl makes it abundantly clear that there have been, at times, difficult internal debates over corporate structure and leadership. This became a major preoccupation again at the end of the turbulent 1980s as it became clear that the company had to be restructured in order to successfully stay on top of its diverse and evolving worldwide business activities and that the ownership structure had to be altered to accommodate the diverging interests of the family owners.

Restructuring

The North American Organization Project (NAOP) was formed in 1990 after Whitney MacMillan had convened a group of 50 managers to talk about their corporate vision and their strategy for the future. They also had to decide how to bring Cargill's North American businesses into line with the way the company's other worldwide businesses were managed – what they call a 'soft matrix' of both 'product line and geography management.'

The outcome, two years later, was a decision to form the Corporate Center, composed of senior management, to concentrate on strategy, asset allocation and personnel decisions, leaving operating decisions to the next level of management, the 'geographies'.[91]

The restructuring was motivated by the realization that personal relations, information-sharing and decision-making capacities were all at risk of being swamped by the company's growth and diversity.

'Twenty years ago most of the decisions in this corporation were made down at the coffee table,' explained Cargill president Heinz Hutter. 'People met every day there and met every day for lunch in the dining room. That's the way information was shared, and everyone knew what was going on. Well, we're too big for that now.'[92]

The basic enterprise that Cargill began with, and pretty much stuck with until the 1930s, was trading, transporting and storing grain and other commodities, commodities being really any bulk material that could be handled as dry generic (undifferentiated) cargo. As it began to move upstream into seeds, fertilizers and feeds, and downstream into milling and processing, and then into a broader and broader range of commodities and products, the centralized structure of the organization was constantly under stress.

It must have been the magnitude of the 1992 restructuring that caused Cargill to have the key trade journal *Milling & Baking News* carry an unusually long story about it. I think it likely that Cargill felt it had to reassure its many customers and competitors that it was not restructuring as a consequence of some form of ill-health or mismanagement, but that it would continue to perform according to its stated goal of doubling the size of the corporation, meaning its equity, every five to seven years. (The company's equity was valued at $4.1 billion in 1992 according to the interpretation of the shares tendered by the family members at the time. See below.)

The major aspect of the restructuring was the designation of North America (including Canada and the US, at least, although neither Canada nor Mexico are ever mentioned) as a 'geography' on a par with the other geographies of Europe, South America, Southeast Asia and North Asia. These are the principal regions within which the company does business, but the business is carried out along product lines as well. The product line and the geography together determine the 'matrix' of activity.

Of course, it is not that simple, because designating North America as a geography carried with it the creation of the Corporate Centre with its responsibility to establish the vision and goals for Cargill on a worldwide basis. 'We want to do less controlling and more strategizing about future directions,' said Whitney MacMillan.[93] He added that Cargill had been 'too inclined to want to measure everything, when we ought to look at something as a continuous belt without focusing on each minute step.'

Interestingly, Cargill's arch-competitor Archer Daniels Midland (ADM) uses a similar imagery in describing how corn processing yields 'an enormous river of dextrose' that flows between the farm and the final products. ADM chairman Dwayne Andreas also describes his very complex company as a 'single business' with the result that 'the increasing complexity of operations makes it more difficult than ever to accurately separate profits and losses of various raw materials from one another. We make arbitrary decisions ... Many costs ... are arbitrarily allocated.'[94]

In other words, ADM, like Cargill, has reached a stage where it is no longer reasonable to speak of isolated 'profit centres' or even 'product lines' and where corporate welfare as a whole supersedes the accounting of its parts.

To end the confusion between Cargill the global corporation and Cargill the North American business (which accounts for more than half the corporation's net worth), the company made another structural change, creating a new Cargill Grain Division (CGD) to replace the old Commodity Marketing Division. The CGD is now the primary source of grains and oilseeds in North America for both domestic and export customers, including its own corn milling, flour milling and oilseed processing. In practice, this means that instead of various Cargill locations competing for the same grains or oilseeds, CGD will make a single bid for each commodity in specific originating locations. This will put an end to 'transfer pricing' between competing Cargill entities. 'The market will rule' is the way this is described.

Rather than acknowledge this as centralized monopoly bidding, the company interprets it to mean that 'merchandisers and product line managers at decentralized locations will be empowered to purchase grain when it is offered at market prices.'[95] Cargill also contends that suppliers (farmers and other) find advantages in dealing with only one buyer who bids 'at the market'.

Cargill may think of this as empowering local managers, but it also explains why local managers have two satellite dishes: one to receive prices from the Chicago futures market, the other to receive orders from Cargill headquarters in Minneapolis. The local managers may be held responsible for their decisions on buying and selling, but the rules they play by are clearly determined moment by moment by the central authority. Marx would love the contradiction.

Another matrix in Cargill's new structure is the trading room itself at Cargill's headquarters. There the three product line heads – food grains, feed grains and oilseeds – sit in one central area with their staffs fanning out around them. This is a good illustration of the attention Cargill pays to communications of every sort, from the face-to-face to the instantaneous global electronic.

In effect, Cargill has now returned to the centralized structure it had before the great explosion of grain trading in 1972–3 and the period of decentralization which followed. Perhaps in the 1970s and 1980s it was simply not possible technically (or technologically) to centralize the burgeoning trade in commodities, but now electronic communications make it a relatively simple matter.

It is, however, more than that. The number of large traders has been greatly diminished and the power of the remaining few magnified accordingly. There are no longer many buyers and sellers, and the few left do not really wish to compete, either intentionally or by accident; Cargill's bid may be the only one at a particular location on any particular day; and a single buyer for a large quantity can exercise considerable leverage on the market. Pity those who believe the propaganda of 'competition'.

The Commodity Marketing Division was not the only piece of the company to be restructured. Cargill's worldwide marketing of all meat and fish products was brought together in a single business unit and is now handled in the same way as oilseed processing and corn milling. This makes their slogan about global sourcing into a concrete reality. Cargill does not simply have Plant A ship x amount of its product to Customer B. If the product of the moment is manufacturing beef for Canadian hamburger fabricators, it might come from a Cargill plant in Australia, the United States or even in Canada itself, depending on local market conditions, what's in the cooler, and transportation logistics at the time.

The new 34-person Corporate Centre, with its responsibility to provide vision and leadership for the company's worldwide operations and corporate strategy, consists of 'senior line managers and five core corporate functions, plus support staff.' One aspect of its mission is to 'manage key constituencies to help shape an environment in which Cargill can prosper.'[96]

When interviewed by *Milling & Baking News* about the company restructuring, CEO Whitney MacMillan stated that: 'There are just too many opportunities within our existing competencies to see any need for a significant change in [corporate] direction.' He said there were three paths that can take the company in its chosen direction: transferring existing competencies to geographies where the company is not currently active; finding other businesses where existing competencies could be applied and where Cargill has an advantage; and moving up the food chain 'at the margin.'[97]

MacMillan used seed corn as an example of the company going outside its core competencies (many years ago at a time when it was strictly a grain trader) to become the leader outside the United States (apparently suggesting that Cargill's sales of seed corn outside of North America surpass those of industry giant Pioneer Hi-bred). It did this, he said, because of seed corn's unique role in providing 'a beachhead to enter developing countries where we might have been unwilling to operate under normal circumstances but where, with seed corn, we can establish a presence.'[98]

As part of its global restructuring, and an indication of new directions for corporate expansion, in 1994 Cargill created a Specialty Plants Products Department for customers who have particular requirements, such as what are now being referred to as 'identity preserved' crops that have special characteristics specified by the end user. These crops include popcorn, organic grains, grains with specific baking characteristics, and oilseeds yielding an oil with particular cooking qualities. Some of these specialty crops are being created through genetic engineering.

These crops are obviously grown from special seed, but that is only the beginning. They have to be identified and kept isolated from planting through harvest and delivery to the end user, including any processing required. In a way, handling these crops is very much like handling grain in the days before the futures market and the commodity exchange, when grain was bought and sold on the basis of actual samples. In the case of identity-preserved crops, speculation is excluded, or held to very narrow margins, by the nature of the commodity and its ownersip. In some cases, the end user, such as Procter & Gamble, specifies the characteristics desired, in a cooking oil, for example, and contracts with a seed company to create (genetically engineer) an oilseed that produces such a product. The seed company then contracts with farmers to multiply the new seed variety to produce enough seed for commercial production of the crop. Then the seed company sells the seed to farmers who grow the crop under contract to the processor that requested the oilseed in the first place. The end user thus owns the seed and its product from beginning to end.

In Nebraska Cargill contracts corn production for Quaker Oats; Cargill supplies the farmers with its own proprietary seed and other inputs, with Cargill perhaps supplying the credit as well, and the crop goes directly to Quaker Oats when harvested.

A Major 'Position': Cargill PLC

Cargill's operation in the UK (Cargill PLC) is one of the corporation's 'major positions' in its current structure, and it provides a good thumbnail sketch of the company's integrated diversity. (In 1992 Cargill had what it called 'major positions' outside the United States in the Netherlands, Canada, Britain and Brazil in addition to the UK. None of them, however, constituted more than 10 per cent of the corporation's business.)

A 1991 handout describes Cargill PLC, with 500 employees in the UK, as active in agriculture merchanting [sic] and commodity trading; oilseeds, starch and glucose processing; molasses distribution; and further-processed poultry. The company is also a supplier of seed, fertilizer and chemicals to British farmers as well as feed grains and non-grain feed ingredients, such as citrus and corn gluten pellets, cotton by-products and soybean meal, according to the handout.

Cargill's UK operations got a big boost when it bought United Agricultural Merchants from Unilever, with its 20 supply depots, in 1990. Cargill said it intended to use the distribution system primarily for seed and fertilizer. The acquisition put Cargill in third place among farm supply companies in the UK.

When Cargill PLC moved out of downtown London and opened a brand new office in the Surrey countryside 20 miles to the south in 1991, it left Cargill Investor Services behind in the middle of London's financial district. Company literature describes CIS as 'a futures and options broker and risk management consultant that is part of the CIS worldwide group.'

Cargill PLC's new 41,000 square foot building in Surrey, set in '50 acres of prime green belt,' has cables laid under the floor to provide more than 600 points for computer and communications hook-ups. A new fiber-optics system cuts the cost of international calls by 40 per cent.[99] The Surrey office pays special attention to trading in cocoa, coffee, rubber and molasses and houses the Financial Marketing Division and the Commodity Marketing Division.

Not surprisingly, given the colonial history of its host country, Cargill PLC has an Africa Division with offices and facilities located in Ethiopia, Kenya, Malawi, Nigeria, Tanzania and Zimbabwe. The activities of this division include hybrid corn (maize) production and research, cotton ginning, oil milling and commodity trading. A long article on styles of corporate management in Africa recently described the way Cargill deals with an alien culture and indentures its farmers to the corporation: Cargill and other multinational agricultural companies provide farmers with financing but require them to have a bank account through which monthly loan payments are remitted automatically to the lender.[100]

Other Cargill PLC divisions are: Intermol, a leading liquid molasses-based feed company; the Malt Division; the Milling Division, which is one the UK's largest corn processors; and the Oilseeds Processing Division, which operates twelve rapeseed and soybean crushing plants and seven refineries in Belgium, France, Holland and Spain as well as the UK. Finally, there is Cargill Technical Services, located in Oxfordshire, which provides:

> management and technical services in economics and marketing, agriculture and rural development and agro-business internationally, [and] is particularly well-suited to developing countries. CTS serves a broad client base, including international development and aid agencies, governments and private companies, and it includes the British Cotton Growing Association.

Ownership

As already mentioned, a change in ownership structure accompanied the internal corporate restructuring (NAOP) – or perhaps it was the other way around, with the need for changing the ownership structure seen as a good opportunity to reorganize.

In 1986 it was reported that Cargill's $2.6 billion in shareholder equity was was held by fewer than 50 descendents of the Cargills and MacMillans, and 450 others, all current members of the company's management, who received about $10 million a year in dividends.[101] In 1992 *Fortune* magazine reported net worth (or shareholders' equity) of the company as $3.6 billion as a result of 'a compound annual rate of growth of 12.2 per cent over the past 50 years.'[102]

Such a concentration of ownership not only results in huge rewards to the very limited number of owners, but also creates a very unusual kind of problem: what are the family members to do with all this money? The logical, and indeed capitalist, response is: 'invest it.' This is the basic reason that Cargill can boast, as it does in almost every country in which it does business, that it reinvests its profits in the country in which it makes them. (I think it actually does essentially this, but there is absolutely no way of knowing the real truth of the matter, as I have indicated elsewhere.) In fact, Cargill says that since 1981 it has reinvested 87 per cent of its cash flow, with only 3 per cent of the company's profits being paid out in dividends. That kind of liquidity provides an awful lot of leverage, particularly when coupled with Cargill's somewhat unusual habit of using its capital to expand or enter into depressed commodity businesses.

This structure also created a problem. What happens if a member of the Cargill-MacMillan clan decides that they really do not need any more money and wishes to bail out? There was no mechanism in place whereby they could receive cash instead of more equity in the company. When senior executive Dwayne Andreas left in the 1950s, his interest had to be bought out by the company, but there was no formal way of doing this and no book value to go by. (In Andreas' case, he actually did have shares in a Cargill subsidiary which could be redeemed, though at a somewhat arbitrary price.)

Cargill finally dealt with this by hiring a team of consultants to come up with a form of Employee Share Ownership Plan (ESOP) for the company that would ensure the security of corporate information, ensure that the corporation would or could never go public, and provide an escape or equity redemption program for family members and, subsequently, senior managers.

In 1992–3 Cargill successfully initiated the resulting plan by inviting family members to offer their 'shares' of the company for redemption. As it turned out, 'Family members tendered 17 per cent of their shares for $730.5 million, or an average of $8.3 million per family member.'[103] Reports at the time indicated that, 'Ownership ranks rose from fewer than 90 family members to nearly 20,000,' but this is misleading because while the family members turned over ownership rights to 17 per cent of the company, this equity remained in the hands of the board of directors, held in trust for employees in the ESOP. At the time, 7800 hourly employees and 12,000 salaried employees were eligible to participate in the ESOP.

In other words, the family still controls the company.

At this point, *Fortune* magazine estimates the wealth of the three MacMillan family members at $2.1 billion, representing 8 per cent of Cargill Inc. (They are: Cargill MacMillan Jr., 66; Whitney MacMillan, 63 and Pauline MacMillan Keinath, 58.)[104]

Forbes' 1994 listing[105] of the wealthiest families in the US contained eight branches of the Cargill-MacMillan clan, assigned family values of $1.7 billion each.*

---

* One of the outcomes of the buyout of some of the Cargill heirs may have been the formation in 1993 of Cargill Communications Inc. by James Cargill (44) and his wife Susan. Possibly reflecting the Cargill tradition of sophisticated utilization of communications technology, they have invested some $5.6 million in a broadcast group and a 24-hour alternative rock music syndication from their Minneapolis base. They also have an in-house ad agency, Creative Services Network, and are looking at other activities such as graphic design and television production. (ST: 21 November 93, City Pages, Mpls, 4 May 94)

A 'Core Competency' Embodied

A successful corporation such as Cargill has to have capable leadership. Imagination, flexibility and resourcefulness have to be combined with an ability to see the big picture – or at least Cargill's big picture. I have met a number of these people, as well as some who do not meet these criteria. I have not met Juels Carlson, but the accounts of his activities offer a good example of Cargill leadership.

Carlson began his career with Cargill in 1965 and worked his way through a variety of positions before moving in 1981 to Geneva, Switzerland, to become manager of the Oils, Oilseeds & Meals Department of Cargill subsidiary Tradax Gestion, SA. From there he went to Tradax in Tokyo in 1983 as manager for Japan, South Korea and Taiwan.* From 1985 to 1990 Carlson was president of Cargill North Asia Ltd and in 1990 became country manager in the Commonwealth of Independent States during the disintegration of the former Soviet political system. Carlson returned to Minnesota in 1992 to become vice president of Cargill Investor Services' Minneapolis regional office.[106]

Cargill's philosophy in entering new markets, such as Russia, is one of extreme caution, and Carlson's mission there was to find something that would suit Cargill. As Cargill's vice chairman at the time, William Pearce, put it, 'We tend to go into businesses that we learned to do well and into areas in which those kinds of skills are needed. We start slowly and learn as we go, from a small base.'

The two projects Carlson focused on and began researching were a small sunflower oilseed processing plant and a hybrid corn seed producing and processing plant that would grow and package seed for local farmers that would double their crop yields.[107] As I discovered, these are the same two crops with which Cargill established its beachhead in India (see Chapter 17). In other words, in establishing a beachhead, both a product and a salesman are required.

---

* See Chapter 14 for more on Carlson's role there.

CHAPTER 6

Transportation and Storage

The development of modern transportation, storage and handling systems has made it possible to move huge quantities of foodstuffs great distances ... Technologically ... it has become possible to depend upon distant food supplies to meet a growing proportion of both basic needs and dietary improvements.

Robbin Johnson, vice president, public affairs[108]

The development of 'modern transportation, storage and handling systems' is a Cargill specialty and a reflection of how the company views the world. Being able to 'source' commodities at will, transport them efficiently to any destination, and deliver them reliably is not only a profitable business in itself; it is also a way of gaining leverage or advantage in the market.

To source, transport and deliver bulk commodities globally, however, requires a rather special view of the world, a view one can only adequately get from a satellite in outer space. Cargill did not, however, start with the satellite view. It started with the economics of water transport and a creative imagination.

A conventional map of North America, for example, displays two coastlines, one on the east and one on the west, and two borders, a long one to the north and a much shorter one to the south. Very few maps reveal the signficance of inland water routes (rivers) and ports, and virtually all distort ecological and geographic reality by imposing political jurisdictions in different colours. W.W. Cargill's successors had the good sense to ignore the political jurisdictions and pay much more attention to water, always by far the cheapest means of transporting bulk commodities.

Since Cargill is most highly developed in North America, we can focus on North America to gain an understanding of Cargill's strategic approach to geography and transportation. Before proceeding with that, however, we must add one other element to the picture. Storage plays an unglamorous but vital role in both the transportation and trading of grains.

Storage

Storage capacity is obviously essential to an effective delivery system. It takes many truckloads to fill one railcar, and many railcars to fill one ship, and transhipping facilities, or terminals, have to have the capacity to store enough truckloads or train loads to fill a unit train or a ship at one go, not over a week or two. Storage capacity, like the reservoir behind a dam, gives the transportation system elasticity and power.

Storage capacity also provides the ability to deliver on demand, or to withhold from market, both of which are essential to successful grain trading. The amount of leverage a company can have on the market, or in negotiations, is in direct relation to its ability to supply at favorable prices or to sit out low prices. This is crucial to the strength of one's hand in playing the futures market. The greater your reserves, the more you can play safely, or at least wittingly. There are overhead charges, of course, but if much of the storage capacity is considered a cost as part of the transportation system, or has been largely paid for by publicly owned port authorities or under one government program or another, the major cost of storage is that of the grain itself. A company may not use all the storage capacity it has, but it is the capacity itself, not necessarily its maximum usage, that provides the financial leverage in dealing in both real, visible grain and in futures contracts for invisible or even nonexistent grain. Grain can materialize, if necessary, before the future contract has to be supplied.

Because it has the storage capacity, Cargill can take advantage of it for speculative purposes. This may explain why Cargill places so much emphasis on the futures market, and expends so much energy propagandizing farmers to use the futures market to maximize their returns. There is a difference in the strength of the players, however. The individual farmer can play this game only within the very strict limits of the crop he or she actually has to sell. And while the farmers may get a higher return by hedging on the futures market, Cargill will still be using that grain for its own speculative purposes.

While Cargill tries to give the impression that its way of doing business is the only one possible, there are alternatives, among them the pooling of grains and single-desk selling characteristic of the Australian and Canadian Wheat Boards. These organizations pool individual farmers' grain to accumulate enough to play in the same league as the Cargills and ADMs. The Wheat Boards also have the choice of staying out of the futures market altogether simply by selling all the grain they are responsible for through negotiation of prices and conditions, such as grade, time of delivery, form of payment, etc. Since this deprives the private traders of large quantities of grain for speculative purposes, the companies expend considerable energy trying to destroy these Wheat Boards.

Cargill's speculative activity is not confined to grains. There is a big futures market in all forms of livestock and livestock products, one of the more well-

Map 1 Major North American bulk transport waterways

known, of course, being 'pork bellies'; Cargill is deeply involved in that market on its own and as an aspect of its livestock operations.

IBP, the largest meat packer in the US and considerably larger than Cargill in this line, has a very different attitude. Not only is IBP 'the most highly focused in the business,'[109] it also stays almost entirely out of the futures market:

> IBP's trading is small because it says it fears the futures market. Chairman Peterson has publicly voiced his dislike of futures. In a 1990 interview with *Cattle Buyers Weekly*, he was sharply critical of the futures' influence on the cash markets.[110]

At the end of 1993 Cargill was still the largest grain company in the US as measured by total grain storage capacity. Second to Cargill was Archer Daniels Midland (ADM) with Continental Grain Co. third, Bunge Corp. fourth, and Peavey Co., a ConAgra subsidiary, fifth.

Whether Cargill will retain its number one ranking is another question. In 1994 ADM reached an agreement with tenth-placed Louis Dreyfus Corp. to assume 'operational control' of most US grain elevators owned by Dreyfus. This will push ADM ahead of Cargill in total capacity, an achievement ADM announced with some glee. It is worth noting that the top two are now very close together, the next three are fairly close together, then there is a considerable gap between number five and number six, the Saskatchewan Wheat Pool. So it is reasonable to say that the trade is controlled, or at least dominated, by an oligopoly of the top five companies.

The *Grain & Milling Annual* for 1994 listed Cargill as having 204 grain storage facilities in the US with a total capacity of 351.7 million bushels; 14 port facilities; 19 river facilities; and eight terminals in North America.

Transportation Systems

Looking at North America as Cargill and the ecologically minded do, one first of all sees that North America really has four coastlines. In addition to the obvious ones on the east and west sides, there is a third, the 3200 km long Mississippi River (6400 km including tributaries) running down the middle of the country, right through the corn and grain heartland, and the fourth, the Great Lakes-St Lawrence River complex running eastward from the centre of the continent. (Cargill actually refers to the St Lawrence Seaway as a 'Fourth Coastline' in its *Bulletin*.)

In the east and the northwest there are also deep-water arteries; the Hudson River in New York state and the 4800 km Snake and Columbia Rivers system in Oregon and Washington states. All of these waterways lie completely within the territory of the US, except for the St Lawrence River and its seaway, and all except the St Lawrence are maintained at public expense, which makes them doubly attractive as transportation routes to a company like Cargill. The St

Lawrence Seaway relies much more on ever higher toll charges, making it an increasingly costly route for the shippers.

Maintenance of inland and coastal waterways in the US, including construction and maintenance of locks, dredging, navigational aids and charting, have been the responsibility of the US Army Corps of Engineers since the passing of the Rivers and Harbours Act of 1824. The cost is both substantial and highly volatile because the choice of projects undertaken by the Corps of Engineers is subject to a great deal of political pressure and patronage: Government appropriations for maintenance of the 11,000-mile system of interconnected commercially navigable rivers in eastern and central US were $16 billion in 1986, $1.6 billion in 1988 and $3.9 billion in 1990.*

While Cargill has always been a staunch advocate of the so-called free market and decried government restriction or interference, it has at the same time always been more than willing to have the public bear as much as possible of the costs of the infrastructure it wishes to exploit. For example, in addition to maintenance of the water routes it uses, many of the port facilities leased or owned by Cargill, from piers to terminal elevators, have been built at public expense by local, regional or state agencies. Water and road access to these facilities is also a public expense.

For a company frugal with its capital, but careful to insist on control, a long-term lease can provide the same kind of private control as outright ownership. Where there are no useful public facilities to exploit, as in Santos, Brazil, or in Kandla Port, India, Cargill is, however, prepared to go so far as to build its own port.

Until the 1930s, Cargill was, as it has said, 'a regional grain merchandiser' with its activities confined primarily to the United States interior. Inland water routes such as the Great Lakes, the Mississippi River and the Erie Canal (the New York State Barge Canal, which had been rebuilt and reopened in 1918), were used where possible for domestic distribution.

When the Hudson River was dredged to a depth of 27 feet in 1931, all of a sudden Albany, 143 miles up the river from New York City, had the opportunity to become a deep-water port. When Cargill got word that the Albany Port Commission was considering the construction of a terminal elevator, John H. MacMillan hastened to propose that the Commission construct, at a cost of $1.5 million, the world's largest terminal elevator, with a capacity of 13 million bushels (353,800 tonnes). MacMillan promised that Cargill would lease the facility long-term if the Port Commission would copy, on a smaller scale, the company's recently completed elevator at Omaha, including the suspended (cantilever) roof.

The Albany elevator was completed in 1932, leased to Cargill Grain Company, and Albany became the preferred destination for Cargill's grain being shipped

---

* For an almost unbelievable chronicle of the politics of water in the US, see Marc Reisner, *Cadillac Desert – The American West and its Disappearing Water*, Viking Penguin, 1986.

east. Grain movement by barge through the canal to Albany might be considerably slower than by rail, but the net cost was lower.[111]

The flexibility and value of the Albany location became even greater when Cargill acquired its own trucks in the mid-1930s and began delivering grain throughout New England. Although the Erie Canal was outgrown and replaced by railroads in the late 1930s, the Port of Albany continued to handle large amounts of grain, particularly corn, from the midwest for export. The Albany terminal today is capable of receiving 100-car unit-trains from the midwest, the grain taking as little as four days to reach the terminal from the farm.

With the success of the Albany terminal, Cargill began to look more seriously at the potential of the Mississippi River, entering into discussions with authorities in St Louis and Memphis about sites for terminal elevators. Memphis won the bidding for Cargill's business when the Memphis Harbour Commission agreed in 1935 to build a terminal, with Public Works Administration (federal government) funds, according to Cargill's specifications – 'Cargill's aversion to big government notwithstanding', as company historian Broehl puts it.[112]

The next move for Cargill was to begin to acquire its own transportation equipment, in this case barges. Cargill first purchased a few old, small wooden barges for use on the Erie Canal in 1937 and within two years had entered the shipbuilding business for itself, constructing steel barges at its Albany terminal for its own use. It also had towboats and barges built for it in Pittsburgh. During the war years of the early 1940s, Cargill even got into building small ships for the US Navy at what had by then become Port Cargill at Savage, on the south side of Minneapolis. More recently the company has been content to take advantage of the skills and resources of others to build its ships and barges to Cargill specifications and with Cargill innovations. The steel, however, more than likely comes from Cargill's steel-making subsidiary, North Star Steel (whose electric mini-mills are, in turn, supplied by its subsidiary, Magnimet, a significant North American scrap metal dealer). The pattern here is strikingly similar to Cargill's other lines of business; Cargill supplies the inputs and buys the product, leaving the riskier segment of the business to independent contractors (growers).

The success of its waterborne ventures, in design and construction as well as in actual use, has continued with many novel and creative projects in water transport and service. These include its sulphur barge operating out of Tampa (see Chapter 16) and its K-2 in the Mississippi River above Baton Rouge (see below).

On the other side of the continent, Cargill had opened offices in Portland and San Francisco and leased a Seattle terminal in 1934 after observing the growing shipment of grain from the West Coast.

Nevertheless, in 1939 Cargill estimated that three firms – Dreyfus, Continental and Norris Grain, in that order – were doing the bulk of North American grain exporting. Bunge y Born of Argentina and Cargill were vying for fourth and fifth place. The company would have to try harder.

The result was that Cargill in two years, 1949–50, increased its terminal elevator capacity from just over 70 million bushels (1.7 million tonnes) to just under 100 million bushels (2.5 million tonnes) by both increasing capacity at existing locations and having new facilities built, often by local port authorities or cities to Cargill specifications. For example, the Greater Baton Rouge Port Commission built a new 4.8 million bushel (122,000 tonne) terminal to Cargill specifications in 1955 and then leased it to Cargill. It was the first private-company terminal on the Gulf of Mexico (actually up-river about 100 miles), giving Cargill a distinct advantage in managing exports.[113]

When the Commodity Credit Corporation (a US Federal agency) was given an increased role in the acquisition and storage of grain with the passing of Public Law 480 (the 'Food For Peace' act) in 1954, Cargill was quick to garner the contracts and provide the storage in its publicly built facilities.

Meanwhile, Cargill continued to expand both its barge fleet and its deep-water freighters, and by 1992 it was reported that through its international subsidiaries and affiliates, Cargill owned, or had under long-term charter, some 20 ocean freighters, ranking the company among the world's largest dry-cargo vessel operators.[114] Cargill also owned or operated somewhere between eight and eleven towboats and a fleet of 682 barges.[115]

This still leaves Cargill a relatively small player compared to American Commercial, the largest barge company in the US, which has a fleet of 3500 barges and about 20 per cent of the market.[116] (American Commercial is a subsidiary of CSX Corporation – see Chapter 16.)

Cargill competitor Archer Daniels Midland (ADM), owning and operating 9800 railcars, 1900 barges and 15,000 trucks, according to its 1993 annual report, is 'the largest transportation buyer in the US.' With its 'partners', ADM also claims to have 'over 100 vessels on the high seas at all times'.

In addition to its duties of maintaining waterways and ports, the US Army also keeps all the records of waterways' traffic. Their voluminous records show that in 1990, 80.5 million tons of 'food & farm products' were exported via the Mississippi River system. Slightly more than that, 82 million tons, was moved in internal commerce.[117] About 60 per cent of the grain exported from the US to world markets is transported by barge and about 90 per cent of the grain transported by barge on the Mississippi is going to the export market.

Table 6.1: 1993 US grain exports (wheat, corn, etc.) by port area:[118]

	bushels	tonnes
Pacific	765,730,000	19.5 m
(Columbia River	597,579,000)	(15.2 m)
Great Lakes	180,308,000	4.5 m
Interior	116,178,000	2.9 m
Atlantic	138,935,000	3.5 m
Gulf of Mexico	2,669,971,000	67.9 m
(mouth of Mississippi	2,124,784,000)	(54 m)

As mentioned above, it was not just water transport that was changing the movement and storage of grain. The growing number of trucks on the road encouraged Cargill to think more creatively about the use and location of its smaller grain handling facilities, the country elevators. It was no longer necessary to be limited by the distance a horse could travel or how much a team could haul. This led Austen Cargill to propose, in 1940, that the company's country elevator business be reorganized around what he called 'trade centers', those elevator locations that farmers seemed to prefer, resulting in a concentration on these 24 or so locations and the designation of the elevators in these locations as profit centres.[119]

The repercussions of this modest, yet radical change in thinking continues to be felt as elevators are closed and consolidated, ownership becomes more concentrated, and farmers have to bear more and more of the costs of getting their grain to a market facility, whether for domestic use or export. The grain companies no longer serve the farmers. The farmers serve the grain companies, even though they may have been so instilled with the ideology of the market that they cannot see clearly the position they are now in.

Cargill continued to expand and integrate its US grain handling and transportation facilities through the 1950s. Integrated barge-towboat units were built and Cargill's transportation services, including trucking and equipment leasing, were integrated into Cargill Carriers Incorporated. In 1960 the 6630 h.p. river towboat *Austen S. Cargill* was launched at St Louis and Cargill's first-ever bulk cement cargo was loaded in Antwerp, Belgium.

With the prospect of the St Lawrence Seaway being able to handle ocean-going vessels when it opened in 1958–9, Cargill became concerned that the advantage it had gained with its Albany terminal would be lost. It decided to protect its export position by building a large terminal elevator at Baie Comeau, at the mouth of the St Lawrence River. At 12 million bushels (300,000 tonnes), this was the largest grain elevator in Canada when it opened in 1960. It was also the largest single financial committment ever made by the company (over $13 million) and was intended to be the lynch-pin of a continental grain transport system. Arrangements were worked out so that the terminal could handle Canadian and US grain separately without duty payments.[120]

At the time, Cargill estimated that it had 28.6 per cent of grain exports from the US while Continental handled 25.4 per cent. Dreyfus was estimated to have 17 per cent of the export market and Bunge 10 per cent.

While positioning itself at the mouth of the St Lawrence, Cargill was also developing a receiving port on the other side of the Atlantic. In 1960 the company acquired terminal facilities in Amsterdam which, like those in Albany and Memphis, were built almost entirely to Cargill specifications by the Amsterdam port authority which then leased them to Cargill.

Building on its bulk transport experience, and always looking for greater efficiencies in the development of its forms of monoculture, Cargill came up with the idea of the 'unit train' to serve the ever-enlarging inland elevators. A unit train consists solely of specially designed hopper cars to be completely filled at one inland terminal and delivered as a unit to either an inland customer or to an export facility, such as Baie Comeau or Albany. Unit trains do create efficiencies in the handling of large amounts of grain, and they do serve the interests of large corporate grain shippers and large inland grain terminals, but they do so at the expense of smaller terminals and customers. With the deregulation of freight rates in Canada and the US, the railroads can offer, or the grain shippers demand, discount rates for loading 75- or 100-unit grain trains at those elevators and terminals that have adequate handling and storage capacity. This puts increasing pressure on the system to eliminate the smaller elevators and forces farmers to travel further to deliver their grain to an elevator.

To ensure that its concept was not limited by the availability of suitable rail cars, between 1986 and 1992 Cargill commissioned 1600 railroad tank cars at a cost of $80 million.

Cargill's railroad cars, for corn syrup, grains and other commodities are often, as the company says, 'the only package our customers see,'[121] and consequently they have to be clean and well maintained. This goes for their trucks as well. Transport Services Co. in Memphis, for example, is a Cargill subsidary dedicated to hauling vegetable oils: corn oil from the Cargill wet milling plant in the Port of Memphis and peanut and soya oils from the recently acquired Kraft plant, on the north side of that city.

The trucks utilized by Transport Services may not actually belong to the company, however; for corporate financial purposes they may be leased from Cargill Leasing. Leasing has advantages for both parties, and there are corporate accountants who earn their living by advising on such matters. Not only are there tax and capital use benefits for both parties in a lease arrangement, there is the issue of control. For example, 'Oakley, Lake Wales, Florida,' is the name one sees on a large number of gleaming stainless steel tanker trucks not only in the yard of Cargill's Frostproof Florida frozen orange juice concentrate (that the industry refers to as FCOJ) plant, but also at their orange juice terminal in Port Elizabeth, New Jersey. While this displays the fact that Cargill is using Oakley to truck orange juice concentrate all over the country, it does not reveal that many of those trucks are owned by Cargill and leased to Oakley. Indian River, a major orange juice supplier in Florida, also leases trucks from Cargill – or so I would assume from seeing Indian River trucks pictured in a company film about Cargill Leasing.

A company brochure describing Cargill's innovation in transporting FCOJ captures the essence of the Cargill approach: 'Cargill pioneered the change from drum shipment to bulk storage and transportation. The result was consistently higher quality at a savings, thanks to a more uniform product, reduced labor, less product loss during handling, and faster delivery.'

Virtually the same thing could be said of the world's largest floating feed products transfer facility opened by Cargill at Mile 158 in the Mississippi River in 1982.

The $16 million 'K-2' export terminal, run by Cargill subsidiary Rogers Terminal and Shipping Co., was designed to transfer soybean meal, grain and grain products from river-going barges to deep-sea freighters at the lowest possible cost to Cargill.

The K-2 is a self-contained facility that generates its own power and produces potable water for sanitation and irrigation. The K-2 is capable of continuously weighing and sampling both ingoing and outgoing commodities, as well as blending to customer specifications, at the rate of 1000–1200 tonnes per hour.[122] Cargill has similar floating facilities in Amsterdam which transfer grain directly from ocean vessels to barges, and there may well be others around the world that I do not know about.

Railroads

With the notable exception of the now-abandoned Erie Canal, it is generally the case that low-cost water routes are naturally occurring and really cannot be relocated, however much the US Army might try. Other means of transport have to be utilized if large quantities of goods and commodities are going to be moved to or from water or between dry land locations. During the past century the railroads arose to fill this need and in spite of the more recent rise in truck transport, the railroads remain second to water for low-cost transport, particularly of bulk commodities. One need only stand in a corn field in central Nebraska within sight of one of the main east–west rail lines to realize how vital the railways are to the continental transportation system. There is literally a continuous flow in both directions of very long freight trains, with one in sight at almost all times.

Along with the centralization of the grain handling system, with small country elevators disappearing along with the branch rail lines that served them, the rail networks of North America have themselves been transformed by integration and reorientation. In Canada the two national lines have turned 90 degrees and shifted from an east–west orientation to a north–south one, while all of the major railways on the continent have pursued amalgamation and rationalization. 'Rationalization', in agriculture, means the abandonment of small farms in the face of the demands of industrialization. In the case of railroads, it means the abandonment of branch lines – and small towns – in the service of the same ideology. The railways claim that the small branch lines are unprofitable to maintain, but that depends on who pays for the alternative, road trucking. In fact, consolidation and rationalization has been applied to grain elevators, rail lines and farms alike, with uniform results: higher costs incurred by the remaining farms for transportation, higher costs to governments for road maintenance, a smaller tax base, and disappearing rural communities.

The CP Rail System, founded in 1880 to link eastern Canada to British Columbia on the west coast, is the seventh largest rail system in North America and includes CP Rail in Canada, the Soo Line Railroad in the Midwest and the Delaware & Hudson (D&H) in the Northeast. CP has had a controlling interest in the Soo Line since 1891 and acquired the remaining outstanding shares in 1990. The next year it bought the D&H. Grain handling accounts for about 27 per cent of CP's revenues and potash fertilizer for 8 per cent.[123]

Burlington Northern Railroad, already operator of the longest rail system in North America with 23,000 miles of track, and Santa Fe Pacific Corp. announced agreement to a merger in July 1994. If it goes through, it would create a rail network with 32,800 miles of track. The Santa Fe goes to Mexico and the BN to Canada, giving the merged companies continental coverage and approximately $7 billion in revenue.

Integrating Mexico

Integration has continued southward as various means have been utilized to extend the rail system into the heavily populated heart of Mexico.

CN North America, another corporate layer of Canadian National railways created in January 1992, joined forces with Burlington Northern Railroad, state-owned Ferrocarriles Nacionales de Mexico and Protexa Burlington International, a rail-barge service jointly owned by Burlington Northern and Protexa, a private Mexican barge company. Under the agreement, BN trains connect at the Port of Galveston, Texas, with Protexa rail barges bound for the ports of Altamira, Veracruz and Coatzacoalcos on the east coast of Mexico. Once in Mexico, the railcars are distributed by trains operated by Ferrocarriles Nacionales.[124]

Burlington Northern also gained direct rail access to Mexico through a connection at Fort Worth with the South Orient Railroad Co., providing BN with a gateway to northern Mexico through the border town of Presidio.[125]

In 1994 Union Pacific Railway received permission from the Government of Mexico to move in-bond truck trailers into Mexico on rail flatcars (intermodal piggy-backing). The trailers will no longer have to be unloaded from the railcars and inspected at the border, but only at their destination within Mexico.[126]

Mexico has not been a trading nation and the country has no major natural seaports. Nevertheless, with the advent of trade 'liberalisation' and the North American Free Trade Agreement (NAFTA), Mexico's transportation system and even its ports have taken on a new importance. As a result, the Mexican government has redefined its role in the management of them. Under a new Law of Ports, each port is to have its own Integral Port Administration (IPA). Each IPA is to be a chartered corporation, with private investors able to hold up to 100 per cent of the shares of the corporation, though foreign participation will be limited to 49 per cent in the IPA itself. Through chartered Mexican corporations, however, foreign investors will be allowed full participation in the operation of terminals, facilities and services.[127]

'The existing port infrastructure, including land and water areas belonging to the port enclosure, will remain in the public domain, but their use, development and exploitation are subject to concession.'[128] This would appear to be an open invitation to companies like Cargill, which already has a lot of experience, to take an active role in the management and use of Mexican ports. IPAs are allowed to contract out the operation of terminals, facilities and related services. The first ports to be privatized under local IPAs were Veracruz and Altamira (both terminals for US rail/barge traffic), Lazaro Carenas and Manzanillo. In 1994 it was reported that the Mexican government would provide $8.9 million and a group of companies will provide the remaining $5.9 million for improvements at the port of Veracruz.[129]

With most of Mexico's population living inland, no amount of seaport improvement is going to meet all its needs for 'port' facilities. Rail traffic can only go so far, and then at least some of it has to be transferred to trucks. This is the purpose of Ferropuerto Laguna, an inland port at Torreon in north central Mexico at the junction of two key rail routes from the US border to the Mexican interior.

The port is equipped with high-speed unloading facilities for both railcars and trucks as well as extensive storage capacity. As under the new seaport regime, Ferropuerto Laguna is a private corporation of Mexican investors. It began operations in 1992 and is still the only grain facility in Mexico that can receive 90-car unit-trains without switching and which can unload them in eight hours.[130] Ferropuerto Laguna does not buy or sell grain, leaving that to the companies like Continental and Cargill.

In 1992, Mexico imported overland from the US; 397,000 tonnes of corn, 425,000 tonnes of wheat, 1.04 million tonnes of soybeans and 2.46 million tonnes of sorghum.[131]

Cargill in Canada

Cargill's development in Canada was very different than its development in the US and provides another example of Cargill's expansionist strategy. From an ecological perspective, Canada's political independence has been, at least historically, an anomaly. Instead of utilizing the water routes to the south, grain transportation has been solely laterally organized, with grain moving either east or west to export terminals, but never south. The future will clearly be different; indeed, the movement of grain has already begun to shift as a result of the increasing role of Cargill and Continental, the restructuring of the rail system, and the development of inland terminals that can clean and dry grain to export standards. This means that in the future a 100-car trainload of wheat might originate in Weyburn, Saskatchewan, and move non-stop to Mexico City.

In spite of having established a beachhead in Canada in 1928 as a grain merchandising company, Cargill remained largely invisible until the 1974 purchase of National Grain.

'You've got to let others do the experimenting before you put your dough in,' is the way Dick Dawson succinctly described a major element of Cargill business strategy. Long a major fixture of the Canadian agricultural scene and Cargill's public presence in Canada, Dawson retired in 1993 after 35 years with Cargill Ltd, the last 19 of them as senior vice president. When he moved up to the vice president position in 1974, he told me that his first accomplishment was to buy National Grain with the $120 million that he had made trading grain in 1971–2 when the Russians went on a buying spree. According to Dawson, when he asked Whitney MacMillan what to do with the money, MacMillan told him to 'buy something.' What he bought was 286 country elevators, five feed mills, a terminal elevator at the head of the Great Lakes at Thunder Bay, and a significant 'originating' capacity in one one the world's major grain-growing regions. When I asked Dawson about his approach to investment, he responded in his folksy way, 'Do the things families don't do, and think hard about doing anything families do.'[132]

On the occasion of Dawson's retirement, reporter Allan Dawson (no relation) wrote in the *Manitoba Co-operator*, 'A good portion of Dawson's job with Cargill involved exercising influence. And some would say he did his job well … In fact, some might speculate Dawson is retiring because the policies he has promoted for years are finally being implemented.' There was another word going around Winnipeg, however: one of the reasons Dawson retired early was that he was just a little too gregarious for the liking of the corporation. This sounds probable to me; we had several conversations and he once spent a whole morning with me discussing the company's business. That was before it was decided, as I was told by another senior executive, that 'It is not a good use of our time to talk with you.'

In spite of the significant physical presence achieved with the purchase of National Grain, Cargill's position in the trading of the major grains (wheat and barley) for export remained confined to that of acting as an agent of the Canadian Wheat Board, not an independent speculator. It is not surprising then that Cargill has labored long and hard, with much deviousness and propaganda, to destroy the obstacle to its preferred position as an unrestricted trader, the Canadian Wheat Board.

Shortly after purchasing National Grain, Roger Murray, president of Cargill Ltd at the time, said that the purchase placed Cargill Grain 'in a unique position to plan efficient future expansion in the handling, processing and exporting of Canadian grain, oilseeds and feed stuffs.'[133] Such a remark would indicate that Cargill saw an early demise for the Wheat Board.

If the Wheat Board was to be destroyed, there were still the Prairie Pools to contend with. Cargill would have to acquire control over, if not own outright, sufficient modern infrastructure to provide the foundations of an alternative grain handling system. Besides replacing many of the old grain elevators it had acquired from National Grain with new high-capacity elevators, such as the inland terminal at Rosetown, Saskatchewan, opened in 1976, Cargill positioned itself to take advantage of a new development. When Canada's first producer-owned inland terminal was built at Weyburn, Saskatchewan, Cargill was designated as sole selling agent for the terminal's grain. This was done with the encouragement of the Liberal Minister responsible for the Wheat Board at the time, Otto Lang, making it clear that Lang himself was working to see the Wheat Board destroyed and Cargill installed in its place.

Two years later Cargill Ltd entered the Ontario market, which is not within CWB jurisdiction, establishing a trading office in London, Ontario and buying Erlin Grain in Talbotville, Ontario, to give it a grain originating capacity. *Business Week* magazine commented at the time:

> Cargill is gambling that Canada's desire to capitalize on the new opportunity in world grain trade will lead it to permit the big private companies to share in the more profitable trading function. 'We're counting on the Canadian system moving more toward free markets,' says W.B. Saunders, group vice-president.[134]

By 1982 Cargill had become the leading private exporting agent for the Canadian Wheat Board, handling 8 per cent of all prairie grain, but for all its efforts to destroy the Wheat Board and to build an alternative infrastructure to the Prairie Pools, by 1994 Cargill had only managed to increase this to 10 per cent. (Total sales for Cargill Ltd, which now has 85 grain elevators and 3100 employees throughout the country, were reported to be about $2 billion in fiscal 1993–4.)[135]

Outside of the Prairie region, Cargill considerably extended its grain buying and farm service activities into Ontario in 1988 with the $40-million purchase of Maple Leaf Mills Grain Division from Hillsdown Holdings of Britain. Maple Leaf Mills Grain Division was only a small portion of Maple Leaf Mills Ltd which Hillsdown had purchased the year before from Canadian Pacific Ltd for $361 million. Maple Leaf had been handling about 10 per cent of marketed Ontario grain (grain not utilized on-farm) through its 23 country elevators in southwestern Ontario and four grain terminals: Midland, Port McNichol and Sarnia, Ontario, and St John, New Brunswick. The three Ontario terminals were situated to receive grain by water from the west and load railcars for further shipment to East Coast deepwater ports in the era before completion of the St Lawrence Seaway. The St John, New Brunswick, terminal was a deepwater terminal at the end of the rail line.

Cargill's next major expansion came in 1991 with the purchase of Alberta Terminals Ltd (ATL) from the Alberta government for the bargain price of $6 million. ATL consists of inland terminals at Lethbridge, Calgary and Edmonton and an off-track loading facility at High Level, in the Peace River region of Alberta. The facilities had cost the Alberta government $17.9 million since it acquired them in 1979. Cargill said the deal, which gives it more than half of Alberta's primary elevator storage capacity, put Cargill in a good position to ship grain into the US.[136]

The success of the Weyburn, Saskatchewan, terminal, combined with the hostility of the private traders toward the Canadian Wheat Board, convinced farmers in the northeastern area of Saskatchewan's grain land that they, too, should build a big 'inland terminal'.* North East Terminal Ltd opened in 1992 with a capacity of 13,600 tonnes. It is supposedly an independent elevator, though Cargill Ltd holds 25 per cent of the company in return for an investment of $500,000 and has a contract to operate the terminal. While the farmers who initiated the project raised $1.8 million in their initial share offerings, because their 75 per cent share is split up among many farmers, Cargill has, whether the farmers realize it or not, effective management as well as operating control.[137]

Currently there are several other big farmer-financed inland terminals either under construction or in the preliminary stages of capitalization. One of the latter, South West Terminals, is to be built in southwestern Saskatchewan, with Cargill as a partner holding 49 per cent of the shares, at a cost of about $1 million.[138]

What is actually being built with these inland terminals, at tremendous cost, is a private alternative to the quasi-public Prairie Pool-Canadian Wheat Board grain marketing system that Cargill will be able to control as the largest private trader. Its only possible competitor is Continental Grain, which is allied with the right-wing United Grain Growers co-operative. UGG provides the infrastructure and gathers the grain, with Continental doing the global marketing. UGG has so far built seven high-capacity concrete elevators and has plans to build 25–30 more, while shedding, one way or another, about half of its current total of 224 country elevators.[139]

The success of Cargill's propaganda campaign against the CWB is reflected in this quote from a letter to the Manitoba Co-operator from a 'Manitoba farmer':

> While it can be said that the CWB has benefitted farmers in the past, it is no longer finding the best markets and prices for its employers – us. Other companies such as Cargill are looking for and finding more lucrative markets and better returns.[140]

This brief sketch of transportation and storage is, of course, an incomplete portrait of Cargill in Canada. Its Nutrena feed division is a major supplier of livestock feed, particularly in the west, and it is involved in the production and distribution of fertilizers (see Chapter 16) as well as handling canola and other 'non-board' crops (crops not under the jurisdiction of the Canadian Wheat Board). Cargill is also the largest meat packer in Canada (see Chapter 8).

---

* Historically, a terminal elevator has been an elevator located at the end of a rail line at a seaport where grain was cleaned and stored before being loaded into a ship. The term 'inland terminal' is now used to describe an elevator located inland that can clean grain to export standards and load unit trains that go directly to a seaport.

West Coast Ports

With the advent of air travel, seaports have lost the significance they once had for most people. Port facilities are now built on the wastelands of New Jersey or on artificial land made inaccessible to the public for security reasons. Like the K-2 in the Mississippi River, out of sight over the levee, the large grain terminals are now built where few people will ever see them. To understand what is happening at a Cargill elevator in a small town in Nebraska, however, one needs to also know what is happening at Pier 86 in Seattle. One can easily observe the loading and departure of a 75-car unit-train of corn from Central City Nebraska, but one is unlikely to observe its unloading in Pasco, Washington, and the loading of the grain onto a barge for a trip down the Snake and Columbia Rivers to Portland where it is stored and eventually loaded into a freighter headed for Japan.

The northernmost grain-handling port on the west coast of North America is 1500 km north of Vancouver at Prince Rupert, British Columbia. Grain moves west from its prairie sources over the mountains and into export position at Prince Rupert. Opened in 1985, the 210,000 tonne grain terminal is a consortium of six companies widely differing in business philosophy: the three Prairie Pools, United Grain Growers, Pioneer Grain and Cargill. Initially, each company put up $55 million and the Alberta Government financed the remaining $220 million, including a $106.25 million mortgage at 11 per cent. Under the agreement, any cash earned goes first to pay operating expenses, then to the participating shippers, and finally to pay off the mortgage. It was not until 1991 that the port made enough to even start paying the interest on the mortgage, which up to then had been accumulating and was added to the mortgage principal. In 1992 discussions were held about the possibility of refinancing the terminal.

To the south of Prince Rupert, in the southwest corner of Canada, lies the Port of Vancouver, a major export terminal for Canadian grains, but only a minor port for Cargill. The company loads and ships containers for export, such as canola and malting barley for China, through Columbia Containers, and probably some grains through Pacific Elevators. The largest terminal elevator in the Vancouver port area belongs to the Alberta Wheat Pool.

Moving southward, the Port of Seattle, Washington, in the northwest corner of the US, is a major container port as well as being the site of a 43-acre Cargill grain terminal at Pier 86 which, as we just noted, receives grain by rail from as far east as Nebraska. (Cargill shipped 1.71 million tonnes through Pier 86 in 1992.)[141]

The largest grain export facility on the US west coast, however, lies a little further south at Portland, Oregon. There Cargill leases one of the Port of Portland's two terminal elevators. (The other is leased by Columbia Grain Inc., a wholly-owned subsidiary of Marubeni Corp. of Japan.) Cargill's elevator has a storage capacity of 220,444 tonnes.[142]

Portland is at the mouth of the Columbia River, which flows westward from its origins in the Rocky Mountains and is joined by the Snake River at Pasco, in eastern Washington state. The 465-mile Columbia-Snake River system is second only to the Mississippi in the US and substantially reduces the cost of moving grain west to export position by shortening the rail journey. Cargill can ship grain by barge from its terminal in Pasco down the Columbia River to its export terminal in Portland. In 1990 Cargill built a new elevator at East Pasco for Tidewater Barge Lines and the Burlington Northern Railroad. The elevator transloads grain from railcars to Tidewater barges for movement down the Columbia River to the export terminals at Portland, including Cargill's. Barge traffic also moves up the Snake River all the way to Lewiston, Idaho. In 1990, about 20 million tonnes of 'food & farm products' were exported from the US interior via the Columbia River system.[143]

The next and last major port area to the south is San Francisco Bay. The Bay's major ports of Sacramento and Stockton both actually lie about 75 miles inland by deep water channel from the San Francisco Bay bridge. Being that far inland puts them in the middle of the central valley, California's irrigated, fertilized and toxified 'Garden of Eden'.

Table 6.2: US Foreign Export/Import Summary 1990[144] (latest figures available): selected commodities in which Cargill is active as trader, processor, or both, by weight:

	Imports	Exports
Wheat	.291 million tonnes	31.294 million tonnes
Corn	.029	57.31
Rice	.168	2.586
Barley/rye	.047	2.224
Oats	.776	.003
Sorghum grain	.003	5.863
Peanuts	.004	.259
Soybeans	.000	16.532
Wheat flour	.041	.946
Grain mill products	.325	.568
Hay & fodder	.005	2.228
Animal feed, prep.	.360	14.052
Meat, fresh/frozen	.850	1.138
Meat, prepared	.229	.065
Fruit juices	1.682	.470
Sugar	2.295	.257
Molasses	1.105	.207
Coffee	1.263	.118
Cotton	.020	1.917

In the Port of Sacramento, Cargill has only a 30,000 tonne elevator, but at Stockton one can find a complete array of Cargill's integrated business activities:

a Nutrena feed mill; a new flour mill located next to the feed mill at the south end of the city; a feed supplement plant located in the port that utilizes molasses from Hawaii to produce 'Mol Mix' liquid feed supplement; a food-grade corn syrup distribution terminal to receive corn syrup in bulk in Cargill's own rail-cars and distribute high fructose corn syrups, sweetener blends and corn-derived products to food processors of all kinds in both Canada and the US; a fertilizer plant (Co-pal Fertilizer) purchased in about 1990; and a terminal elevator to handle the import and export of grains.

While visiting the Cargill facility at Stockton I noticed that the weathered name on the silos of the Nutrena feed mill was Kerr Gifford, the name of the company Cargill bought in 1953 when it first expanded to the west coast. This mill draws grain from Idaho, Nebraska, Wyoming and Montana and serves the west coast – mostly dairy herds numbering 400–500 head – plus exporting to the South Pacific.

South America

Cargill can be found on the rivers of South America, as well the waterways of North America, and for the same reasons: water is the cheapest way to transport bulk commodities; and, it is common practice for waterways to be maintained largely at public expense. This may be partially explained by the fact that historically rivers have served as political boundaries, thus falling into a situation of shared/no responsibility. Or it may be simply that it was better to have the cost of mainenance borne by the state than to have feudal barons demand tolls for passage through 'their' water. In Europe, the Rhine River is an obvious example, and opportunities for toll collection can be observed by any river traveller. Today freight traffic on the Danube, which comprises a 2500 km system administered by The Danube Commission, is free except for pilot fees on the lower 270 km of the river. Costs of maintaining the river, including the locks, are borne by the bordering (riparian) states.[145]

A look at some of Cargill's water-related activities in South America reveals a familiar strategy regarding the construction, leasing and maintenance of facilities, both port and water route: utilize as much public money as possible while gaining or maintaining control.

In 1986 Cargill worked out a deal with the Sao Paulo state railway in Brazil to minimize travel and turnaround time between Cargill's inland facilities and the port of Santos where Cargill had built a private bulk terminal. The terminal was built on land leased from the state port operating authority. The result was, in effect, a private export corridor expected to move 440,000 tonnes of citrus meal, soybean meal and soybeans annually[146] (see Chapter 10).

From Cargill's grand ecological satellite perspective, Brazil has to be considered a major resource, if not market, of the global food system. But it suffers from an inadequate transportation infrastructure that is, in part, the consequence of a difficult topography. Its major growing areas lie inland with mountains between them and the ocean. For the growing areas to join the ranks of global commodity sources, rail and water connections to the ocean and the global market must be improved.

Then a news item about straightening a river caught my eye. The Hidrovia project of Argentina, Bolivia, Brazil, Paraguay and Uruguay calls for a five-nation inland waterway that will, by the end of the decade, allow barges to travel 2143 miles down the Paraguay and Parana Rivers from eastern Bolivia to the South Atlantic.[147]

Map 2 Major Rivers of South America

Why would five governments want to straighten the Paraguay River? To answer the question, I got out my maps and my magnifying glass and discovered that the Paraguay River really begins in the Mato Grosso of Brazil, which is one of the largest areas for soybean production in the world. The Paraguay River flows south, demarcating a number of national boundaries, and then joins the Parana River to meet the Atlantic Ocean at Buenos Aires. I suspect that it is probably not the five countries who want the project, but TNCs such as ADM, Unilever and Cargill.

As it is, the Mato Grosso lies thousands of kilometres from the coast and shipping soybeans by truck to Brazil's southeastern ports, including Paranagua where Cargill has facilities, can cost $70 per tonne or more, while shipping south by water to ports on the River Plate might cost half as much. 'There's a very large output in Brazil's mid-west that needs an outlet. That's why we believe that the River Paraguay will come to represent for us the same that the Mississippi does for the United States,' said a Brazilian shipper. Particularly if it can be developed with World Bank and state financing and maintained at public expense like the Mississippi. Of course this would please Cargill, and, who knows, it might have been Cargill's idea.[148]

The $1 billion project seems to be getting underway, though now it has the name 'Paraguay Parana Waterway'. There is talk that it should be operational by early next century and that it 'will save countries in the region beytween $800 million and $1 billion dollars a year.' Project advisors (unnamed) say that should allow 17 million tonnes of produce now being shipped to Atlantic ports by truck or rail to switch to barges and ships sailing down the Paraguay and Parana Rivers to sea.[149] No mention has been made of who who is to pay for maintenance, and, of course, neither has it been mentioned that the savings will go to the shippers – Unilever, ADM and Cargill – not to the countries.

In the meantime, the soybean interests are eager to tap the Mato Grosso, and transport routes through Brazil only can eliminate international negotiations and conflicting interests. This may explain the Brazilian plans to inaugurate a different and separate system of river locks that will allow barges to travel 2400 km from Paraguay to Sao Paulo.

Two locks were opened in March, 1994, in the Parana-Tiete waterway linking Brazil's prime soybean-growing area in the Cerrado of Mato Grosso state with the Atlantic Ocean. Soybeans are moved by truck to the Parana River port of San Simao, then by barge in a northeasterly direction up the Parana River to the Tiete and then east on the Tiete to the Piracicaba region of Sao Paulo state where they again have to be trucked the rest of the way to Santos port.[150] Not an easy route, but water transport is cheap.

With relatively inexpensive water transport, the Cerrado, the central plains of Mato Grosso, could quickly be incorporated into the Cargill system of global sourcing.

CHAPTER 7

Policy

Cargill's task is to monitor the political landscape, maintain its hegemony, and head off pesky legislative proposals that emerge from time to time. The company's power in Washington ... is undeniable. But its style of influence is subtle.[151]

Congressional aides and USDA officials often describe Cargill's Washington office as more of a listening post than a lobbying nerve center. The company prefers to work through influential trade associations [whose] state-of-the-art lobbying techniques offer Cargill the advantages of Washington influence without the costs of close company identification with controversial proposals or overt political tactics.[152]

Cargill has a full array of policy advocacy (lobbying) styles, all of which are highly sophisticated and of varying degrees of subtlety. In recent years it has developed effective grassroots lobbying techniques to enhance its higher-level activities and achieve favorable local business climates.

What might be described as Cargill's highest level of lobbying is its tried and true use of the revolving door of public service, where (usually) senior Cargill executives take leave of Cargill for a stint in government advisory and policy positions and then return to the company when their mission is accomplished. In Canada, this is called an 'executive exchange', though as far as I know, it is not really an exchange since there is no record of a government bureaucrat working in Cargill's offices (see below).

The next level of policy advocacy is the slightly academic 'impartial' consultant's 'policy analysis' which usually recommends the policies advocated by those paying their fees, such as Cargill and other agribusiness allies. It is then possible for the corporations to cite these 'independent' studies to support their arguments. It works, too, since the media, who take the corporate side anyway, go along with the ruse and quote the 'studies' as well, seldom identifying the studies' sponsors.

The third level of activity is through the myriad associations that represent some commodity or processing interest, such as the turkey growers, flour millers, soybean processors, peanut council or feed industry (there are 77 pages in one directory of US agricultural associations with several per page).

Finally there is the monthly *Cargill Bulletin*, which for decades prior to 1993 was the sole public report by the corporation about its activities. The end of this era of keeping the public at least minimally informed was marked with the freshly designed January 1993 issue. Instead of information on corporate activities and developments, there is now a more 'scholarly' approach to global agricultural policy, as defined by Cargill, along with a Cargill *Commentary* providing the company's policy recommendations on the subject of each issue. There is of course, no more favorable way to solve a problem than to first identify it according to one's interests, and then provide the solution according to one's means. The problem is defined to suit the answer one has to offer. Since the *Bulletin* is the official voice of Cargill, I have used it extensively in this study.

Lobbying at the Grassroots

Grassroots political action is one way to improve the operating climate for business. Cargill has its people both at the bottom and the top.

The Cargill Community Network (CCN) is the name of a grassroots program 'aimed at improving Cargill's reputation and success in communities where it is doing business.' The CCN is 'designed to help win Cargill's public-policy objectives at every level of government' by spreading the word that Cargill is 'a solid corporate citizen' while 'building a reservoir of community goodwill that ensures we have friends when we need them.'[153]

From a computer database, network members get information on state and federal issues as well as help in identifying their state and federal legislators; in some cases the network also negotiates group memberships 'with leading business organizations.'

The Ohio Circle is one example of the CCN in action. One successful grassroots campaign that achieved the results Cargill wanted was a fight in Ohio in 1992 against a 'right to know' initiative ('Issue 5') that would have given Ohio consumers and neighborhoods more information about toxic substances used in the state. Polls showed Ohioans supported the measure by a margin of nearly nine to one, according to Cargill's own account. 'Because Issue 5 was a product of a grass-roots movement, it required a grass-roots movement to defeat it. That effort took shape in a group called Ohioans for Responsible Health Information.'[154]

In June 1992, Cargill managers from 20 locations met together for a 'Circle Meeting'. Circle Meetings, initiated by Cargill Chairman Whitney MacMillan in 1984, are special gatherings of senior Cargill managers to learn what's new at corporate and local levels and to share ideas and information. That first meeting produced the Ohio Circle Council which organized asset management, marketing, origination and public policy subgroups. The public policy group set about organizing a campaign 'to educate the voters of Ohio' about Issue 5.

Cargill used its sales channels and trade associations to carry its message that the proposal would hurt Ohio businesses and the economy. 'We as a coalition of Cargill businesses in Ohio aggressively educated our employees, our customers and suppliers, and the communities in which we live and work.' The initiative was handily defeated as a result of Cargill's intervention.[155]

In another example, in 1991 the fertilizer division used grassroots techniques to help turn a political tide that was running against the building of Cargill's new nitrogen fertilizer plant in Saskatchewan. Radio commentaries, a video, and a series of newspaper columns were used to convince legislators that the plant was a good thing for farmers and the environment.

Cargill also used its grassroots techniques to lobby for the North American Free Trade Agreement (NAFTA). After members of the Cargill Community Network had done their organizing work, employees at Cargill's 600 locations in the US were given information about the trade agreement and given cards to send to their congressmen. Cargill figures that well over 50,000 cards may have been sent to Washington.[156] As Cargill told its employees, 'NAFTA is important to Cargill because it clears the way for what we do.'[157]

Like businesses large and small, Cargill has also been known to use contributions to political campaigns in judicious amounts at crucial moments to further their objectives. In 1993 a piece of legislation went through both chambers of the Minnesota legislature with little opposition. It went to Governor Arne Carlson for signing into law but was vetoed instead. The bill would have imposed an assessment on Canadian wheat and barley coming into Minnesota and sold in Minnesota markets. The assessment would have extended to Canadian wheat sold in the state a charge for research and promotion already levied on domestic grains. Farm groups put the blame on Cargill for applying pressure on Carlson to veto the bill and said that the reasons given by Carlson for his veto were virtually identical in wording to a memo from Cargill that was circulated to those potentially opposing the bill.

Supporters of the proposed levy revealed that the MacMillan family was the second largest contributor to Carlson's campaign funds in 1991 and 1992. In 1993, Duncan MacMillan and Whitney MacMillan each gave $3000 to Carlson's campaign committee during the last ten days, before such contributions were limited to $500.[158]

Lobbying at the Top – the Personal Approach

Cargill is not spending millions [on a corporate advertising campaign] for the sake of ego. Like everything it does, this is part of a well-thought-out, long-range plan. Since the early 1960s Cargill has become increasingly active in attempting to influence US grain trade and farm policies.[159]

When William R. Pearce retired as vice-chairman of Cargill in 1993, Cargill's home-town newspaper, the Minneapolis *Star-Tribune*, carried an unusually frank report on Pearce's career and provided a rare insight into how Cargill works.

'Perhaps he has had more influence on public policy than most elected officials, save presidents,' comment staff writers John Oslund and Tony Kennedy:

> but despite a lifetime spent influencing the private affairs of Cargill Inc., the domestic affairs of US agriculture, and the foreign affairs of the United States' most powerful friends and enemies, most Minnesotans have never heard of Cargill's retiring vice-chairman.[160]

Pearce started work with Cargill as one of its four lawyers in 1952, moving to the Public Affairs Department in 1957. By 1963 he was vice president of public affairs.

Kennedy and Oslund relate how, as the Watergate scandal was crippling the Nixon administration in 1973, Pearce was on leave from Cargill to serve as a deputy special representative for trade negotiations, an appointment made by President Nixon in 1971 that gave him the rank of ambassador. In this position, Pearce steered a trade bill through Congress that set the stage for US international trade policy for a generation. Kennedy and Oslund report former Secretary of State George Schultz as saying of Pearce, 'He had an easy way of getting things done, and he got them done the way he wanted them done.' Cargill's own comment on this aspect of Pearce's work: 'As a member of the administration, Pearce shaped international trade policy.' Pearce rejoined Cargill in 1974.[161]

Pearce also recognized that Cargill's policy of 'meeting fiery criticism with icy silence was, in the end, bad for business,' and Pearce began to see to it that 'positive stories about Cargill began to appear in small-town weeklies, farm magazines and larger dailies.'

When the Soviet Union invaded Afghanistan in 1979–80, the Carter administration imposed an embargo on the sale of agricultural goods to the Soviet Union. Pearce argued that if the government insisted on an embargo, then it should buy the grain already sent on its way to the Soviet Union by the grain companies. The government agreed, but on the condition that the government would cover the companies' costs, but not their anticipated profit. President Carter also asked Cargill to halt all grain sales to Moscow through its foreign subsidiaries. Kennedy and Oslund report that 'after rigorous internal debate, led by Pearce, Cargill subsidiaries from Canada to Argentina honored the embargo.'

Cargill's own telling of the story does not mention Pearce's role in obtaining the compensation, due or not. In a later issue of the *Cargill Bulletin*, the company simply reported that:

> By the fall of 1980 ... the government was in the process of assuming the contractual obligations for 13 million tons of corn and 4 million tons of wheat once destined for the Soviet Union. Eventually, most of the corn contracts were sold back into the marketplace. The embargoed wheat, however, was purchased outright and the 4 million tons were placed in reserve.[162]

Those with less of a financial stake in the affair had other comments:

The USDA compensated Cargill and its colleagues for grain they had agreed to, but could no longer, ship. A 1981 report by the Agriculture Department Inspector General ... described possible manipulation by unnamed companies. Large amounts of grain were reclassified as bound for the Soviet Union and thus made eligible for compensation.[163]

A similar windfall had occurred in 1971–2 when the Soviet Union made surprise and unprecedented purchases of massive amounts of US-subsidized grains. According to Richard Gilmore, the sale of wheat to the Soviet Union in 1972 cost the US $300 million in subsidies, most of which went to the largest private exporters:

> The windfall came from the fact that several firms, having made sales to their foreign affiliates before the government's notice of the forthcoming termination of the subsidy program, subsequently registered these sales at the peak subsidy rates.[164]

Cargill's sales (the figures include subsidies) went from $2 billion in 1971 to $29 billion in 1981. Figures are not available for the intervening years. One can draw one's own conclusions.

The most high-profile Cargill executive to directly shape US policy as a member of the administration has been Daniel Amstutz. Unfortunately his name recurs all too often to the exclusion of others who have probably served Cargill's interests equally faithfully, not only in the US, but in many other countries.

Amstutz started his career with Cargill in 1954 as a grain merchant, moving up to the position of assistant vice president for feed grains in 1967 and then on to the position of president of Cargill Investor Service in 1972 where he remained until 1978 when he left Cargill to become a partner in Goldman, Sachs and Company developing their commodities trading business. In 1983 Amstutz became US Undersecretary of Agriculture for International Affairs and Commodity Programs and president of the Commodity Credit Corporation, all of which made him chief policy officer for US farm programs. From 1987 to 1989 he held the rank of Ambassador as chief negotiator for Agriculture in the GATT negotiations. Since 1989 he has been a private investor and consultant. Need one ask for whom he is consulting? In 1992 Amstutz was appointed executive director of the International Wheat Council. The Council's mandate is to foster co-operation between its members, which are grain importing and exporting countries.

David Gilmore offers a good Canadian example of Cargill's policy of shifting senior management through key public policy positions. Gilmore, as a Cargill vice president, moved to Agriculture Canada in 1985 under the executive exchange program just after the Tory election victory to become coordinator of commodity strategy development. He had an office on the 9th floor of the Carling Building next to the deputy minister of agriculture. I was told at the time that of course Gilmore was not advising on grains policy – just everything else! He rejoined Cargill in 1987.

Another Canadian example is Phil de Kemp who went to work for Cargill in the commodities marketing division in 1983 when he finished university. He worked in three locations getting to know Cargill and western grains and oilseeds. In 1986, as a Cargill employee, he went to work in the Grain Marketing Bureau of the Department of External Affairs. When the Bureau was moved to Agriculture Canada, de Kemp went with it, still on Cargill's payroll. His term under the executive exchange program expired in 1988, but de Kemp stayed on as an employee of Agriculture Canada. A year later he was 'loaned' to Charlie Mayer MP, Minister for Grains and Oilseeds, as special assistant for western grains and oilseeds.[165] De Kemp is now executive director of the Canadian Malting Industry Association.

A slightly different kind of example is Barbara Isman, vice president of corporate relations (public relations) for Cargill in Winnipeg. Isman was Executive Director of the Western Canadian Wheat Growers Association when it was created out of Palliser Wheat Growers Association in 1985. She remained in that position until she resigned abruptly at the end of 1987. In 1985 the new WCWGA launched a glossy magazine, *Pro-Farm*, with Barbara Isman as Senior Editor. In her first editorial, Isman explained that the name stood for 'progressive' and 'professional'. In that same issue there was a bold-headed ad which read, 'A Partnership That Works' in which 'Cargill Ltd congratulates *Pro-Farm* on its first issue.' Since its founding, Western Canadian Grain Growers has been one of Cargill's most aggressive and reliable commodity group supporters. It has walked lock-step with Cargill in advocating the destruction of the Canadian Wheat Board.

The corporate-government-lobby interchange occurs at the board level as well. On the eve of the Clinton inauguration in 1993, Walter Mondale, a former Democrat US Vice President, was elected to Cargill's board of directors. Whitney MacMillan said of the appointment: 'His experience in national and international affairs is a perfect complement to the interests of an expanding global company.'[166] Mondale was subsequently nominated by US President Clinton as ambassador to Japan in 1993, at which time he had to leave the Cargill board.

As the push was on to conclude the Uruguay Round of the GATT negotiations in the last months of 1993, Cargill shared its vision with the readers of its *Bulletin*: 'There is only one direction to go: forward ... Seven years of talk and paperwork, after all, have been aimed at one worthy goal: to improve human welfare within a sustainable, growing global economy.'[167] At the same time, the chief executives of two of the country's largest agriculture-related companies, H.D. Cleberg, of Farmland Industries, and Whitney MacMillan, were appointed to a GATT advisory group to 'to help congressional leaders monitor the final phase' of the GATT negotiations.[168]

The Collective Approach

The public can certainly be excused for confusing the agricultural lobby with a farmers' lobby. TNCs like Cargill certainly do nothing to ease the confusion. On the contrary, agribusiness corporations are highly skilled in representing their corporate interests as the interests of farmers.

Whether at the level of farm commodity group or the GATT negotiations, agriculture is not the homogeneous, undifferentiated industry that agribusiness talks about. When agribusiness talks about agriculture, it is talking about a very specific form of capital intensive, industrial commodity production. Each commodity is described as an industry – the sugar industry, the cotton industry – and the categories are considered inclusive of everyone from grower to trader to processor to manufacturer. This results in a wonderful mystification of reality that legitimizes an unacknowledged power structure.

Most agricultural organizations, such as the commodity and industry associations, may sometimes technically be farmer organizations, but functionally and financially they are industry organizations. In many cases, the membership of these asociations is composed of farmers, processors and traders, and, as should be expected, the wealthy industry/processor sector can easily dominate the interests of hundreds, or hundreds of thousands, of farmers. The legitimacy of these groups depends on acceptance of the premise that processors and growers share common interests. Of course they do to some extent, but they also have other, diametrically opposed interests: farmers obviously want the highest price possible for their crop; the processors equally obviously want to pay the lowest price possible for their industrial inputs.

Such distinctions are crucial when dealing with 'farm' or 'agricultural' lobby and policy groups. For example, Cargill is readily identifiable as a sponsor of the Agricultural Policy Working Group (APWG) or a member of the US Wheat Associates, but it is not organizationally identifiable with the work of Dennis Avery and the Hudson Institute, even though their ideological kinship is evident; Cargill quotes Avery in its *Bulletin*, which is equivalent to a papal blessing. Even less readily identifiable as a Cargill agent (or agency) is an organization like Women Involved in Farm Economics or the American Soybean Association, unless you go to their meetings and banquets and take note of the displays, or who has paid for participants' travel and their drinks.

The Agricultural Policy Working Group

Some years ago the *Washington Post* described how:

> some of the country's biggest and most profitable agribusiness companies have mounted a campaign orchestrated by two former Reagan administration agriculture officials to defeat legislation that would raise farmers' prices by reducing

crop production. [The campaign] could generate earnings of $250,000 for one-time Agriculture Department officials William G. Lesher and Randy M. Russell, now partners in an agricultural consulting firm (Lesher & Assoc.).[169]

The *Post* identified Cargill, Continental Grain, Monsanto and IMC Fertilizer as being behind the campaign. When Russell and Eugene Moos subsequently joined Lesher & Assoc. its name was changed to Lesher, Russell & Moos. Moos is now Undersecretary for International Affairs and Commodity Programs in the US Department of Agriculture.

When the corporate consortia formed their lobby contracting group in 1986 they gave it the name Agricultural Policy Working Group (APWG), and this name continues to appear on the joint policy advocacy papers. The group's 1993 policy document, *The Impacts of Environmental Protection and Food Safety Regulation on US Agriculture*, bears the names of Cargill, Central Soya, IMC Fertilizer Group, Monsanto, Nabisco Brands and Norfolk Southern as members of the APWG.

This paper is attributed to Bruce Gardner (who served as Assistant Secretary of Agriculture for Economics under Clayton Yeutter). The tone of this paper is captured in these sentences from the executive summary: 'Farmers and the food industry are concerned that prospective regulations will be based more on emotion than fact, causing significant economic harm, while generating few environmental or food safety benefits.' The explanation that follows stresses that regulations, particularly on biotechnology, 'delay or prevent innovations that could otherwise occur' and that 'each year that innovations are delayed from commercial adoption, billions of dollars in productivity gains are lost.' To broaden the appeal of their argument, the study then casts it in terms of environmental responsibility: 'Slower productivity growth may mean greater stress on the environment as farmers use more resources to meet world food needs.' (This is exactly the same party line and language currently being broadcast by Dennis Avery of the Hudson Institute, which got its start under Herman Kahn as an extremist advocate for nuclear deterrence.)

The first line of argument is simply 'productivity' and therefore prosperity, the second is environmental responsibility, and the third is 'international competitiveness'. Then all three are joined: 'Productivity growth is the key to agriculture's future international competitiveness, and hence, to the prosperity of US farmers.'

The next step is to argue that reduced farm subsidies 'need not have ill effects on farm incomes' because 'the main risk to farm incomes is reduced exports.' The loss of 'export competitiveness' is the consequence of 'losing the edge in controlling production costs.' What all this comes down to is that Cargill and others say they have to be able to buy grain at prices low enough that they can sell the grain on the world market at a profit to them. The consequences for farmers and rural communities are simply not part of the equation, apart from the ideological conviction that a high volume of sales at any price is better than a low volume.

Cargill and its colleagues want to see commodity production freed from any quantity limitations and any limitations resulting from what they consider to be undue public regulation, for whatever reason. Farmers must not only be free to produce as much as possible, but must be able to utilize whatever 'technology' may be available to assist them in this project. From the corporate perspective, there is no such thing as surplus food. Comparative advantage should rule, not land conservation measures or a need for adequate farm incomes. Any country that can grow food 'competitively' should do so unhindered, with distribution left to the market.

It is not hard to see the corporate rationale for such policy recommendations. Transnational agribusinesses, including the corporations that make up the APWG, all profit according to the volume of commodities produced regardless of the actual prices of the commodities themselves: the higher the production, the more agro-toxins (Monsanto) and fertilizers (Cargill and IMC Fertilizer) required; the more transportation (Norfolk Southern) and trading (Cargill) required; and, the more processing possible (Cargill, Central Soya, Nabisco).

In the US and Europe this maximum-production demand is aimed at the variety of agricultural land set-aside programs that have been put in place for purposes of conservation of marginal and fragile lands, to reduce surplus production, and to increase farm incomes. The Gardner 'study' provides a concise summary of the US Government farm program and income assistance mechanisms that Cargill objects to:

> The US government supports farm income for the major crops through loan rates and deficiency payments. Loan rates are essentially floor prices, which the government agrees to pay for a farmer's crop should market prices fall below the loan rate. Deficiency payments are paid to farmers based on the difference between the loan rate (or market price) and a higher target price multiplied by a farmer's program acreage ... In many years, farmers have produced more output than could be marketed at the support levels. In those years, the Commodity Credit Corporation (CCC) has been obliged to purchase and store commodities ... In an effort to control these storage and acquisition costs, the government implemented 'supply control programs,' such as mandatory set-asides and the Conservation Reserve Program (CRP) that came in with the 1985 Farm Bill.[170]

Gardner's evaluation of these programs is curiously at odds with the policy recommendations of the study as a whole and its sponsors. Gardner writes that, 'With 10% of the nation's wheat and corn acreage base in the reserve, the program has been attractive because it conserves soil, while helping reduce surplus production and supporting farm income.'

Such results might seem reasonable enough, even laudatory, but the reduction in marketable commodities that results runs directly counter to the self-interest of the APWG corporations, namely, maximization of commodity production. One-tenth less acreage is, after all, 10 per cent less pesticides, fertilizers, seeds and so on. While at the time it apparently was politic to let Gardner speak for them, they have since done away with such misrepresentation of their position.

Able, Daft & Early

Cargill's policy position and recommendations were also presented in 1993 in an 'impartial' study prepared by the consulting firm of Abel, Daft & Early (AD&E) entitled, 'Meat, Poultry and Dairy Product Exports: A Silent Revolution – Implications for US Grain and Oilseeds Policies.' Whether the provocatively named firm is real or a pseudonym for the sponsors really doesn't matter. This study was 'supported by' the American Feed Industry Association (which has a $2 million annual budget for educational programs for members and 'legislative and regulatory representation'); the American Meat Institute (which has a $5 million budget 'to create a consumer, legislative, and regulatory environment'); American Poultry International (representing poultry exporters); American Poultry USA Inc. (with a $5 million budget to represent 16 companies); Cargill; ConAgra; Continental Grain; National Cattlemen's Association (with a budget of more than $5 million 'to represent beef cattle producers in national and public affairs' – which includes Cargill, ConAgra and Continental by definition); National Pork Producers Council ('a commodity group' with a $2 million budget); and National Turkey Federation ('a commodity group established to serve the best interests of the turkey industry').[171]

The intent of the AD&E report is to document the importance to the US economy of unrestrained livestock and livestock feed exports and hence of grain and oilseed production. This is the same policy recommendation as the Lesher/Gardner 'study' described above:

> A key to remaining competitive and experiencing rapid export growth in the future lies in having an abundant supply of feedstuffs that are internationally competitive and that support stable growth in US production of meat, poultry, and dairy products.

As I point out elsewhere, Cargill makes similar policy recommendations everywhere it operates, which has to make one wonder how every country can be the winner in a competitive struggle. The AD&E study, for example, points out that 'as the rapid emergence of Thailand as a poultry producer and exporter indicates, the United States must continue to pay attention to being price competitive in order to sustain growth in poultry exports.' The study does not mention that Cargill has a significant presence in Thailand as a feed producer and exporter of cassava (manioc) and as an integrated poultry producer (Sun Valley). The implication of such a recommendation is that Cargill should be able to – indeed, must – lower its effective wage rates in its US poultry operations and squeeze more out of its growers in order to be competitive with its low-wage poultry operations in Thailand. This is the policy rationale for short-weighting its growers, presumably – it's in the national interest! (see Chapter 8).

The argument of the AD&E report is that meat, poultry and dairy products have had the highest rate of growth among agricultural exports in recent years. This growth is being driven by increases in consumer income abroad and trade liberalization. The cumulative result of increasing exports of meat, poultry and dairy products is significant gains in domestic employment, but this meat production requires an unrestricted supply of cheap feed. Therefore the US Government must adopt policies that remove limits on the production of feed gains and oilseeds (reversing the policies of the 1980s and, so far, the 1990s) and encourage their production.

That 'production must be allowed to expand to meet growing feed demand' is the first 'critical element' the paper identifies for such a policy. The second is that the US must 'maintain adequate stocks of grains and oilseeds to prevent sharp fluctuations in grain and protein meal prices.' In other words, it should be national policy to maintain a reserve (oversupply) of feed grains and oilseeds that is sufficient to keep prices 'competitive' (i.e. depressed) so that the livestock and livestock processing industry can afford to produce and export more meat and poultry – at the expense of the grain and oilseeds growers. AD&E offer this non-sensical definition of 'competitive' prices:

> Competitive prices are those levels that over time maintain US shares of world markets for grains and oilseeds deemed reasonable by historic standards, given relative production efficiencies among exporting countries, and taking into account trade distorting measures employed by other countries and the United States as well.

Because the US, as far as food is concerned, is a 'mature' market, the only place increased domestic production can go into is increased exports. The moral justification for this is that 'the United States has a comparative advantage in world trade that encompasses the bulk of agriculture's output' and that 'policies that support competitiveness of these products will yield substantial long-term benefits for the agricultural sector.' Exactly who in the 'agricultural sector' will benefit is not mentioned, nor is the impact of larger meat exports on the importing countries.

In discussing global competition, the report, as is customary in discussion of transnational commerce, mentions only states – Australia, the US, Canada, Japan – just as the term 'agricultural sector' is used without identifying who or what in particular is being referred to. In reading that 'Australia is increasing production and exports of beef' one is encouraged to overlook just who that might, in fact, be. In reality, it may be a Japanese company, such as Nippon Meat Packers, which is increasing the number of cattle on its Australian ranches and processing in its Australian-located plants for export to the Japanese market. In the same way,

'Canadian' beef exports may well have been fattened on contract and processed in Cargill's Alberta plant.

The report casually mentions another factor behind the push for increased US production: 'Some markets are too small to support an efficient domestic industry such as in the many nations that make up the Caribbean and Central American region.' Such a casual dismissal of small-scale economies and self-reliance is, of course, itself a major policy position, yet it too goes unexamined, probably on the assumption that the TNC definintion of 'efficiency' is scientifically beyond debate.

Yet at the same time, 'efficiency' can make allowances for government subsidies, and federally backed export credits and loan guarantees are cited approvingly as tools for enhancing export opportunities and 'to increase US export competitiveness.' The paper suggests that applying export subsidies to 'value-added products such as meat, poultry and dairy products can lead to increases in output and more economic activity, including growth in employment.' With increased production, grain producers are able to 'use their land and other resources more fully and thus reduce per unit production costs.'

The paper then suggests that part of the public policy to build and maintain feed stocks should include interest-free loans to farmers on stored grain. In other words, the industry is calling for public subsidy of grain storage via loans to farmers against the crops they are storing (the current commodity loan program). This would free the business sector from having to purchase grain and store it at their own expense. One might call this a 'just in time' delivery system as developed in the auto industry: the traders, cattle feeders and meat processors, which are in many cases the same companies, would be able to call for grain only when they have a deal, either to sell/deliver the grain, or to feed it to the animals in their feedlots, rather than having to build and pay for storage facilities and the interest on the stored grain.

By having stocks on hand, by which they really mean a surplus to current needs, and by having the public pay for the storage of these stocks, the price of grain can be kept under pressure, that is, down, and the cost of grain utilization as cattle feed likewise kept low. The AD&E paper does not consider the effects of this on the grain and oilseeds growers, except to say that in growing more they can become more efficient and, apparently, more willing to produce for lower prices.

Finally, citing the fact that 'developing oveseas markets for US farm products has been part of US agricultural policy since the mid-1950s,' the paper suggests that meat, poultry and dairy export products 'should continue to receive foreign market development support.' One must remember, of course, that Cargill is a trader in feed grains, a feed manufacturer, and a meat processor and exporter. Allocations for the Market Promotion Program of the US Department of Agriculture for 1993 were $147.7 million.[172]

A second AD&E study, done this time for the National Grain and Feed Association (as opposed to the meat industry sponsorship of the first, though many of the players, like Cargill, are in both) reflects the growing sophistication of the industry argument. Cargill uses this study, which it helped pay for, to argue that the acreage and cropland reduction programs have hurt rural America by drastically reducing the economic activity they depend on, and by increasing the price of their agricultural output, thereby reducing production even further.[173] Cargill's answer: maximum production and minimum prices.

Cargill argues, citing a USDA study, that 'the incomes of rural people and the economies of rural areas each year are becoming less affected by changes in farm prices and the incomes from farm sources,' that only about 20 per cent of the families living on farms received more income from farm sales than from off-farm sources in 1991 and that the percentage continues to drop: therefore lower prices will bring new vitality to rural America through increased production. It is a logic I cannot explain.

In its official *Bulletin*,[174] Cargill says that US federal farm policies over the past few years have 'waged war on American productivity' and cites as one casualty the United States' grain storage and handling capacity which is 40 per cent idle. This reveals that although Cargill may have patience, it also has a short memory: it was the grain industry that urged the US to greatly expand, at public expense in most cases, its grain handling capacity in the 1970s in response to the short-term increase in market (USSR) demand. Now Cargill is blaming public policy for underutilization of facilities for which there never was a real need but which Cargill and other traders wanted as a way of increasing their trading leverage.

The most interesting new twist to its policy position, however, is its explanation of how lower prices and increased production of grains will benefit everyone:

> Progrowth agriculture policy is one of the best strategies for breathing new life into rural America, and into cities and suburbs as well ... A progrowth farm policy becomes an instrument for healthier, more self-sufficient farms and for rural development, job creation and general economic expansion. Americans need to embrace that broader definition of agriculture.[175]

Finally, in a broad attack on commodity groups that continue to lobby for high prices, the *Bulletin* asks, 'Is the US Department of Agriculture basically a farmers' department? Or is it a department to assure that the agricultural economy operates in a way that serves not only the interests of farmers, but also the broader interests of society?'

The demon of idle crop land that Cargill would like to exorcise was described by Whitney MacMillan in a speech to the American Feed Industry Association. Since the 1985 farm bill, he said, the US has idled 440 million acres, an area 'seven times the size of the corn belt'. Consequently, grain exports have declined 20 per cent from 5 billion bushels (1.27 million tonnes) in 1980 to 4 billion bushels (1 million tonnes). 'Farm policy is inviting competitors to step into the breach' in meeting world demand, warned MacMillan.[176] The president of the National Grain and Feed Association put the same sentiments this way: 'grain that is never grown is never planted, never fertilized, never sold, never processed, never fed, and never exported.'[177]

'By locking up millions of acres of productive land for 10 years,' writes the *Cargill Commentary*, 'the Conservation Reserve Program (CRP) has contributed to a drain on rural jobs and economic vitality, shrinkage of the farm-to-market infrastructure and lost exports. Like many other agriculture businesses, Cargill has suffered the consequences.'[178] The *Commentary* then tries to broaden its appeal to include those concerned about the environment:

> The CRP also has had unintended adverse environmental effects on a global level. Idle US farmland that could have been farmed sustainably created a void that other countries filled by cultivating rain forests, deserts and other fragile areas.[179]

I have never seen any references cited that might actually document this argument.

In calling for lower crop prices and higher production levels, Cargill also calls for 'decoupling', the separation of commodity prices from farm income. Farm incomes should be considered as a combination of farm-gate returns for what is produced, off-farm income and deficiency payments. The deficiency payments would really be a form of welfare based on some sort of needs test for those who fail to reach an adequate income level by some combination of farm-gate sales and off-farm income. (Cargill never says where it puts speculative income from playing the futures market.) Cargill now tends to refer to such deficiency payments as 'income support'.

Cargill has been arguing for decoupling for many years. Vice president for public affairs Robbin Johnson said in 1987 that the long-term goal should be 'to have market forces guide resource allocation' while 'farm incomes should be supported directly rather than through price guarantees.'[180]

The ironic twist in this is that there would no longer be a meaningful market price, or price-setting mechanism, because supply and demand would be decoupled and prices would be set solely by the buyers. Of course, this has always been Cargill's objective.

Though offered as a moral solution to the ills of rural America, the hungry of the world, and the growing populations of the 'newly industrializing countries of Asia and the Pacific Rim,' Cargill never explains how the unfettered growth of agricultural production in the US will actually address these problems. Instead of a policy or an explanation, what it offers is a heavy dose of ideology, highly uncharacteristic of Cargill's functional pragmatism:

> Agriculture cannot afford solutions that pit efficiency against ecology. Farmers must produce more while producing better ... Policy makers will be more successful at fulfilling those twin tasks through the deployment of market forces and incentives ... Markets have proven the best means of coordinating our complex food system.[181]

'Development'

In recent years Cargill has elaborated, in public, what it feels to be its proper place and responsibility in addressing the problem of hunger in the world. At first I thought this was a rather novel and sophisticated way of furthering its corporate interests. How better to position itself than as the most efficient delivery vehicle for sustainable development? Cargill Chairman Whitney MacMillan has been saying this since 1988 at least:

> We believe we can contribute to rural development by investing in the services necessary for successful agricultural production. Providing seeds, feeds, fertilizer, storage, distribution and marketing services are obvious and important examples. We also could be a source of production credit, farm implements, harvesting services and insurance. And we can offer plenty of plain old good advice accumulated from our worldwide experience.[182]

Then I discovered that Cargill adopted this policy from Nelson Rockefeller in 1947. W.G. Broehl records that in 1947 Cargill entered into a business arrangement with Nelson Rockefeller in Brazil, where Rockefeller wanted 'to demonstrate that private capital organized as a for-profit enterprise could also upgrade the economics of less-developed countries.'[183] To do this, Rockefeller had formed the International Basic Economy Corporation (IBEC) in Brazil as a family-held business. Among the enterprises intended for this business were a hybrid seed corn company, a hog production company, a helicopter crop-dusting company and a contract farm machinery company.[184] This was, of course, even before all the Rockefeller Green Revolution initiatives of the 1960s and 1970s.

The 'plain old good advice' offered by Cargill is really very simple, and it is based on the economic theory of comparative advantage: those regions that can produce a surplus of food efficiently have a responsibility to do so. Those regions with conditions adverse to the 'efficient' production of food should pursue other economic activities and purchase their food with the money thus acquired. Cargill's role in this is as trader, broker, processor, distributor – in short, middleman – making the whole system function. Whitney MacMillan again:

> There is a mistaken belief that the greatest agricultural need in the developing world is to develop the capacity to grow food for local consumption. That is misguided. Countries should produce what they produce best, and trade ... Subsistence agriculture ... encourages misuse of resources and damage to the environment.[185]

Maximizing production and allowing the market free play may be Cargill's solution to world hunger, social justice and good ecology. But first the problem has to be properly defined:

The United States holds a reserve of highly competitive resources that the world needs ... It would be wise policy to eliminate acreage reduction programs quickly rather than stand by and watch this opportunity pass to less efficient competitors.[186]

In his address to the Columbus, Ohio, Council on World Affairs in 1993, Whitney MacMillan addressed the question, 'Why can't we feed hungry people?'. He first defined the problem and then outlined the public policies he thought necessary to deal with the causes and not just the symptoms of hunger.

Our problem isn't a shortage of food supplies ... The real problems occur when people don't have money or access ...

There is no guarantee that charitable organizations or foundations will ever have the luxury of enough resources to meet relief needs, let alone adequately address the larger and more fundamental issue of generating economic growth ...

I believe this century has seen the emergence of another institution ... capable of playing a major role in attacking the world hunger problem, if allowed to do so. That institution is the modern global company.

Companies like Cargill ... do things that go to the heart of our hunger problem. We bring goods and services needed by people that are fundamental to their well-being. We create markets that otherwise might not be available. We bring needed capital, and we transfer technology and expertise that adds to the efficiency of the marketplace, and we transfer the economic gains from that added efficiency to both the people we buy from and the people we sell to.[187]

The government policies that would make all this possible, according to MacMillan, included: enhancing the ability of the developing world to move from subsistence agriculture to commercial systems; trade liberalization; greater reliance on market-based economic principles; economic and tax policies that encourage investment; and using the productive capacity of the United States 'to meet the food needs of a hungry world.' MacMillan stressed that, 'Our job at Cargill is to help build better sustainable agricultural systems ... Our task is made much more complicated, much more difficult, and sometimes outright impossible if we don't have the kind of public policies that foster the kind of long-term, sustainable economic growth on which all our aspirations for this world are based.'[188]

Cargill public affairs vice president Robbin Johnson delivered a similar message to the USDA Outlook '93 Conference:

Breaking the poverty cycle means shifting from subsistence agriculture to commercialized agriculture. Subsistence agriculture locks peasants out of income growth; it leaves populations outside the food-trading system and therefore more vulnerable to crop disasters, and it harms the environment through overuse of fragile land resources.

Agribusiness must wring excess costs and waste out of the food system, largely through the use of productivity-enhancing technology ... To promote innovation while protecting health, sound science needs to be the foundation of both domestic and international regulatory policy.[189]

A Private Sector Approach to Agricultural Development is the title of an informal document, apparently published by Cargill in late 1993, that contains a list of countries where Cargill has operations, a list of Cargill products worldwide either traded or produced, a partial listing of the *Fortune* 500 companies for 1993, and a list of 'Potential Dynamic Contributions of Agricultural Development to Overall Development':

- Labor for an industrial workforce
- Raw materials for an agricultural processing industry
- More/better quality food at lower cost for an expanding population with rising incomes
- Saving/capital for industrial investments
- Export earnings to pay for imported capital goods
- Increased rural income and employment as a market for industrial output as well as for its own sake.

Among the tables in this curious document is one for 'Cargill Argentina Financial Contributions 1948–75,' including sales figures and net worth and a similar table for Brazil covering the period from 1968 to 1983. There are also tables for 'Cargill Argentina job creation 1960–1993' and 'Cargill Brazil job creation 1960–1993,' a table of Cargill Brazil's profit (loss) for the years 1966–78, and a table for Brazilian corn and soybean exports 1963–68.

The document also lists Cargill's Asian operations in 1983, provides a table of 'Cargill Southeast Asia job impact 1993' by country, and, in a separate box, the following:

Our main problem in investing in Asian host countries has been the host government approval process to make an investment in the first place. How can we convince the host country to let us take all the business risks normal to that of a host country entrepreneur?

Times spent by us have been:

Indonesian Feed Expansion	1.4 years
Indonesian Hybrid Seed	1.5 years
Indonesian Hybrid Poultry	4.5 years
India Hybrid Sunflower Seed	4.0 years
Pakistan Frozen Orange Juice	3.0 years
Japan Feed	1.0 year
Korea Feed	1.0 year
Thai Poultry	3.0 months
Philippine Copra Crushing	2.0 years
Malaysia Feed	4.0 months

Finally, the document gives tables of capital contribution and accumulation and balance of payments contribution by Cargill in Brazil, Argentina, Southeast Asia and Africa for 1993.

Because the dates or periods covered by the figures vary, and because there is little meaningful description of how the figures were arrived at, the document in fact provides much less real information than it appears to. There is no reason to think that this is accidental, given Cargill's very great reluctance to reveal any kind of financial or strategic information. But the intent of the document is clearly to buttress Cargill's arguments that it is a most worthy agent of 'development' if only given the chance. Hence the comment about government approval process. One suspects this document might have been prepared after Cargill's strategic defeat/retreat in Kandla Port, India, in 1993 (see Chapter 15).

Later, James R. Wilson of Cargill Technical Services in England sent me a copy of a paper he had presented to an international gathering on development (The Salzburg Seminar) in January 1994. The title of the paper: 'A Private Sector Approach to Agricultural Development.' Clearly the document described above was the raw material for Wilson's presentation, and equally clearly it must have been circulating through the company in one form or another for some time and can, therefore, be taken as the Cargill line.

The outstanding feature of Wilson's paper is the use of the language of military strategy. In fact, this sort of military terminology is used throughout Cargill's corporate information, but never in sufficient concentration to be really obvious. The terminology and the strategic thinking that it expresses must be what the corporation means by the term 'Cargill Culture'. It is a culture dominated by militarism and aggression. I found that a brochure describing 'Career Opportunities at Cargill' asks, 'Who are we looking for? ... We seek talented and aggressive individuals ...'.*

Wilson's paper provides a brief statistical and policy review of agriculture's role in development since World War II, and then states that 'a partnership and a balance between government and private companies and individual entrepreneurs – between public sector and private sector – is necessary for successful development effort.'

In reviewing Cargill's 'Development Strategy', Wilson points out that 43 per cent of the company's investment and 30 per cent of its workforce are outside the USA and that as Cargill has developed, its 'job creation' in the US has increased at about the same rate as its foreign employment, at least from the mid-1960s.

Wilson then explicitly describes Cargill's approach to starting a business in a developing country – or almost any other place, for that matter:

---

* The military fascination does not seem to be unique to Cargill. In the ConAgra Inc. annual report for 1994, chairman and CEO Philip Fletcher says that 'strategic war gaming ... is a significant investment to sharpen management's strategic skills ... We brought together about 60 senior operating and corporate staff officers to wage a strategic war game. ConAgra and competitor companies battled for nine years (in three days) to win in the marketplace of the future.'

Cargill speaks of beachheads. Much of business strategy has its origins in military strategy. Historic product-line beachheads for the company have been hybrid seeds (primarily corn), commodity export marketing, and animal feed milling. The strategy has been: create the beachhead with inputs of capital, technology and a management nucleus; get the cash flow positive; re-invest the cash flow and expand the beachhead … The company generally insists on majority ownership in beachhead companies because it needs to be clear who is responsible for the management of an individual company.

Wilson then provides four regional illustrations of Cargill's 'development' practices. He describes Argentina in the 1960s as Cargill's 'first major beachhead'; the product-line used was hybrid corn seed. With an initial capital input of $175,000 in 1948, by 1975 nearly $5 million in dividends had been taken out of Argentina 'to protect working capital from inflation and devaluation.' The value of the investment had, at the same time, increased to nearly $20 million. Wilson emphasizes that from 1948 to 1966 no dividends were taken out, and that this distinguishes Cargill from most public sector aid and development programs that have a time frame of three to five years. In addition to Argentina, Wilson says, Cargill used hybrid seed as a beachhead in India, Pakistan, Zambia, Zimbabwe, South Africa, Tanzania and Malawi.

Brazil was 'the site of Cargill's second major development effort.' Here the company established 'a commodity export beachhead' and from 1967 to 1975 invested $9.3 million, taking out in dividends of only $773,000. However, this policy led, by 1975, to capital formation inside Brazil of $87.8 million. Without explaining what happened in the intervening years, Wilson says Cargill's exports from Brazil in 1993 were $294 million. Given Cargill's activities in Brazil, these exports were probably composed largely of soybeans, soybean oil and meal, and frozen orange juice concentrate.

Wilson's paper includes a statement of Cargill Brazil's 'formal strategy' that includes among its goals and objectives: 'Donate 1 per cent of our net income before taxes to the Cargill Foundation to carry out its program of providing for agricultural scholarships, scientific meetings, etc.' Some of the 'etc.' is, in all likelihood, used to sponsor the work of commodity and other organizations that will advance the Cargill policy agenda.

In terms of 'development', says Wilson, Cargill had created 4505 full-time jobs by 1993 'plus 3280 full-time equivalents for orange harvesting, seed planting and seed detasseling.'

In addition to Brazil, Wilson writes, 'Commodity export marketing has been used as a development beachhead in Thailand (tapioca/cassava), Philippines (copra), Malawi (cotton), Peru (fishmeal/fishoil) and Ivory Coast (cocoa).'

The third region Wilson looks at is Southeast Asia. Cargill did not set up a regional management team in Singapore until 1983. Since then $155.3 million in capital and 'inter-company loans' has been invested in the region. By 1994 the net worth of Cargill companies in the region had grown to $60 million, but only in 1993 did the region finally 'turn a profit'. 'Animal feed milling was the domestic market beachhead in Southeast Asia as well as in Central America, Korea, and most recently, Poland,' writes Wilson.

Africa is the fourth development region cited, and is focused on six countries. Capital inputs up to 1994 have been $9 million, with loses incurred overall in the region until 1992 and only $354,000 taken out as dividends. Cargill has 1250 full-time employees in the region.

Wilson's summation of his research paper is that 'although the bottom line of business long-term is certainly to make a profit, the private sector, in patient pursuit of profit, can have a significant role in agricultural development.'

Cargill's corporate consistency in its interpretation of reality and in its policy advocacy can only come from strong, highly centralized leadership. In recent years Whitney MacMillan has provided that leadership and articulated that policy. A 1993 profile of MacMillan reported that he was 'remembered as having said that Cargill is in the global economic development business. Cargill enters a country, perhaps selling seed. It may then invest in a plant, creating jobs. It implements efficient methods of processing and distributing agricultural products. And it leaves profits there, to be reinvested.'[190]

Cargill was not able to establish a beachhead in the old Soviet Union, however much it might sell to the country. It has suffered a similar confinement with Japan, though in the case of Japan it has been the *zaibatsu* (large industrial combines) that have imposed the confinement, not the government itself (see Chapter 14). With the collapse of the Soviet Union, however, Cargill, along with every other agribusiness TNC, has sought to establish a presence and carve out a territory. Prospects for big business remain dim, however, since the countries of the former Soviet Union have not transformed themselves brightly and successfully into so-called free market economies.

Cargill has no intention of giving up, however. The situation just calls for a different strategy, which Cargill articulated, as usual, in its *Bulletin*. First it suggested that adequate and possibly subsidized credit facilities for the farmers in the region would make it possible for them to buy seeds, fertilizer and machinery. Then:

> Direct help is needed with technical assistance and farm management. That means more than short-term advice. It will take a generation to reeducate people to think in terms of entrepreneurship and markets ... Needed now are policies that encourage competition and reward the survivors.[191]

Apparently this is what Cargill means by 'development'!

This sounds very much like the project in Brazil many years ago with the Rockefellers and the strategy that Cargill has pursued in Thailand and Taiwan (see Chapter 8). If the Cargill scenario is implemented, then it could expect to be the supplier of inputs and advice, as well as the buyer, if not also the processor, of the commodities produced. The outcome, Cargill says, would be that 'Western

Europe and the United States could find themselves competing in third country markets with added value products from Eastern Europe and the former Soviet Union. Such are the opportunities of capitalism.'[192]

In fact, Cargill has, over the years, worked at putting in place the infrastructure for such policies. In 1987, along with 18 other TNCs with offices in Switzerland, Cargill formed the International Enterprise Foundation of Geneva (IEFG). A year later businessmen in Zimbabwe founded a sister organization (IEFZ). Its first major project was a business training program for small farmers, funded by the Danish relief agency Danida. Cargill established an office in Harare, Zimbabwe in 1991 and planned to work closely with IEFZ.[193]

The International Centre for Agricultural Science and Technology (ICAST), established by Cargill Ltd (Canada) in 1992, is strikingly similar in structure and intent. ICAST, with offices in Innovation Place, the 'campus' of biotechnology promotion and practice at the University of Saskatchewan, is 'an alliance of all of the players in the agri-food industry ... to accelerate the utilization and commercialization of value added products and technologies.' In practice this is an alliance of agribusiness interests to ensure that private corporations capture every possible benefit from publicly funded research and development.

To get off the ground, this free market industry organization apparently required Can$11 million of public money: Can$6.5 million from the Government of Canada through the Western Diversification Fund and Can$4.5 million from the Saskatchewan Agricultural Development Fund. The Chairman of its board of directors is none other than the president of Cargill Ltd, Kerry Hawkins.[194]

ICAST itself describes its mission as one of:

> forging and maintaining strategic alliances among farmers, industry, government, and institutions to create a culture enabling technology development, ensuring substantial economic prosperity, and enhancing product quality and safety.

ICAST claims that it will achieve for:

> the regions of Canada ... a regional/international investment capacity with a strong focus on market opportunities, facilitating world class project networks, and increasing farm-gate value added and agri-food manufacturing at the local level.[195]

ICAST vice president Frank Gleeson reassured the public in 1994 that although ICAST was created with government funding, it operates in a business-like way. All the staff are from business, as are the board of directors, from major companies including Cargill, Monsanto and McCain Foods. As he said 'ICAST is above politics ... What we're about is enhancing competitive advantage.'[196]

When one gets sensitized to such ideological and organizational approaches, a news story in the Mexican business weekly *El Financiero International*[197] that might otherwise go unnoticed catches one's eye, as did a report of the establishment of The Mexican Foundation for Innovation and Technological Transfer in Small and Medium Businesses, or 'Funtec'. The board of the foundation consists of Mexican businessmen, including some who work for foreign transnationals. The report suggested that it was the World Bank that provided the $20 million with which the new foundation acquired the testing laboratories of the federal government. It all sounds familiar, and very similar to ICAST or IBEC.

CHAPTER 8

Feeds and Meat: Feeds, Beef, Poultry, Pork and Catfish

Feeds

For an aggressive company in the business of trading, transporting and storing – 'merchandising' – grains, to move upstream and downstream in 'value added' activities would seem logical and, indeed, inevitable. But it wasn't until the late 1930s that Cargill moved into the formulated feeds business and not until the 1960s that it moved downstream into slaughtering and processing cattle, hogs and poultry. When it fully integrated its extended lines of business, from seed to feed to slaughter, Cargill could take full advantage of the resulting synergies and financial efficiencies. The process appears to be a combination of the rational pursuit of profit and growth combined with skillful analysis to identify new lines of opportunity.

Will Cargill had sold simple feeds – milled grains, essentially – as early as 1884, but a more serious start was made in 1934 in Montana with 'Cargill' brand feeds. Five years later Cargill entered the formula feed business with the construction of new buildings in Lennox, South Dakota, specifically for the purpose of feed manufacturing, marketing the product under the brand name 'Blue Square'. This business expanded rapidly into Minnesota and Iowa and was run for some time quite separately from the Montana feed division.

At the end of the war in 1945, Cargill made two big acquisitions in feed milling and oilseed processing: Honeymead Products Co. of Cedar Rapids, Iowa, which included a feed plant and a soybean processing mill, and Nutrena Mills in Kansas.

Honeymead was owned by the Andreas family, and when it was bought by Cargill it was being run by a young member of the family, 27-year-old Dwayne. Dwayne Andreas stayed with Honeymead and Cargill, soon becoming a vice president. He left Cargill in 1952 in a dispute over management styles and went to work for the Grain Terminal Association.[198] In 1966 Dwayne Andreas and his younger brother Lowell were invited by the Archer and Daniels families to become majority shareholders of their company, Archer Daniels Midland (ADM), and to run it. In 1971 Dwayne became CEO of the company.[199] Under the leadership of Andreas, ADM has become a major competitor to Cargill in oilseed processing, flour milling, grain handling and other activities, though with a very different management style. Andreas, 75, was still head of ADM, as chairman of the board, in 1994.

The purchase of Nutrena Mills, then a major midwest milling company centered in Kansas and offering a complete line of poultry, dairy and hog feeds, cost Cargill $1.6 million and took the company directly into the retail world.[200] Nutrena became Cargill's feed division and Cargill's Montana-based Blue Square brand was replaced by the Nutrena label.

The company's next expansion in the feed business came six years later with the acquisition of a major interest in Royal Feed and Milling Co. of Memphis in 1951. Cargill rolled it into Nutrena and in the years following continued its expansion in different regions of the country, acquiring Beacon Milling in 1985 and buying ACCO from Quaker Oats in 1987. Beacon serves the East and ACCO serves the Southwest.

Cargill extended its Nutrena feeds business into the US northwest with the purchase in 1989 of Hansen & Peterson, Inc., of Burlington, Washington, including their feed mill. This gave Cargill a total of 58 mills in Canada and the US. The Washington State acquisition complements Cargill's big mill in Stockton, California, and suggests that Cargill believes that the dairy and cattle business will continue to be concentrated in the West. Further evidence of this is the company's construction of a $10 million feedmill at Hanford, California, in 1992. With a planned capacity of 180,000 tonnes per year of dairy feed primarily, this will be the biggest feedmill Cargill has ever built.

In the same year Cargill began building a $5 million feed mill at Wooster, Ohio, with an annual capacity of 60–70,000 tonnes of livestock feed,[201] and completed the purchase of its first feed mill in Louisiana. The 60,000 tonne capacity mill serves the aquaculture industry as well as supplying bagged animal feeds.[202]

Cargill's expansion in the feed business in Canada paralleled that in the US. When it purchased National Grain in 1974, the package included five feed mills. In 1985 or 1986 it purchased Kola Feeds in Brandon, Manitoba, and then Southern Feeds in Lethbridge, Alberta, where it already had a molasses-based liquid feed supplement plant. This made Cargill the top feed supplier in the major cattle producing region of the country, but it did not stop there. Cargill expanded its fertilizer services by adding four small blending facilities, starting 11 others, and buying two fertilizer sales operations in Saskatchewan and Manitoba.*

Cargill continued its relentless expansion in the retail feeds business, establishing a beachhead in Ontario in 1987 with the purchase of Ayr Feeds, primarily a supplier of feed to the poultry business. At the time, Cargill owned nearby Shaver Poultry, a major source of laying hen 'genetics', otherwise known as

---

* When Cargill decided to close the Kola mill in 1990, the former owner of the plant, which specializes in steam-rolled grain, bought it back rather than see it close. Mill manager Sharon Walker said that the area does need the mill and with it locally owned again, any profits from the business will remain in the area. (*Virden Empire Advance*, 5 December 90)

breeding stock. The next year it gained a lot of new territory with the purchase of the feed mills of Maple Leaf Mills from Hillsdown Holdings for $40 million. (Hillsdown had bought Maple Leaf Mills from Canadian Pacific the year before.) Cargill then sold Ayr Feeds to Maple Lodge Farms, Ontario's own *Integrator* (the company supplies chicks and feed and buys the birds for killing and processing) in the poultry business, because, as Cargill troubleshooter Ian Gillies put it, 'the poultry business does not really appeal to Cargill and the plant could not easily be upgraded to serve the purposes of Cargill. It was a mistake but it did help us to understand the Ontario market.'[203] The acquisition of Maple Leaf Mills also made Cargill Canada's largest soybean handler.

Cargill's next move in Ontario was to purchase Arkona Feed Mills in Arkona, Ontario, from the Brown family in 1989. Cargill spent $1.5 million upgrading the plant so that it could serve the specialized hog and dairy industries of Michigan and Ontario with its Nutrena feeds. The Arkona management now reports to Cargill's feed plant in Mentone, Indiana, which was itself expanded in 1994 to process 100,000–120,000 tonnes of feed annually. This transnational integration was not a fruit of free trade agreements, since feed grains already moved freely across the US-Canadian border, but simply one expression of Cargill's long term continental strategy and its 'ecological' perspective. Southwestern Ontario, southern Michigan and northern Ohio and Indiana constitute a kind of bioregion.

Today Cargill has 60 feed mills in the US and another 60 outside the US. It is also a major producer of feed supplements, based on the products of its molasses division, and it operates the fourth largest feedlot enterprise in the US, Caprock Industries. Caprock, located in Texas, has the capacity to feed 293,000 head of cattle at one time. (The largest cattle feeder in the US is Continental Grain with a one-time feeding capacity of 373,000 head.)[204]

Cargill also owns integrated chicken and turkey operations in the US southeast that utilize its Nutrena feeds.

Moving in the other direction, Cargill is the third largest beef packer in the US, the third largest poultry processor and the fifth largest hog slaughterer. Much of the livestock that it kills and processes is raised under contract, and these contracts often specify the use of Nutrena feeds. Cargill also supplies advisory and veterinary services, and may also finance the cattle that are fed under contract.

Beef

In one of his more ebullient moods, Cargill Canada's long-time vice president Dick Dawson, who retired in 1993, once said of Canada and the meat business:

> More people all over the world are living better today. Our challenge is to grow more tons, value add to more meat, value add again to more further processing and selling into a rising market … More people live at even higher

standards the world over. More people also starve. All the graphs point upward. We are in an irreplaceable business on a growth trend.[205]

Meat is big business. World production in 1993 was estimated at 164 billion kilograms. The largest component of this is pork, with 1993 output estimated to be 69 billion kg. Beef ranks second at 48 billion kg and poultry third at 41 billion kg. Production of beef and veal has remained fairly stable, though it has dropped as a percentage of global meat production from 36 per cent to 29 per cent since 1983. Poultry, on the other hand, increased from 20 per cent to nearly 25 per cent. The US accounted for about 22 per cent of global beef production in 1992, with the EC second with 17 per cent.[206]

Most of the beef cattle in the US are in the central plains, with 65 per cent of cattle marketed coming fron Nebraska, Kansas and Texas; 80 per cent of these US cattle are sold through feedlots, with 210 feedlots marketing half the cattle. There are 840,000 beef cattle operations in the US with 780,000 of them having fewer than 100 cows. The beef cattle population itself is estimated at 100 million, down from 132 million in 1975. In 1992 the US exported 1.2 billion pounds of beef. Carcass weights average 710 pounds.[207]

In 1980 there were 78,000 feedlots in the 13 major cattle-feeding states. By 1992 this number had dropped to 46,450, although the number of cattle on feed remained relatively constant as the feedlots got bigger. The location of the slaughter industry has shifted from the centres of population to the centres of production due to the ease and lower cost of shipping boxed meat as opposed to live cattle or even carcass beef. Boxed beef is itself a relatively modern concept, dependent on recent transport and packaging innovations such as vacuum packing and adequate refrigeration. Prior to the era of boxed beef and massive trucking, beef was shipped by rail as 'swinging' beef (split carcasses hanging from a hook) in refrigerated railcars. The rail journey from western slaughter-house to eastern market provided time for ageing of the meat.

Nebraska Corn and Beef

The scale of contemporary North American beef production is hard to imagine. It is also hard to see. Getting a tour of a large packing plant to get a first-hand view of the deconstruction of a large animal is a virtual impossibility for reasons of health and safety and corporate trade secrets. Beef feedlots are visible and visitable, but are located only in very particular geographies and beyond the traveling reach of most people. The only more or less ubiquitous and visible aspect of beef production are the fields of corn and grains that constitute the bulk of feedlot cattle feed. (The feedlot conversion ration is 8–9 pounds of grain to produce one pound of beef.) Fortunately, feedlots and packing houses are not the totality of the beef industry. There are the cow/calf farms (the source of feedlot cattle) and there are farms that raise essentially grass-fed beef. The feedlot, though assumed to be immortal, was, in fact, only invented in the 1950s as a mechanism to use up the surplus grains that were no longer welcome in Europe and became the foundation of the current highly concentrated beef industry in which Cargill is a very major player. There is no better place to get a view of this activity than in the corn and beef country of central Nebraska, so I spent a few days there looking around.

As of January 1 1993, Nebraska ranked second to Texas in number of cattle and calves in the state (5.9 million to 14.3 million in Texas) and number of cattle on feed (2.13 million in 6400 feedlots to 2.46 million in Texas). It ranked first in number of cattle slaughtered in the state with 6.58 million head killed in 46 plants in 1992.

In 1992 the top three states in production of corn for grain, i.e., livestock feed, were Iowa, with 1.9 billion bushels, Illinois with 1.66 billion bushels, and Nebraska with 1.06 billion bushels. The US total was 9.48 billion bushels, or 241 million tonnes.[208]

Nebraska corn is grown and utilized by feedlots or it is shipped westward by rail, either for export from Cargill's Pier 86 terminal in Seattle or to chicken and turkey growers in California or Monfort (ConAgra) beef feedlots in Colorado. (The corn is shipped in 75-car trains, one train carrying 6732 tonnes.) The fact that ConAgra might buy feed from its arch competitor Cargill simply illustrates that competition has its limits and that there are class interests that bind big to big.

The railroad west from Omaha, where ConAgra has its baronial headquarters, passes through Central City, Wood River and Gibbon, three of the ten locations in the state where Cargill has grain elevators. All the elevators are on railway lines, none far from the main line west, the only direction Cargill moves grain from Nebraska. Because of the intensity of corn production – 'continuous corn' on 97 per cent of the land – each elevator can draw on farms within something like a 20-mile radius. Most corn is grown under contract to a company like Cargill or a consumer products company like Quaker Oats.

Wood River is an older facility with both upright silo and horizontal shed grain storage, the latter requiring a day and a half to load a 75-car train. When the grain comes in by truck it is dumped and then pushed into piles in the sheds by means of front-end loaders. Loading a train requires the same loaders to move the grain to a point where it can be conveyed (elevated) upwards and then flow into the rail car.

The woman running Cargill's Wood River elevator, which handles about 2 million bushels (51,000 tonnes) per year (she said) has been working there 17 years and clearly knows her business, which is buying corn from the farmers and selling it for domestic food and feed use. She does this with the help of two satellite hook-ups, one to the futures market at the Chicago Board of Trade and the other to Cargill's own network. Export sales, however, are handled by the Cargill traders in Minneapolis, who forward orders for her to fill.

The Cargill facility in Central City handles fertilizer in addition to grain. The large amounts of anhydrous ammonia and other fertilizers that the facility distributes are acquired by Cargill's head office, which tells the Central City staff where they have to go to pick it up, either by truck or rail car.

Bradshaw is not quite on the main line, but that does not hinder the Cargill elevator there from handling about 6.5 million bushels (165,000 tonnes) of corn per year split between yellow corn for export and white corn grown under contract for Quaker Oats at St Joseph, Missouri. Bradshaw also handles 100,000–200,000 bushels (2,500–5,000 tonnes) of soybeans and a like amount of milo (sorghum). These volumes reflect the domination of corn (with yields of 200 bushels per acre) in the region.

Despite the fact that Nebraska raises 25 per cent of all the beef in the US, and that it is all slaughtered in Nebraska, Cargill sells very little corn for cattle feed in the state because the feedlots grow their own. Caprock Industries, Cargill's feedlot subsidiary, is centered in Texas, and draws its feed requirements from the southwest. The Nebraska feedlots do purchase feed supplement, usually a custom blend of minerals and vitamins in a molasses base, or with a molasses glue, from Cargill's plant in Grand Island. Molasses is one of Cargill's global product lines.

One 14,000-head capacity feedlot I visited had four different grades of supplement, one for heifers, one for steers, one for lighter animals and one for heavier animals. While there were only 7000 head of cattle on feed in the lot at the time I was there, there was a constant cycling of mixer-feeder trucks that would make a run down a long feedbunk and then return to the storage area for another load. I asked the loader operator where the cattle went for slaughter, did any go to Cargill? No, he said, they went to IBP, Monfort and Excel, all of which have very large plants in the region. He was surprised when I told him that Excel *is* Cargill![*]

Miles of feedlots are situated on a south-facing slope that follows the wide arc of the Elkhorn River in the northeast quadrant of the state. The flat bottom land of what was once a much bigger river is now corn, while the feedlots utilize what was once the river bank. The uplands are corn again. There is not much 'wasted' space, unless, of course, you count that taken up by the feedlots themselves. It is all a stunning example of monoculture.

The Cargill feed and feed supplement business in the region is carried on both under the Cargill/Nutrena and Walnut Grove names. Cargill's big supplement plant at Grand Island supplies hog and cow/calf farms as well as feedlots directly as well as other Cargill and Walnut Grove locations for distribution to smaller users.

---

[*] After putting a metered amount of supplement in their mixer tank, the driver would position the truck for loading – 8000 lbs at a time – by means of a front-end loader, with more or less one scoop of grass silage, one scoop of corn silage, one scoop of hot-rolled grain corn. While the truck was going up the hill to the feedlot, the agitator would mix the feed and then auger it out into the feed bunk as the truck moved along at a pretty good clip. No personal service there.

Walnut Grove was a local feed company for many years. The three warehouse locations and one feed plant give no visual or print clues to Cargill ownership, having been purchased by Cargill from W.R. Grace in 1991. (In the same deal, Cargill also acquired Farr Better Feeds in Colorado from W.R. Grace.)

The men I talked with in the Walnut Grove office were not happy about working for Cargill. They thought working conditions were bad under W.R. Grace, compared to when it was a local company, and worse under Cargill. They said that Cargill is arrogant and that salesmen have to have a university degree to get hired, but you can't sell feed just because you have a laptop computer, which is now mandatory. The men said they are not supposed to talk baseball or family with customers, just 'business'. But that does not sell feed – which is why they try to keep invisible their Cargill ownership.

Company caps – the kind of baseball caps with corporate logos that company salesmen give away to their customers and that every farmer has at least six of – used to cost the Walnut Grove salesmen a dollar. I was told that Cargill raised the price to $5 and then gave the salesmen a 4 per cent raise, which just about covered the extra cost of the caps. They also told me that business went down when Cargill bought Walnut Grove because the local people don't like doing business with Cargill. Cargill is just too big, has too much power, they said.

When Cargill bought the business, they told me, it fired more than half the management. No-one can understand the accounting systems they are now forced to use. I later discovered that Cargill feed dealers around the world are supposed to be using the same system. There is resistance, however, in very disparate places. I heard a very similar story in Taiwan! (see Chapter 12). No-one at the retail level may understand it, and it may not sell grain, but the uniform accounting language insisted upon by head office has another purpose: 'One of the challenges in running a worldwide business is making sure employees are talking the same language when it comes to reporting on business performance.'

In 1990 Nutrena standardized its reporting forms throughout North America, but separate computer systems were being utilized, in the local language, in other 'geographies'. 'Not only was it impossible for these locations to do all their business in English, but cultural differences and a large variety of local business practices made a common system seem impossible.' By 1993, however, Cargill could report that 'in the fishing village of Shibushi, on the southernmost island of Japan' and in Nakom Pathom, Thailand, local employees are working in their own languages but the figures they sent to Cargill headquarters in the USA were all in the same format thanks to special computers that translate the information and store it in a file from which it can be retrieved in any language, providing Cargill with 'a flexible system that is the same throughout the world.'[209]

Months after my Nebraska visit, I heard that Cargill peremptorily fired the Walnut Grove salesmen, with a pittance of severance pay.

In looking at any aspect of Cargill's activites, one has to work with limited information. Many requests for information have gone unanswered; and while I could travel to Nebraska and India, I could not also travel to every other location in which Cargill is active, such as Warsaw and Moscow where Cargill opened offices in 1990 and 1991 to prepare the way for future investments. Even this limited bit of information, however, gives an indication of Cargill's strategy in the region.

Based on the intelligence gathered from these advance listening posts, Cargill used its stock weapon, feed milling, to establish a beachhead in Poland. In 1992 it opened a $750,000 poultry and pig feed mill in the province of Plock with plans to triple the plant's current capacity of 30,000 tonnes per year. Consistent with its principle of holding a controlling interest in any joint venture, Cargill holds 60 per cent of the new company, Cargill Pasze SA, with the remaining 40 per cent held by the provincial government of Plock. Roger Murray, president of Cargill Europe, described the move as, 'a major step in our long-term strategy of becoming a significant presence in Polish agriculture.'[210] Cargill is also building a second 100,000 tonne capacity feed mill in Siedice, southeast of Warsaw.

Meat Packing

You want to go back to the 19th century? You want to have a packinghouse in every little town and deal with 21st century marketing? There's no way! … There is no stopping it. This is an evolution that's going to take place in spite of whoever is in the way.

Robert Peterson, chairman and CEO of IBP Inc.[211]

Table 8.1: Meat & Poultry's top 100, July 1992, 1993 and 1994 (US meat and poultry results only)

| | Sales in $ billion | | | No. of |
	'91	'92	'93	employees
ConAgra, Inc.	12.5	16.2	12.7	83,975*
IBP, Inc.	10.4	11.1	11.7	29,000
Cargill Meat Sector	6.0	8.0	8.0	18,500
Tyson Foods, Inc.	3.9	4.2	4.7	50,000†
Hormel Foods Corp.	2.8	2.8	2.8	10,400
Sara Lee Corp.	2.8	2.8	2.9	14,000
Oscar Mayer Foods	2.3	2.1	2.1	10,000
John Morrell & Co.	2.1	2.1	1.5	5,700

* 1992 figures are total sales, 1991 and 1993 figures are estimate of meat only. ConAgra's employee figure reflects a lot of further processing, such as prepared dinners.
† The high employment figure reflects Tyson's concentration in poultry processing, which is labor intensive.
The purchase of National Beef and Hyplains Beef by Farmland Industries in 1993 will move Farmland into fourth place ahead of Hormel.

In terms of commercial cattle slaughter only, the market share of the top three companies has increased from 52.9 per cent in 1988 to 61.5 per cent in 1993, with IBP holding 27.9 per cent, ConAgra (Monfort) holding 17.1 per cent, and Cargill (Excel) holding 16.5 per cent.[212]

The concentration indicated above is also expressed in the growth of large plants. In 1982 there were 12 plants in the US with an annual capacity for slaughter of 500,000 or more beasts and they accounted for 28 per cent of the cattle slaughter. Ten years later there were 20 plants in this category handling 60 per cent. In comparison, there are just two plants in Canada with a capacity of 400,000–500,000 beasts per year, Cargill and Lakeside Packers, both in Alberta.[213]

ConAgra is the number one packer by far. Its US-based companies processed about 6 million cattle and more than 9.5 million hogs in 1993–4. Their poultry sales were more than $1.6 billion on about 10 million dressed pounds of broiler chicken. In 1994 ConAgra increased its holdings in Australian Meat Holdings from 50 per cent to 91 per cent. AMH is Australia's largest meat company by far, with 10 per cent of the country's capacity and annual sales of more than (US) $1 billion, and exports 85 per cent of the production of its eight processing plants. Monfort markets AMH beef in the US.[214]

Concentration in hogs, both raising and killing them, is rising even faster than in beef. The number of hog farms in the US has dropped from 653,000 in 1980 to 235,840 in 1993. Now one 50,000-sow unit replaces 1000 50-sow units.[215] The hierarchy of hog processors is slightly different than that for beef, but the degree of concentration is similar.

Table 8.2: Commercial hog slaughter, 1993 market percentages of top five companies[216]

IBP	17.4
ConAgra	12.8
Smithfield Foods	8.8
John Morrell	7.5
Excel	7.0

Cargill launched itself into beef slaughter and processing in a big way in 1968 with the purchase of MBPXL for $68 million. The company was renamed Excel.

By 1991, Cargill owned 31 meat and poultry processing and further-processing plants throughout the world. It operated 14 beef and pork plants and three broiler chicken and three turkey processing plants in the US plus the largest beef packing plant in Canada at High River, Alberta.

Cargill meat and poultry brands that one might find in the US are: Emge, Excel, Honeysuckle White, Medallion & Riverside, Sterling Silver, Sunny Fresh and Double Diamond; and in Canada: Canada Choice.

By 1991 Cargill was also operating a broiler processing plant in Bangkok, Thailand; a beef and sheep plant at Wagga Wagga, NSW, Australia; a pork processing plant in Taiwan; a beef and chicken processing plant in Saultillo, Mexico; a beef plant and a broiler plant in Honduras; and a broiler plant in Argentina. Its Sun Valley subsidiary operates a broiler processing plant in England and a turkey plant in Wales.[217]

In addition to being the third largest beef packer, Excel is the fourth largest cow (beef and dairy) slaughterer. Lest Cargill be given credit for doing it all on its own, it is good to note the public assistance it has received for just one project in Nebraska:

> In 1993 Cargill decided to replace its existing meat processing plant in Nebraska City with a new $15 million facility. Unwilling to finance this small project on its own, it asked the Nebraska department of economic development for a $1.55 million grant, the highways department for $304,000 in road improvements, and the Federal Economic Development Administration for $445,000. It then asked the residents to vote themselves a $2.63 million tax hike to finance the plant.[218]

Of course, Cargill is not unique in demanding and utilizing public assistance in the pursuit of free enterprise; it is simply following standard operating procedures for successful – and unsuccessful – corporations.

Mexico

In 1991, in anticipation of the NAFTA, Cargill's Excel division purchased a modern meat processing plant in Saltillo, Coahuila, Mexico, from Alimentos Colonial with the intention of selling beef cuts and portion-control chicken products to the Mexican middle class. Instead, the plant is taking advantage of 300 low-wage employees to produce labor-intensive deboned chicken legs and to process offal, shipped in from Cargill plants in the US, for export to Japan.[219]

All of Excel's plants are involved in business with Mexico: the beef facilities in Plainview and Friona, Texas; in Dodge City, Kansas; Sterling and Fort Morgan, Colorado; Schuyler, Nebraska; and High River, Alberta. Pork plants in Ottumwa, Iowa and Beardstown, Illinois are also involved.[220]

In 1992 the US exported nearly $382 million of beef, veal, pork and lamb to Mexico,[221] while imports of feeder cattle from Mexico rose to an annual average of 1 million head. It would be nice to know Cargill's share, but market share figures are virtually impossible to obtain, unless a company releases them itself.

Australia

Thanks to its climate, land base and sparse population, Australia has become one of the few global beef sources, and as such it has also become highly integrated into the global beef system dominated by the few large US packers, including Cargill. In the case of Australia, Japan assists in the domination of the industry by foreign-based TNCs.

Many of the feedlots and meat processing plants are owned by US and Japanese companies, including ConAgra, Cargill, Itoham, Nippon Meat Packers, Japan Food Corp. and Mitsubishi. Cargill operates a beef and sheep plant at Wagga Wagga in the state of New South Wales that it purchased from Metro Meat Ltd in 1991. In 1994 Cargill announced the building of a $A20 million feedlot. The rest of Metro Meat, which processed nearly one-quarter of Australia's lamb and mutton and had 3 per cent of the cattle slaughter, was purchased by a Chinese government investment company in late 1993.[222]

Nippon Meat Packers, Australia's fifth largest meat packer, is particularly significant because it is a Cargill partner in Thailand but a competitor in Japan. Nippon Meat recently purchased the cattle interests – a slaughter plant and feedlot – of Louis Dreyfus, bringing its total to five processing plants and two feedlots. Cargill is ranked 23rd in size among packers in Australia. With CanAgra's 1994 purchase of Elders IXL's share of Australian Meat Holding (AMH), foreign ownership of Australia's meat processing industry reached 30 per cent.

Beef consumption in Australia has fallen steadily since the mid-1970s and is now about one-third (35 kg per person per year) of the country's total production of an estimated 1.77 million tonnes. Australia has been trying to make up for that drop in domestic consumption by increasing exports. The number of cattle is remaining fairly steady but actual meat production is increasing as larger numbers of the herd are being grain fed to higher weights in feedlots. Feedlots now provide about 10 per cent of the cattle going to slaughter.

In spite of the size of the companies that own them, beef plants in Australia are much smaller than those in North America and the line speeds are slower. This allows more time to be spent on each carcass and results in a considerably higher level of hygiene. This in turn leads to a longer shelf-life of 100 days compared to the North American standard of 30 days, a distinct export advantage.[223]

Table 8.3: Australian beef and veal exports, major destinations: (kilo-tonnes)[224]

	1985	1987	1989	1991	1992	1993	1994
United States	273.7	361.9	277.2	361.5	369.4	274.4	n.a.
Japan	94.1	119.9	176.5	183.4	217.7	279.1	296.0
Korea	0.1	0.2	58.9	94.5	97.3	52.9	n.a.
Canada	20.8	35.8	21.8	38.6	51.8	84.3	n.a.
Taiwan	21.3	26.0	26.1	29.9	36.5	32.6	n.a.
Total exports:	690.0	908.0	872.0	1079.0	1192.0	790.4	795.0

Canada

Canada is treated in some detail here because Cargill's development has been more recent and I have been able to document it because I live there.* Cargill's entry into the Canadian beef sector provides a good portrait of the company's strategy and practices.

> The natural advantages of the foothills terrain, the millions spent on irrigation systems for forage cultivation and rancher-friendly government land-leasing and feed grain policies have all helped nurture the Alberta cattle business.[225]

> The pending shakeout would be the first since 1927 when most meat plants in Canada were all but bankrupt when commodities markets worldwide collapsed. Five years later, the Depression forced consolidation of four major meat processors into Canada Packers Inc.[226]

The pending shakeout referred to above was the consequence of Cargill building a $55 million beef packing plant in High River, Alberta, (with the help of $4 million from the Alberta Government), and running it with wage rates about $2.50 per hour below the rates in other western Canadian plants at the time.

The plant opened in 1989 with a kill rate of 1600 per day five days a week, single shift, without a union. The next year the 430 workers in the bargaining unit at the High River plant voted for UFCW (United Food and Commercial Workers) certification. The agreement with Cargill was for a starting wage of $8 an hour, rising to $9.60 after one year and up to $10.95 as the top wage for a skilled worker. By mid-1993 Cargill's base wage rate had risen to $10.25.[227]

By the time Cargill opened its plant, 700 workers at four Canada Packers' plants in Alberta had accepted a $1.50 per hour rollback in their basic wage to $12.51, the average of wages at other Alberta plants, including Cargill's. Canada Packers had forced this concession from the workers in 1988 under threat of closing the plants altogether. In other words, Cargill had effectively set the basic wage rates for the packinghouse workers in the province of Alberta a full year before it was actually in business.

To give credit where credit is due, however, Cargill has a better record than many companies on the environmental front. In building the plant at High River a creative solution was found to deal with the half-million gallons a day of waste water that would be produced by the plant – after Calgary sports fishermen had objected to the plan to dump the waste into the Bow River upstream of their favorite fishing holes. Eventually an agreement was reached with the Government of Alberta, the town of High River and Ducks Unlimited to pipe the waste water, after treatment, about ten miles south east to Frank Lake, which had become a dry lake bed in recent years. The shared costs of this part of the project were

---

* See Brewster Kneen, *Trading Up*, NC Press, Toronto, 1990, for the full story of Cargill in Canada.

estimated at between Can$7.4 and Can$8.9 million, but the project did, apparently, fulfill the promise of being an ecologically sound solution.

Once the High River plant was in operation, Cargill wasted no time making its attack on the big Ontario beef market. It found ways to get its product distributed in the lucrative Ontario market, including the use of the distribution system of Maple Lodge Farms, a large privately owned poultry processor just west of Toronto. Maple Lodge distributed Cargill Foods' boxed beef, trucked in from High River, throughout Ontario.[228]

Cargill continued its expansion and solved the problem of eastern Canada distribution with the purchase of the Trillium Meats Ltd plant in Toronto from Steinberg, Inc. (Soconav) of Montreal in 1993. Trillium was a meat-cutting and distribution operation that had been used to supply Steinberg's Miracle Food Mart stores before Steinberg's financial desperation forced the sale of its stores to A&P earlier in 1993.

Maintaining a corporate tradition, Cargill closed the deal with Steinberg only after the members of UFCW Local 633 agreed to a substantial wage reduction rather than lose their jobs. Cargill was after a cut of $6–7 per hour, according to Cargill vice president for corporate affairs, Barb Isman. The hourly rate at Trillium had been $17–18, while at Better Beef in Guelph the wage rate averaged $15. Under the contract the workers finally ratified, Trillium meat-cutters would make about $16 an hour after three years, about $2 less than they earned under the Steinberg contract while some reclassified workers would earn about $6 less than previously. Cargill retained about 225 of the 400 who had worked for Steinberg's. Viewing the plant as an extension of its High River operation, according to Cargill's food division vice president, Bill Buckner, Cargill trucks sides of beef and boxed beef from High River to the Trillium facility for further processing into 'case-ready' retail cuts.

A lot of the offal and by-products from the High River plant, but little meat, have gone to the Pacific Rim from the very beginning. Hides have been going to Korea and Taiwan.

A Canadian trade journal, reporting on Cargill's quality improvement process in its High River plant, provided an insight into the Cargill concept of market-defined social relations. The Cargill Quality program, which they tout in many of their trade magazine ads,

> is based on the theory that every employee … is both customer and supplier. For example, on the fabrication line, the person up the line is supplier and the person down the line is customer. If the person downstream is dissatisfied with the quality of the product he receives, he sends it back up the line until it meets his standards.[229] ('Fabrication line' does not refer to where the animal is put together, but where it is taken apart and the cuts of meat 'fabricated'.)

When Cargill announced it would build the plant at High River, it was already the major feed and feed supplement manufacturer and supplier in southern

Alberta, and if a feedlot operator was short of cash, they could get financing to buy cattle through Cargill's Financial Services Division. The stipulation is that the cattle that are financed by Cargill have to be raised on Nutrena feeds. There really is no choice since no bank is eager to lend money for feed when the cattle are already assigned to Cargill as collateral for the loan with which they were purchased. If Cargill is then also the cattle buyer, it can tell the grower what specifications the cattle have to meet, when they will be shipped, and how much will be paid for them. The outcome is that the 'independent' cowboy/rancher or feedlot operator is, in reality, little more than a franchise operator.

The impact of Cargill's presence on Canada's beef industry has been immense. Alberta's share of fed cattle production in Canada rose from 34 per cent in 1980 to 43 per cent in 1993, while Ontario's share dropped commensurately from 26 per cent to 17 per cent. In the same proportion, Alberta's share of cattle and calves slaughtered in federally inspected plants rose from 37 per cent to 47 per cent while Ontario's dropped from 31 per cent to 24 per cent.[230]

XL Foods of Calgary, a relatively small beef processor, was one of the victims of Cargill's determinative presence. It placed the blame for its financial woes on Cargill, saying that, 'The marketing strategy employed by Cargill, when matched with other packers attempting to retain market share, has totally destroyed margins, resulting in severe losses to the entire Canadian industry.'[231] XL sought to salvage its own finances by restructuring wages by means of a lock-out. Its workers were allowed to return to work only after accepting an average roll-back in wages of $2.39 per hour and a shorter work week. The company justified the cuts on the ground that it had to be competitive with Cargill.[232]

Cargill also put tremendous pressure on the other packers in 1989–90 by paying top price for cattle in order to fill its plant capacity. In the short-term, bidding-up cattle prices doesn't seriously hurt a company with Cargill's resources, but it may help drive its competitors out of business, particularly if the current wholesale price of beef is undercut at the same time. Buyers as far east as Nova Scotia reported that Cargill was 'low-balling' the wholesale market in late 1989 in order to get established. Cargill simply paid more for cattle and sold for less until it had the market share it wanted.

When Cargill opened its High River plant, Canada Packers was still the largest beef processor in Canada, with three plants in western Canada killing 12,000 cattle per week. Then in mid-1990 Hillsdown Holdings PLC purchased Canada Packers for a reported $700 million and the next year shut down two of its three beef plants. The third was sold to Burns Foods Ltd. Burns Foods did not fare well, and it too blamed Cargill for its troubles. Cargill, said Burns president Arthur Burns, 'is offering carcass beef at 10 to 14 cents a pound below the market, when normal profits are only 3 to 4 cents a lb.'[233] Cargill vice president Bill Buckner responded: 'It's not true. North America is a very competitive marketplace. We've been pricing to make sure we can compete in it.'[234]

By no coincidence, the Calgary-based Canada Beef Export Federation was incorporated in 1989 as a non-profit federation representing beef packers, processors, exporters and provincial and national beef associations. The Federation engages in market research and sponsors trade missions. Provincial cattlemens' associations have made contributions in the $35,000–$100,000 range to the Federation, substantial support comes from public sources, such as the British Columbia provincial government and the Western Diversification Fund (a federal Tory patronage pot), which contributed $1.25 million in 1990. Industry contributions, if any, are unpublished, but as the major exporter, Cargill is clearly the major beneficiary of the organization's activities, which parallel those of the US Beef Export Federation.

By 1994, with the 'shakeout' pretty well completed, the only major 'Canadian' beef packers left were: Cargill Foods, killing 2200 per day six days a week; Lakeside Packers, killing 1600 per day, Better Beef in Guelph, Ontario, with 1200, XL Foods of Calgary with 1000 per day, and Intercontinental Packers in Saskatchewan with 600 per day capacity.[235]

Lakeside Packers, a unit of Lakeside Farm Industries Ltd, of Brooks, Alberta, remains Cargill's only potential competitor, although it is a slaughter-only facility. Until October 1994, Lakeside was a non-union, private company, killing 11,000 cattle per week (550,000 per year) and operating a 40,000-head feedlot.[236] Then IBP, the world's largest fresh meat processor, purchased Lakeside from its current owners, which included Mitsubishi Canada Ltd and Vencap, an Alberta government venture capital fund. It is IBP's first acquisition outside the US and makes Alberta the stage for direct competition between Number One and Number Three in North America. It also means the almost-total takeover by foreign transnationals of one more segment of the Canadian food industry, following similar developments in flour milling and oilseed crushing. Cargill was not long in counter-attacking with the announcement that it would expand its facilities in High River and double shift the plant in 1996, allowing it to kill about 4000 per day, or one million per year.

From Cargill's standpoint, it's a great system. Being the feed supplier, the banker, the buyer of the finished cattle, their butcher and their wholesaler creates a tidy system that gives the company maximum control and return with the major risks – weather and animal health – being shouldered by others. It is also a very good way to market cheap grain, as long as you are not the farmer who grows it.

Cargill tried to implement such a system with pigs in Manitoba in 1979 with its Cargill Pork Systems (CPS). A 'qualified applicant' could enter into 'a production agreement with CPS under which he agrees to supply the land, buildings, equipment and production management.'[237] Cargill, under this contract, agreed 'to provide the breeding stock, feed, veterinary assistance [advice], health aids [drugs] and ongoing technical and managerial support'. 'Production management' is more commonly known as labour. In retailing, this type of arrangement is known as a franchise. But, for reasons unknown, Cargill has since dropped all its hog operations and is now simply the supplier of Nutrena Feeds and advice. Although at one time Cargill operated a 27,000 hybrid hog breeding farm in Mount Lehman, British Columbia, from which it supplied growers, Cargill currently has no presence in the pork industry in Canada.

Poultry

Virtually all poultry in the US is grown under contract to one or another processor. The Integrator, as these companies are called, provides the grower with day-old chicks, usually from a company hatchery, and supplies the feed, the medications, and the specifications of the required buildings. When the birds reach market weight the integrator buys back the 'finished' birds at a price and under conditions established by it. The growers provide the building and the labour and take the risks of the birds doing poorly or dying.

Cargill entered the poultry processing business with the purchase of a processing plant in Ozark, Arkansas, in 1967. It is now about the 25th largest broiler chicken processor in the US, with a processing plant in Georgia and three broiler chicken 'complexes' in Florida and Georgia producing more than 4 million pounds of ready-to-cook (RTC) chicken per week. (In comparison, the largest broiler company, Tyson Foods Inc., produces 81.5 million pounds of RTC chicken per week.) Cargill is number 5 in turkeys, with two turkey complexes in Arkansas and one in Missouri, processing more than 400 million pounds of live turkey in 1993. (Butterball Turkey Co. is the largest processing with about 700 million pounds annually.)[238]

To give an indication of the scale of these complexes, after a \$25 million expansion of Cargill's Buena Vista, Georgia, broiler chicken complex, the plant could process 750,000 chickens per week with a workforce of 1000. The expansion included additions to the company's feed mill and hatchery around Oglethorpe, Georgia, and construction of company-owned breeder farms to produce the chicks required to supply the 70 new contract growers that would raise the chicks to a 6-pound market weight in addition to the 65 existing Cargill contract growers. The Buena Vista plant debones chicken and ships the meat to a Cargill plant in Dawson, Georgia, where it is transformed into a variety of chicken items.[239]

At about the same time it was expanding its Buena Vista plant, Cargill announced plans to build a \$38 million broiler production and processing complex in Vienna, Georgia, that would employ approximately 1000 people and require a network of 80 to 85 independent contract growers.[240]

The exploitation of both chickens and chicken farmers, characteristic of the 'modern' broiler industry – 'industry' is indeed the appropriate term – has generated its own opposition in recent years as the power of the Integrators to silence the growers' complaints has finally been broken by skillful organizing by the growers.

For example, in March 1992, Cargill settled with the US Justice Department, agreeing to continue contracting with Arthur Gaskins, president of the National

Contract Poultry Growers Association, after canceling his contract in 1989 when he and 30 other growers sued Cargill for allegedly underweighing their birds over a period of eight years.

Cargill agreed that 'it may not terminate the contract of any poultry grower because they participate in grower association activities, seek legal redress against Cargill, contact state or federal regulatory agencies or retain an attorney to represent them in any matter.' Previously, Cargill had held that it could terminate growers for any reason, or even for no reason at all.

On the underlying issue of a suit against Cargill charging false weights, a federal magistrate has allowed the growers to file a class action complaint which could more than triple the number of Florida and Georgia growers seeking monetary and injunctive relief.[241] Such legal actions tend to be lengthy and these cases (and others) were continuing at the end of 1994.

With concentration and integration the golden rule of the poultry business, the number of companies processing chickens in the US dropped from 127 in 1982 to 56 in 1993, and these 56 were processing 56 per cent more chickens. The eight largest companies had 54 per cent of the processing volume and the top 20 had 79 per cent.[242]

Cargill tried poultry in Canada, but in 1981 it shut down its Panco Poultry division in Surrey, British Columbia, after three years of operation. Panco was processing 2 per cent of the chickens sold in British Columbia and Cargill had just completed a $2 million modernization of the Panco plant. Cargill laid the blame for closing the plant on the failure of the BC Chicken Marketing Board to give it more birds and said the business was not sufficiently profitable.[243]

From 1965 until 1988, Cargill had major or total control of Shaver Poultry, Cambridge, Ontario. (Shaver's hybrid poultry, according to the company, are responsible for one-third of all white eggs produced in the world.) In 1988 Cargill sold Shaver to l'Institut de Selection Animale (Merieux Group) of France that already had the biggest share of the world's brown egg market. According to the press release, Cargill had concluded that poultry breeding is out of the mainstream of its integrated poultry operations. 'Cargill will concentrate future resources on live production, processing and marketing of poultry products.'

As indicated above, Cargill has expanded its poultry operations in the US, but given the highly concentrated character of the US poultry business and the near-saturation of the market, it is hardly surprising that Cargill looked elsewhere for more rapid expansion in one of its 'core competencies'. As early as 1970 Cargill was attracted to Indonesia by the country's large population and its agricultural economy and sent one of its experts to study the situation. The recommendation of Cargill scout Kees Nieuwenhuyzen was that Cargill start a feed company and a small breeding hatchery, and build from there. 'For a company of Cargill's size, the start was very circumscribed: a small labor-intensive factory 60 km outside Jakarta that cost $250,000 with a capacity of 200–300 tons of feed per month.' At the time Cargill owned Shaver Poultry in Canada which could supply the breeding stock for the poultry operation, thus enabling Cargill to supply farmers with the chicks and their feed.[244]

By 1982 the operation had grown to two feed mills, three chicken breeding farms and a hatchery with an annual production of 4.5 million broiler and layer chicks. Hybrid corn seed, which had been developed by Cargill in and for Thailand, had also been added to the company's products. The seed, it was said, worked so well in Indonesia that the government decided to subsidize 30 per cent of the cost of the seed to farmers. 'We didn't ask for it, we wouldn't have asked for it ... but we can't say no. So we make the best of it. And the important thing is not the subsidy itself but that the government indirectly becomes a vehicle for us to get the seed sold,' said Nieuwenhuyzen.[245]

From there, Cargill opened an Indonesian office to allow better contact with the regional office in Singapore which had been opened in 1983 'and to ease Cargill into a stronger position as an exporter of Indonesian products, primarily copra (coconut), tapioca, rice bran, and other grain substitutes, to Taiwan and Korea.'[246]

At the time, James Spicola was president of Cargill. He described the strategy Cargill applied in Indonesia:

> It's similar to the development we've followed in other countries. We start out with a reasonably small capital investment in a field to which we think we can bring some expertise and technology and management, then grow the business from there. We reinvest the profits and move into other opportunities as the situation develops ... We've found that our welcome to the country is much more productive on a long-term basis if we've started small and grown.[247]

Cargill's activities in Thailand reflect another aspect of its global integration. There it has interests in cassava (tapioca) processing for animal feed which it utilizes in local poultry production, but, much more importantly, exports in very large quantities to Europe as a protein supplement in livestock feed. In fact, the highly intensive production of pork in Denmark, for example, would not be possible without importing large quantities of feeds such as cassava.

Globally, most cassava (also called tapioca or manioc) is produced on small subsistence farms for local consumption. The largest commercial producer of tapioca in 1990, according to the *International Bulk Journal*,[248] was Brazil with 25.4 million tonnes. Thailand was the second largest producer with 21.9 million tonnes, and over 80 per cent of the tapioca traded internationally is shipped from Thailand, with 70 per cent of that going to the EC in chip and pelletized form for animal feed and alcohol production, with 12 per cent being turned into flour and starch for food and industrial uses.* The major traders in 1990 were Khron,

---

* The planting and harvesting of tapioca occurs all over Thailand. The tapioca root normally takes 12 months to mature. Dried chips are transported in bulk to pelletizing plants. The majority of exports are carried in lighters and barges to export facilities midstream in the Gulf of Thailand. The busiest facility is Thai Bulk Services, established in 1978 by German and Dutch interests. Toepfer (ADM) and Krohn are now shareholders along with Thai interests. (IBJ: April 91)

exporting 25 per cent; Toepfer (ADM), 20 per cent; Peter Cremer, 15 per cent; and Cargill.[249]

Cargill's strategy in Thailand has been somewhat different than in Indonesia. Rather than starting very small and growing, Cargill formed a joint venture in 1989, Sun Valley Thailand, with Nippon Meat Packers Inc. of Japan to produce, process and market fresh-frozen chicken. The facilities are located in the Lopburi and Saraburi provinces of Thailand.

The fully integrated business has its own parent-stock chicken farm, hatchery, broiler chicken farms, feed plant and broiler processing plant. Operations began in 1990 and Sun Valley Thailand started exporting more than 600 tonnes of frozen chicken monthly to Japan. The company put out something like 175,000 chicks weekly to the farms that grow them out, with hatchery capability to triple the rate of placements as market conditions dictate. That was in 1991, when Cargill was planning for Sun Valley Thailand to begin developing export markets in Hong Kong, Singapore, Belgium, Germany and Holland within the next two years.[250] No figures are available on what has actually happened.

Sun Valley Thailand's parent is Sun Valley Poultry Ltd of Britain, which Cargill acquired in 1980. Sun Valley sells one out of every four 'further-processed poultry products' eaten in the UK and provides McDonald's with all of the chicken nuggets and sandwich patties sold in the UK and most of Western Europe. It also markets chicken under such well-known private labels as Sainsbury's and Marks & Spencer.

Sun Valley supplies one-third of all chilled processed poultry in the UK, maintaining quality by maintaining control over every aspect of its poultry business, from egg to finished product. The chicks and turkey poults produced at its own hatcheries are farmed out to 200 independent growers and are raised on Cargill's own feed, which Cargill supplies. To deliver this feed, as well as to deliver the final 'value-added' poultry products, Sun Valley operates its own fleet of trucks.[251]

Sun Valley Foods employs 3700 people in its chicken and turkey processing plants in Wales and in Hereford, England, producing poultry products for both the domestic and export markets. Altogether, Cargill employs almost 10,000 people in its international poultry operations located in five countries on four continents.

While not ranking among the top 20 processors in the US, Cargill's Sun Valley was 18th in Europe in 1993, processing about 65,000 tonnes annually. (The top European processor, Doux of France, was ten times larger.)

The US – Eggs

Hens were once able to fend for themselves pretty well (except for the foxes), feeding in the barnyard and garden, pecking for fresh grubs and table leftovers. The farmer's job was to collect the eggs. By 1970 that quaint, though efficient, model had been replaced with industrial production and one worker tending 10,000 laying hens. Twenty years later that number was up to 100,000 hens, thanks to automatic feeders and egg-gathering equipment. US consumption, on the other hand, had dropped from 390 eggs per person per year in the late 1940s to 243 in 1989, with only 1481 large-scale producers remaining. Cargill, which had been aggressively expanding in the fresh egg business in the previous decade, was described in 1987 as the largest egg producer in the US with 12 million layers under contract. Second at the time was Rose Acre Farms with 7.7 million layers, according to *Egg Industry* magazine.[252]

Cargill, like the other integrators, contracted with farmers to grow Cargill-supplied chicks and then contracted with another set of farmers to look after them as layers. The feed, which accounts for about 60 per cent of an egg's production cost, was supplied, as part of the deal, by Cargill's Nutrena division, itself one of the country's five largest feed companies. 'Cargill literally makes up on volume what it loses on every chick because it makes a profit producing the egg' (referring to the money it makes on the feed it sells to the farmers) reported *Forbes*, which figured Cargill had 4 per cent of the US egg market at the time. Cargill claimed it hadn't driven the price of eggs down, just adapted to a changing market. At the time there were rumors of Cargill selling out, possibly to Cal-Maine Foods. There were also rumors that Rose Acre Farms, the second largest egg producer, might also be sold, to Michael Foods.[253]

In May 1989, Cargill did sell the egg production division of Sunny Fresh Foods, which was then reported to control egg production from more than 12 million hens, to Cal-Maine Foods of Jackson, Mississippi, making Cal-Maine the biggest egg producer in the US with control of some 18 million hens. According to the feed industry trade magazine *Feedstuffs*, Cargill was selling its shell egg operations because shell eggs no longer fitted its long-term strategy. The president of Cargill's Worldwide Poultry Operations explained that the company had been repositioning its poultry operations away from commodity products to further-processed, value-added products, such as liquid pasteurized eggs and cooked egg products that are sold to food manufacturers and institutions.[254] These products, which bear a striking similarity to many other 'invisible' products that Cargill manufactures for the food industry, continue to be produced by Cargill's Sunny Fresh Foods division processing facilities in Minnesota and Iowa.

At its Minnesota plant, Sunny Fresh also makes an egg patty that appears to be a poached egg, but the yolk, while designed to look like the real thing, contains no cholesterol. Customers, like H.J. Heinz, McDonald's and Sara Lee, 'often come to Sunny Fresh with a basic concept or idea for a product,' and Cargill's design team will work with the customer's technical staff to make the product practical for mass production.[255]

Such products, however, still require protection from predators just as chickens require protection from foxes. In 1992 Cargill filed a suit against Michael Foods in an effort to abrogate patents covering Michael Foods' ultra-pasteurization process for manufacturing liquified eggs. Cargill charged, in effect, that Michael Foods patented a process that it knew Cargill was already using.[256]

Apparently pleased with the financial results of its egg product strategy, in 1994 Cargill purchased a third egg processing facility (Herbruck Foods in Michigan) that was constructed in 1989 and produces products similar to those of its other two plants.[257]

Catfish: A Tactical Retreat

Cargill's catfish story is not unlike its experience with shell eggs in the US or pork production in Canada: a tactical retreat from what Cargill had considered a promising venture.

Cargill entered the seafood business in 1989 when the Fishery Products Department was created to buy farm-raised shrimp overseas and sell them to food-service customers in the US. Two years later Cargill entered the US domestic fish industry when it began operating a leased catfish processing plant at Wisner, in northern Louisiana. In order to get more control over the input side of the business, it added 1200 acres of catfish ponds in southern Louisiana bayou country near Lebeau to the operation in 1992.

In its employee magazine, Cargill described how it worked with about 100 independent catfish growers while providing a buffer supply in its own production ponds at Lebeau, where there are 100 ponds each covering about 10 acres. The fish are fed twice a day with puff pellets of feed mechanically sprayed onto the ponds surface. As many as 50,000 to 70,000 pounds of fish can be caught in a single net. They are trucked live, in a tank, to the processing plant at Wisner.[258]

It is not hard to understand the attraction Cargill felt for catfish. In 1992, catfish production in the US totaled 457 million pounds compared with just under 100 million in 1982, and consumption in the US is a mere 1 pound per person per year.

Immediately after leasing the Wisner plant in 1991 Cargill began an expansion of its automated processing capability, and ended up spending well over $2 million on new equipment to get the plant up to the sanitary level that would give fresh product a guaranteed shelf-life of 10 days, while the frozen product had a shelf-life of 120 days.[259] The Louisiana Commissioner of Agriculture announced that he was pleased and that this was 'an indication of a real commitment on the part of Cargill.'[260] Cargill said that if the venture proved to be a success, the company might expand into other popular types of fish, such as salmon and trout.[261]

To most of us, $2 million might seem like a significant commitment, but two years after Cargill made that investment, in November 1993, SF Services announced that it was going to purchase Cargill's catfish processing plant in Wisner for $3.2 million. It wasn't really a purchase, however, because Cargill wasn't really the owner. Cargill had acquired the plant in the first place on a lease-purchase agreement with the Louisiana government, agreeing to pay $2.16 million for the plant over a 10-year period. SF then obtained a lease-purchase agreement with the Louisiana government similar to the one Cargill had given up.[262]

Cargill had apparently not attached enough importance to the existing relationships between processors and suppliers or fish growers. According to the trade magazine *Meat & Poultry*,[263] the catfish industry in the US is unique for its concentration and organization, with four companies processing 90 per cent of the catfish. In addition, many farmers have a stake in the company which processes and markets their fish. 'The supply situation is probably the main reason Cargill got out of the business. Everyone had high expectations of Cargill becoming a major player, but it didn't work out,' says Bill Allen, president of The Catfish Institute. Cargill's Mark Klein said, 'We got into the business as an experiment to determine if opportunity existed for us. We found we would have had to invest significantly more capital into the project and we couldn't justify it.'[264]

Cargill encountered similar social dynamics when it tried to enter the wholesale beef trade in Japan on its own account. It found that it simply could not break into the network of established relationships. It was a matter of more than product and price, which Cargill seems to have difficulty understanding at times. It has faced similar situations when trying to impose its will on the feed business, where customer relations are crucial. Others are not always as impressed with Cargill's brand of rationalism, or pragmatism, as its own executives are.

CHAPTER 9

Subsidies and Charities

The principal impediments to achieving food security through imports now involve trade policies.

Robbin Johnson, vice president public affairs[265]

Cargill's fortunes appear to run parallel to the major export subsidy programs (trade policies) of the US. I have to say 'appear' because there are no consistent and reliable statistics to draw upon. Aggregate figures for trade and aid are available from government sources, but they do not give, and are not allowed to give, any indication of corporate shares. From the other side, private corporations are under no obligation to reveal financial results, and what numbers they give are those that suit their own purposes. So we are left having to observe correlations and draw inferences.

The government of the US really entered the grain business in a serious way in the immediate post-World War II years, first through UN Relief and Rehabilitation Agency programs and then directly with the Marshall Plan. These programs moved mountains of grain aid to Europe, with the result that US wheat and flour exports jumped from 48 million bushels in 1944 to 503 million in 1948. The grain majors, including Cargill of course, were the agents of these programs on behalf of the government, and as such they did well storing and delivering grain for a fee.

By the early 1950s, however, Europe was on its feet, determined to become self-sufficient in food production after the trauma of hunger and food insecurity during the war and immediate post-war years, and grain imports were replaced with domestic production. The dumping of US grain in Europe was no longer welcome foreign aid, but unwelcome competition and an obstacle to the European goal of self-sufficiency.

The ingenious response of the United States and its grain lobby was the passage of Public Law 480 – the Agricultural Trade Development and Assistance Act, known as 'Food For Peace' – in July 1954, that set US grain exports on an upward path again. PL 480 'combined and extended the use of surplus agricultural products for the furtherance of foreign policy goals ... The funds could also be used to develop new markets for United States farm goods ... That it was a boon to the American grain traders goes without saying,' wrote W.G. Broehl in his history of Cargill.[266]

As an agent of the government, Cargill has always been one of the prime beneficiaries of PL 480 financing. At the same time, as a private trader, Cargill has benefited handsomely as Food For Peace grain exports whetted the appetites of many new potential customers for subsequent commercial sales (see Chapter 11).

In fact, the promise of eventual commercial purchases was often a specific precondition for the food aid in the first place. Food aid, particularly wheat, was utilized much like infant formula: to create a taste and a market for a company's products for a lifetime.

Between 1955 and 1965, Cargill's US grain exports increased 400 per cent, with sales rising from $800 million to $2 billion. By 1963 Public Law 480 had generated sales for Cargill and Continental of $1 billion each. (This was for storing and transportation, not for processing or manufacturing.)

In addition to its increased sales under PL 480, Cargill also benefited from the government's grain storage program. Between 1958 and 1968 it received some $76 million for storing grain, often in leased publicly owned terminals or terminals built with public funds. Cargill's reputation in the trade for manipulating government programs to its advantage is extensive. As an executive in a competitor company put it, referring to Cargill: 'The big don't get that way by waiting around for something to happen.'[267]

In 1964 US policy shifted from subsidizing the storage of grain to subsidizing grain exports only. Subsidies were paid to the grain companies so that they could discount the price and sell grain below both the domestic price and the prevailing world market price. While the savings from reduced storage costs were expended in subsidizing exports, the government, or national budget, benefited by the increased foreign exchange earnings.

Dan Morgan, in *Merchants of Grain*, pointed out that officially all this was called 'making American agricultural products more competitive abroad.' Even the conservative London *Financial Times* was explicit about the dependency of the private companies on public subsidies:

At the height of US 'grain power' in the 1970s, companies like Cargill Ltd and Continental Grain Co. made fortunes out of US agricultural exports. Privately owned and secretive, they are the two largest members of a group of five companies that controls between 85 and 90 per cent of US grain exports … Fierce advocates of a free market for agriculture, they have become overwhelmingly dependent on Government efforts to increase their sales.[268]

With PL 480 still in place and in use, in 1985 the Congress of the United States passed the Export Enhancement Program (EEP) of the Food Security Act, putting in place the most notorious of the publicly funded corporate assistance programs. While it is explained publicly as a program to aid US agriculture, it is not the EEP but the federally set domestic target price and the federal loan rate on commodities that benefits American farmers and isolates them from so-called world market prices.*

Under the EEP, elegible countries are designated year by year by the Secretary of Agriculture. Individual sales are then negotiated between the eligible country or its designated agency and one of the trading companies on the basis of the subsidy available at the time for that particular country. The subsidy is then paid, in one form or another, to the company making the deal.

In its first four years of operation (1985–9) the EEP had 'targeted' 65 countries with 12 commodities, including flour, under 104 'export enhancement initiatives'. Sales under EEP in this period totalled $8.5 billion. In addition, $2.57 billion in Commodity Credit Corp. stocks or payment-in-kind (PIK) certificates[†] were given out as bonus rewards.[269]

Clayton Yeutter, who at that time was US Trade Representative, explained on many occasions that such programs were necessary to counter the subsidized exports of the European Community and to subsidize US farmers so they could compete on world markets.[‡] Regardless of the rationalization, the effect of the EEP has been to pull down the 'world market price' and, consequently, often with great damage to their domestic agriculture, the prices received by farmers in the recipient countries for their grains.

Who really benefits? In 1987 it was reported that wheat sales to China under the new EEP netted Cargill bonuses worth $2 million, while Dreyfus and Continental each benefited by half that amount.[270]

During these years of the pro-business free-enterprise Reagan regime, grain traders Cargill, Dreyfus, Continental and Artfer Inc. (owned by Ferruzzi Group), collected $1.38 billion from the US Government, more than 60 per cent of the subsidies through the Export Enhancement Program in its first four years.[271]

In other words, while continuously condemning the 'trade distorting practices' of, for example, the Canadian Wheat Board, Cargill is happy to cooperate with what has, in the United States, become a subsidized *de facto* state trading corporation.

To dispel any doubt as to the intent of the Export Enhancement Program, new guidelines issued in 1989 made it quite explicit who is to benefit. The US

---

* The government makes up the difference between target price and actual selling price, while the loan rate is the amount that the government, through the Commodity Credit Corporation, will 'lend' the farmer against the collateral of the farmer's grain. If the grain actually sells for a price higher than the loan rate, the farmer keeps the full amount. If the selling price is below the loan rate, the farmer can forfeit the grain to the CCC and keep the loan. The farmer wins either way.

† The PIK certificates enabled the holder to draw on grain stocks held by the CCC, including the grain that farmers had forfeited against their CCC loans as described above, which the corporations then sell as their own. In addition, CCC stocks were granted directly to the companies to sell.

‡ The office of The US Trade Representative was created in the Trade Expansion Act of 1962 to represent the US in trade agreement negotiations and to administer the trade agreements program. The Trade Act of 1974 expanded the Special Trade Representatives' responsibilities, gave the office Cabinet-level status and gave the trade representative the rank of ambassador.

Department of Agriculture grouped the guidelines into four areas, the first two being;

1 Trade Policy Effect: EEP proposals must further the US negotiating strategy of countering competitors' subsidies and other unfair trade practices by displacing exports in targeted countries.

2 Export Effect: All EEP initiatives must demonstrate their potential to develop, expand or maintain markets for US agricultural commodities.[272]

In its first year, the Export Enhancement Program accounted for only 12 per cent of the 25 million tonnes of US wheat exported, but by 1987–8 this had climbed to 70 per cent of the 45 million tonnes exported. During this same period the debt of the Third World or 'less developed' countries was growing and they were increasingly unable to afford the grains that the US needed to sell. Since 'the market' was unable to play its part in moving US grain surpluses, government intervention was a growing necessity.

Three extensive articles in the *New York Times* in 1993 evaluated the EEP:

The agriculture Department's $40 billion campaign to bolster crop exports, begun a decade ago to help beleaguered farmers, has instead enriched a small group of multinational corporations while doing little to expand the American share of the world's agricultural markets … An examination of the subsidy programs highlights the symbiotic relationship between one of the biggest and least scrutinized federal departments and some of the politically influential companies it regulates.[273]

Altogether, the US government doled out $4.26 billion to 95 corporate trading companies from 1985 to early 1992 to move $14 billion worth of commodities under the Export Enhancement Program. The top winners in this public lottery were:

Table 9.1: Total amount received from US Government 1985–92[274]

	US$ (million)
Cargill Inc.	800.4
Continental Grain	702.1
Louis Dreyfus	591.0
Ferruzzi Trading	180.6
Peavey Co. (ConAgra)	177.0
Artfer Farm Mgmt (Ferruzzi)	140.7
Pillsbury Co.	132.7
Bunge Corp.	132.4
Union Equity Co-op Exch.	124.6
CAM USA Inc.	118.8
Garnac Grain Co.	107.1
Richco Grain Co.	95.1
Toepfer Intl. (50% owned by ADM)	74.9

For fiscal 1994–5, 74 different countries were 'invited' to bid on the total EEP subsidy budget of $850 million. This was $150 million less than what was offered in 1993–4. It would be more accurate to say that these are the countries allocated EEP quota by the US Government, on the basis of criteria that are not public, and that they are 'invited' to submit offers for subsidized grains. When a country is 'invited' to bid, it makes an offer for an amount of grain at a subsidized price. The US government then has to decide if it is willing to accept that bid. If it does, the subsidy ends up being the difference between that amount and the price the company handling the deal says it has to pay to buy the grain. In other words, it is a complex, highly political game played largely under the table at public expense.

PL 480 and the EEP are not the only publicly funded programs that have benefited the grain processors and merchants in the name of US market share and global competitiveness. Programs such as the Targeted Export Assistance Program administered by the Foreign Agricultural Service of the US Department of Agriculture are often channeled through non-profit industry foundations and associations to render them relatively invisible to the public.

US Wheat Associates and the US Feed Grains Council are among 46 organizations that have received suport from the Targeted Export Assistance Program, and US Wheat Associates has been involved in several wheat foods product promotions.* One such project sent 100-tonne samples of various classes of US wheat to mills around the world along with US specialists who worked with the potential foreign users. Mills in Senegal, Burkina Faso, Colombia, Taiwan, and many other markets have participated in this program. In 1988 more than 1000 small bakeries in Korea participated and ten new baked foods were introduced.[275]

In 1989, The National Association of Wheat Growers Foundation developed a project called 'The Developing World: Opportunities for US Agriculture' with the intent of increasing oportunities for US wheat exports to less-developed countries. 'The project will train up to 30 growers to make presentations to state and local groups, and through the media, on economic development and trade and the potential of less developed countries to enhance the US economy [sic].'[276]

Another publicly supported program which operates to the benefit of Cargill and others is the USDA Market Promotion Program (MPP), established under the Food, Agriculture, Conservation and Trade Act of 1990, 'to counter unfair foreign trade practices.'[277] This program provides funds or commodities owned by the Commodity Credit Corporation to trade organizations, companies and cooperatives to implement foreign market development programs. It has come under criticism for having provisions to assist promotion of branded products in foreign markets, thus assisting individual large companies.

---

* US Wheat Associates and similar groups are 50 per cent financed through the US Department of Agriculture to promote commodity exports. The industry itself pays the other half of its costs.

US Wheat Associates has used MPP funding for a number of years. Its projects have included flour milling schools in Egypt, Venezuela and Morocco and baking schools in Thailand, Costa Rica and Algeria. Such projects have proved important 'in developing markets for US wheat.'

US Wheat Associates have also supplied equipment for use in a new milling school in Venezuela to provide training in flour milling and related subjects for millers from throughout Latin America. 'The US presence in the school will broaden familiarity with US wheat and maintain relations with Latin American milling industry representatives in the face of aggressive competition from Canada and other world suppliers,' said Winston Wilson, USWA president.[278] There is no way of knowing why Venezuela in particular was picked for this program, but Cargill, as the major player in the flour and pasta industry in Venezuela, will certainly be a primary beneficiary of this program.

Another set of assistance programs is what are generally known as the General Sales Manager (GSM) 102/103 programs of the Commodity Credit Corporation (CCC). The GSM program guarantees 98 per cent of principal and a portion of interest payments on loans (for three years under GSM 102 and ten years under GSM 103) provided for purchase of US agricultural products by foreign buyers. When the US General Accounting Office (GAO) examined these programs to determine whether they had actually helped increase US exports worldwide, it found that as of June 30 1992, there was approximately $9.04 billion outstanding in guarantees on loan principal and $4.5 billion in accounts receivable, with a cumulative cost of the programs at about $6.5 billion if they were terminated immediately.

The GAO subsequently responded to the US Department of Agriculture's defense of the programs stating that:

> Since there is no convincing evidence that these programs have increased US agricultural exports worldwide, it is difficult to justify these programs' high costs based on their market development in particular countries. These programs may simply reroute US agricultural exports ... We also note that CCC has sometimes granted much larger guarantees than its credit analysts recommended, giving market development as the reason. We also note that certain program officials have told us that in the past the reasons were sometimes for political or foreign policy purposes.[279]

In other words, apart from shifting sales from one place to another, the people of the US gained nothing for the $6.5 billion net cost of the program. Since it is highly unlikely that the money simply ceased to exist, it probably became somewhat invisible for a time, later to appear on corporate balance sheets.*

---

* The cost of the GSM 102 program is currently $5 billion per year. Eligible banks in countries that purchase US farm products can obtain US government guarantees (through the CCC) for loans made to importers of US goods.

While Cargill was, typically, utilizing the good offices of the US Government under the guise of the EEP and other programs to intervene in the world grain market for the sake of sales and market share, it was also trying to destroy other state trading companies, such as the Australian Wheat Board (AWB). As a member of the Australian Grain Exporters' Association, a coalition that included ConAgra, Continental Grain and Louis Dreyfus, and with the encouragement of the Australian Government, Cargill sought to break the export monopoly of the Australian Wheat Board by promising higher grain prices to the farmers and lower costs to the government if the trade was deregulated and thrown open to the private traders. Bob McCarthy, executive director of the Exporters Association, said the traders only wanted the right to compete against the board, not its abolition. McCarthy claimed the private traders could trim $20 to $30 per tonne off wheat handling costs because their infrastructure and handling costs would be less than those of the AWB. AWB chairman Clinton Condon said the new group sought 'the opportunity to get their hands on the most significant supply of white wheat in the world with a reputation for quality built over 50 years.'[280] It is exactly the same game Cargill and the others play in Canada against the Canadian Wheat Board.

The efforts of the Exporters Association failed, however, and the Australian Government announced in October 1992 that the AWB would retain its export sales monopoly until June 1999 and that the government would continue to guarantee 85 per cent of the Board's borrowings to finance export sales of grain.[281]

China

In January 1994, the US granted a $65.6 million EEP subsidy to grain exporters to sell nearly one million tonnes of US wheat to China. The $65-per-tonne subsidy was larger than subsidies on grain sales to Africa or the ex-Soviet republics and enabled the grain companies to sell to China at about half the US domestic price.[282]

It is hardly surprising then, that Cargill showed some ambiguous sensitivity to the hot (at the time) political debate about China's human rights record. It suggested that 'the debate is complicated by the growing awareness of the need to help China's 1.2 billion people achieve their human rights aspirations while taking advantage of the tremendous economic opportunities for the US in this huge, growing market.' Cargill's corporate conclusion was that, 'Trade sanctions can cause long-term market losses for American farmers.'[283]

The same Commentary also cited the American Enterprise Institute to the effect that, 'Human rights and economic interests are compatible because economic growth is raising living standards and, with that, internal pressure for political and civil reform.' Showing a particular concern for the commodities in which Cargill has major interests, the right-wing policy institute cited by Cargill pointed out that Florida fertilizer and Florida citrus could be especially hard hit by any trade sanctions on China. 'US fertilizer companies did $293 million worth of business with China last year [1993, and] over the past five years, China has purchased approximately one-quarter of all US phosphate production.' The institute also reported that 'the Florida citrus industry' was concerned that China might attempt 'to export citrus to traditional US export markets to earn hard currency.'[284]

A long-term replacement for the withered market of the Former Soviet Union (FSU) is obviously needed by the US and Canada. China is the only possible one, thanks to its sheer magnitude. For this market to be exploited however, it must not be offended. But it must also have more adequate infrastructure to handle large grain shipments – just the sort of project that the World Bank favors.

True to its purpose of financing agricultural 'modernization' and infrastructure for use by transnational corporations, in 1994 the World Bank announced a $1 billion (said by China to be $1.75 billion) investment program, the largest such undertaking in history, for construction and installation of modern grain storage depots and handling equipment at 370 interior and export-import sites throughout the country. The largest port facility is to have 300,000 tonnes of grain storage capacity. One of the major aims of the project is to convert grain handling in China from sacks to a bulk system. Many of the new port facilities are to be designed for both import and export movements.[285] What more could Cargill ask for?

The northeast of China is reported to be extremely fertile and capable of producing large quantities of maize and soybeans. Port facilities are to be built on the northeast coast to facilitate export of these crops and import of wheat. Port facilities are also to be built at the mouth of the Yangtze River so that maize and soybeans can be imported from the northeast along with wheat from around the world. Port, storage and distribution facilities will also be built in the southeast to serve the heavily populated 'southeastern corridor.' Once these facilities are in place, China will be thoroughly integrated into the global grain system of the 'grain majors', as the Japanese describe Cargill, Continental and others.

Carrying on the tradition of his Republican predecesor and responding to the powerful lobbying of agribusiness, in 1994 US President Clinton lifted the 19-year-long embargo against trading with Vietnam. The grain trade licked its lips in anticipation, particularly those in the flour milling business. With wheat consumption a very low 5 to 10 kilograms per capita annually and a population of 70 million, Vietnam is viewed as a tremendous growth market for wheat and wheat flour. The day the embargo was lifted, in fact, representatives of US Wheat Associates were in Vietnam meeting with senior officials of the Ministry of Agriculture and Food Industry. 'Hopes were pegged on the US Department of Agriculture targeting Vietnam for flour and wheat allocations under the Export Enhancement Program and qualification of that country to purchase wheat and flour under Title I of PL 480,' reported *Milling & Baking News*.[286]

Charity

Cargill is highly experienced in the art of invisibility, particularly as the recipient of public charity, but it also has its own program of public visibility and charitable activities. When it is visible, it wants to be seen as a benevolent family of good-citizen individuals, not as one of the most powerful corporations in the world. As the company reported to its employees:

> Community projects such as the current family literacy effort are giving Cargill locations a higher profile in the towns and cities in which they operate ... It's hard for people to hold to sterotypes of The Big Controlling Corporation once they see Cargill people as individuals involved at the grassroots level in making the community a better place.[287]

Being in the food business, or at least the business of making money from agricultural commodities, it is not surprising that Cargill supports food charities. It's this kind of charitable activity that enhances Cargill's presentation of itself as an international development agency.

As part of its 125th anniversary celebrations in 1990, Cargill focused on the company's volunteer community service activities to which it gave the collective name 'Cargill Cares'. The kickoff was the presentation of a $100,000 cheque to the Second Harvest National Food Bank Network in Chicago by Whitney MacMillan, chairman and CEO of Cargill, and Peter Kooi, president of its Commodity Marketing Division. Cargill also urged employees at each of the company's approximately 500 locations to support local food shelves and feeding programs during 1990.[288] As a result, locations nationwide raised an estimated $500,000 in cash contributions and in-kind donations for Second Harvest.[289] On a cost-benefit basis, such tax-deductible contributions are certainly a good investment of advertising budget dollars, though Cargill's generosity somewhat pales when this is put alongside the $100 million it lost in derivatives trading in 1994 or the billions it has received in public subsidies.

When Peter Kooi was named a director of the Harvest Food Bank of Greater Minneapolis in 1992 he announced that: 'Hunger is with us in summer as well as in winter, and its presence is growing in the country and in the suburbs as well as in the city.' Such a statement serves the useful purpose of assigning to 'hunger' an anonymous, demonic character as an unwelcome stalking presence in the land, with the implication that Cargill will do its best to drive the demon out but bears no responsibility for its presence.

In 1993, just in time for Christmas distribution, Cargill donated 150,000 lbs of rice, that it said was worth $27,000, from its recently acquired mill in Greenville, Mississippi, to Second Harvest. 'As a major food products company, Cargill is interested in what it can do to stem hunger in this country,' said Peter Kooi.[290] Earlier in the year, a division of Excel, Cargill's beef division, had contributed 17,000 lbs of meat to shelters and soup kitchens in Indiana.[291] (That is about 1 per cent of one day's production by a single Cargill packing plant.)

In 1992, Cargill initiated a high-visibility Partners for Family Literacy Project with the American Library Association (ALA), in the words of a press release:

> to encourage the development of community partnerships among Cargill locations, public libraries, literacy providers and other community organizations ... Cargill's gift [of $100,000] to the ALA follows the Cargill Cares tradition of emphasizing information and education to address major social problems.[292]

In a response to criticism of the ALA from librarian Sanford Berman and the Social Responsibilities Round Table for being the handmaiden of Cargill, Julia Peterson, director, Cargill Information Center, wrote: 'These projects are partnerships between Cargill and local libraries – many in rural communities where library services have suffered from major budget cutbacks and where our support can make a real difference.'[293] The irony in having Cargill return to the rural community the money it previously extracted from it through its business operations apparently went unnoticed. Surely, though, someone must have wondered why it is that Cargill can afford to support library activities in rural communities when public funding of such essential community services is being cut back, partly as the result of pressure from corporations such as Cargill.

Providing college scholarships to high school seniors from farm families is another favorite form of Cargill charity. Since 1986 the company has awarded scholarships worth some $2 million.[294] Compare that figure to its net profit of $0.5 billion in 1994 alone.

In Canada, Cargill Ltd and Saskferco (its Canadian nitrogen fertilizer company) donated a portion of revenues from the sale of agricultural chemicals and fertilizers in 1993 to 13 rural Manitoba hospitals as well as $6500 to the Health Sciences Center Research Foundation for spinal cord, physical therapy and respiratory research.[295] It is hard not to take a cynical view of such charitable activity.

CHAPTER 10

The Americas

Argentina

There is actually a large group of Argentine farmers known as *Cargilleros* – farmers who are loyal to Cargill brands and services, whether it be feed, seed or grain marketing.[296]

Due to its volatile politics and persistent, and times rampant, inflation, Argentina has not been an easy place for a company like Cargill to do business. The presence of its Financial Markets divison has helped make the enterprise profitable by buying and selling currencies and other financial instruments while the commodity divisions buy and sell beans, grains and fertilizer. Cargill itself makes the point that its Financial Markets division has been able to learn from its branch in Argentina how to make up in the financial markets 'the money we would normally expect to make from the commercial side' during inflationary times. As a result, the Argentine Financial Markets division of Cargill 'developed a reputation for gutsy financial trading that resulted in winning big.'[297]

Argentina *is* beef, and so is Cargill, but Cargill's notion of beef production is not what the Argentinians have been doing. Cargill has said that it intends to transform the traditional practice of the cow/calf operators in the northwest of shipping their calves to the pampas for fattening on grass into one of fattening cattle in feedlots. More control can be exercised this way, more manufactured feed sold, and more dependency created. To this end, Cargill has introduced feed formulations and ingredients developed in the US. Cargill has a broiler chicken plant in Carabassa, Argentina, that can also utilize its feed products.

The company has been active in Argentina since 1947, and has stayed in Argentina despite the political and economic turmoil in the country that prompted Cargill's Argentinian competitor Bunge y Born to move their headquarters to Brazil.

When a 1979 change in government regulations made it possible, Cargill built a private port and terminal elevator at San Martin, near Rosario on the Parana River, about 250 km north of its mouth at Buenos Aires. It expects that these new facilities will help draw wheat farming to the central region of the country.

At the same time it also built a soybean crushing plant – 'the largest in the world of Cargill' – at San Martin.[298] The location was chosen in order to serve the growing region to the south.

Cargill also plans to build two country elevators in the same region that will be able to funnel grain, via the newly privatized railways, to its $24 million export elevator at Bahia Blanca, Argentina's best deep-water port southwest of Buenos Aires. Cargill has a second soybean crushing plant on the coast above Bahia Blanca at Necochea. The company is currently able to crush 5400 tonnes of soybeans a day at these two facilities.

Soybean monoculture requires fertilizer, which Cargill can supply from its plant in Tampa, Florida, landing it in bulk at its warehouse at Necochea where it is bagged. Farmers delivering soybeans can return home with a load of fertilizer. Out of its 'concern for the environment', Cargill also provides support to a foundation that educates farmers about 'ways to conserve soil through modern farming techniques.'[299]

In addition to helping to introduce hybrid corn in 1954, Cargill is now developing a dwarf sunflower while its staff of agronomists continues to work with farmers, 'explaining how hybrid seed offers greater disease and drought resistance as well as higher yields.'[300]

Cargill established its Argentinian Juice Division in 1989 to operate a plant to process apples and pears at Neuquen, in the valley of the river by that name in the west of the country. There the company processes and blends juices for Motts, Minute Maid (CocaCola) and Tropicana. Fruit juices, like the vegetable oils Cargill produces, are almost exclusively export products going to the US and Japan (see Chapter 11).

While Cargill is virtually unknown and invisible in North America as a supplier of consumer products, in Argentina, as in Venezuela, the company is involved in 'further processing' and distributes its products under its own Granja del Sol (Farm of the Sun) label as well as under supermarket private labels.

Having gained fruitful experience in pasta manufacturing in Venezuela (see below), in late 1994 Cargill SA was making a bid for a controlling interest (75 per cent) in Argentina's third largest flour miller and fifth largest pasta maker, Minetti y Cia SA.[301]

Brazil

Brazil, with an area slightly less than that of the US, is the world's fifth largest agricultural exporter, the world's largest producer of oranges and coffee, the second largest producer of cocoa and soybeans (which it has only been growing since 1970), and third largest producer of corn. Brazilian coffee is widely used to provide bulk in coffee blends because of its lack of special taste while more expensive coffees, like Colombian, supply the flavour.

One fifth of Brazil's population of 160 million has less than an adequate level of nutrition and 90 per cent of the population lives on less than $100 a year.

In 1948, Cargill Agricola e Comercial was established in Brazil as a joint venture with Nelson Rockefeller's International Basic Economy Corporation (IBEC).[302] In its company literature, however, Cargill has identified 1965, when it invested $9 million in a hybrid seed breeding program and plant, as the beginning of its presence in Brazil.[303] From 1967 until 1975 Cargill invested $9.3 million in Brazil, while taking out only $773,000 in dividends, leading to capital formation inside Brazil of $87.8 million by 1975.* As with all information about Cargill, one has to work with what there is, and I have no figures for post-1975.

Cargill claims that it reinvests everything it makes in a country, but there is no way of knowing whether that is true or not, since there are no public financial statements. If, as a result of investing only what is available from its own internal cash flow, Cargill Brazil has achieved the status of being second only to Cargill's US operations in size, one must conclude that Cargill Brazil has been a highly profitable operation.

Cargill Agricola claims to be Brazil's largest agricultural company, with 20 production plants and 59 other locations in the south and east of the country, and 4500 employees. Cargill Agricola is the fifth largest (or ninth, depending on which Cargill figure you believe) exporter of Brazilian coffee, accounts for 20 per cent of Brazilian soybean exports, processes 25 per cent of Brazil's cocoa, is the country's third largest orange juice producer, behind Cutrale and Citrosucro, and the second largest seed company. Cargill also processes corn and soybeans, supplies feed, seed and fertilizer, and trades in corn, soybeans, wheat, coffee and 'financial instruments'.

Cargill is best known in Brazil for its soybean oil, which it sells under the brand name 'Liza' and which now carries the Cargill logo. It was launched in 1975 and has been the market leader since 1980 in spite of being a premium oil with a premium price 10 to 40 per cent higher than other brands. All the soybean oil that Cargill produces in Brazil is sold domestically, as is most of the soybean meal.

Cargill Agricola's latest (of five) soybean processing plants is located in Uberlandia along with its large modern corn milling plant. 'Much of the corn that farmers bring to the plant is sold on a barter basis,' reported *Cargill News*. 'Cargill gets the corn: farmers get seed or fertilizer ... It's good for the farmers because buying seed on credit means paying 15 per cent or more a month in finance charges. Plus, they're getting paid with tangible goods, not cash that will quickly devalue.'[304] Corn milling is relatively new in Brazil and there are only three other companies in the business. About 25 per cent of the mill's glucose output is sold to Brazil's largest brewer, Brahma, for use in beer production in place of rice or malt. Brahma is also a producer of soft drinks and as such is one of Cargill's orange juice customers.

---

* J.R. Wilson, Cargill Technical Services, UK. Wilson's account differs from other company accounts. See Wilson in Chapter 7.

It almost goes without saying that Cargill has a big feed business in Brazil, and its feed division sees a big market in pet food. It works closely with Cargill Argentina, which has already developed a thriving pet food business. Mercosul, the developing South American common market, will enable the pet food businesses to be developed as a single multi-country operation, in Cargill's view.

One of Cargill's major enterprises in Brazil is orange juice. The story of orange juice illustrates some of the difficulty I had in writing this book: does one examine all of Cargill's operations in one country, or does it make more sense to follow one commodity around the world? And if one does take a commodity like orange juice, one has to begin with reclaimed land and citrus pulp and work it through to the tanker trucks, leased by Cargill to an independent company, which haul the concentrate around a continent.

Cargill's two Brazilian orange-juice plants, one acquired in 1977 at Bebedouro and the second built at Uchoa in 1985, between them process about 45 million 90-pound boxes of oranges per year out of Brazil's total production of about 300 million boxes (1994 estimate). They process 170,000 tonnes per year, at the rate of 40,000 oranges per minute. By comparison, total US production for juice is about 175 million boxes, but Florida production is expected to reach 250 million boxes during the next ten years. With production increasing this rapidly, Brazil may soon become a residual supplier to the US market, which may explain Cargill's aggressive push into the Japanese market in recent years.

Cargill exports its frozen orange juice concentrate in bulk from its private terminal at Santos, the largest port in South America. (Santos is, in effect, the port of Sao Paulo.) Refrigerated trucks carry the concentrate from the inland processing plants to Santos, where 15,600 tonnes can be stored (at −5°C) while awaiting shipment on one or the other of Cargill's two custom-built bulk tanker ships for delivery to its terminals at Amsterdam (built in 1980) or Elizabeth, New Jersey (just outside New York City, built in 1986).

Once it reaches Amsterdam or New Jersey, the orange juice is shipped out either by tanker truck or in 55-gallon drums or 300-gallon bins to food service companies, institutions or companies that package it for retail, not under the Cargill name, but under just about any other well-known brand name. There are only six employees in the New Jersey office/terminal, including the manager.

In a break from its customary strategy of avoiding primary production, Cargill owns four citrus farms in Brazil totaling 25,000 acres. The largest – Vale Verde – with 1.37 million trees on 13,260 acres of reclaimed ranch land and tended by some 400 employees, is probably the largest single orange grove in the world. Cargill hopes that eventually its own groves will be able to supply 25 per cent of its needs in Brazil. Now, however, most of the oranges the company processes come from 'independent' growers with whom Cargill contracts to 'own' the trees for the season. At harvest-time, the company hires 4000 pickers and moves them from grove to grove.

Because of the location of the orange groves, it is possible for Cargill's contractors to drive around and pick up day-laborers in the nearby cities, returning them after a day's work. This provides Cargill with the lowest cost and most flexible labor-force possible and virtually eliminates any kind of labor organizing.

The company's direct involvement in orange production may be comparable to its involvement in fattening cattle. Both are highly industrialized agricultural sectors with a degree of flexibility that reduces their risk factor compared to poultry or vegetable production. Oranges can be held on the trees and cattle in the feedlot if there are problems in the system.

A by-product of orange juice processing is peel oil, which is used to add flavour and aroma to juice as well as in the production of cosmetics and pharmaceuticals. The final remains of the peel are then turned into pellets, 99 per cent of which goes to the EC for animal feed. It was estimated that about one million tonnes of citrus pellets would be exported from Santos in 1992 through the facilities of Cargill, Corredor and Cutrale.[305]

In addition to oranges, since 1986 Cargill has been developing pineapple production in Brazil in order to try to balance out the orange processing season at its two plants with pineapple juice production.

Already established as a cocoa trader, in 1980 Cargill decided to move on into the processing of cocoa. It then took the unusual step, for Cargill, of actually building a new plant in Bahia. The enterprise was not a great success and the output was of poor quality until 1986 when Cargill acquired Gerkens of the Netherlands, one of the world's largest cocoa processors, and put Gerkens' people in charge of the plant. It now produces top-quality cocoa for the world market. Gerkens/Cargill processes 110,000 tonnes of cocoa beans annually, almost 5 per cent of the world crop.[306]

Cargill's coffee operations, including those in Brazil, began with the acquisition of Dutch coffee and cocoa trading firm ACLI in 1983. ACLI International was described in 1986 as one of three trading companies dominating the Central American coffee business.[307]

Cargill also has significant coffee interests in Colombia, where Cargill Cafetera of Colombia has five mills in the heart of Colombia's coffee growing region. Cargill has not missed the opportunity to cash in on the current fashion for fancy coffees. In 1992, Millstone Coffee in Everett, Washington, signed an exclusive contract with Cargill to buy 12,000 bags per year of the special label *Casa de Lorena* beans which are among the harvest's richest, largest and highest in acidity. Millstone pays $1 per pound for Cargill's coffee (which sells for $7.99 in the supermarket). This is 20 cents more than Cargill would get on the commodity exchange. Cargill has invested $500,000 in new silos for each of its mills and labs so that small samples of the beans can be tested regularly to maintain quality and detect any of the 14 common faults in coffee beans.[308]

I found one of the places where Cargill samples coffee in Liberty Corner, New Jersey, about an hour's expressway-drive west of New York city in pleasant ex-urban countryside. There Cargill maintains a staff of coffee traders, but the only real coffee they handle is the samples that are tasted for quality. Apparently this particular global trading system still has to rely on the arbitrary and arcane practice of actually tasting the commodity that one is buying and selling. Unfortunately the staff were away trading on the coffee exchange in New York and thus unavailable to answer questions, but on the wall of the reception area the 'Cargill Coffee Code of Behaviour' caught my eye. Among the eight points of proper behaviour were: '1) We all know, understand & are committed to our organizational objectives; 2) All our communications are 100 per cent truthful and open without fear of consequences; 3) We expect to have fun; 4) We RHaTal each other; 5) We overcome fear to take risks … .' This last sounds very much like a slogan from the much maligned Little Red Book of Chairman Mao! (I couldn't find out what RHaTal stood for.)

Venezuela

While Cargill had been trading in Venezuela since the 1950s, it only settled there and began operations inside the country in 1986 when it first entered into a joint venture and then purchased pasta-maker Agri-Industrial Mimesa. Three years later the company purchased a Pillsbury pasta and flour plant near Caracas, giving it two more brands of pasta, each targeted to a different consumer group. Since Venzuelans eat more pasta – 11.8 kg per person per year – than people in any other country except Italy, it's a good business to be in and a good place for Cargill to gain experience with branded consumer products. Cargill itself says that Venezuela 'may be unique in the world of Cargill for its emphasis on branded products' and the new president of Cargill Inc. has said that 'We've targeted Venezuela for a brand strategy.'[309] Given the similarities of Cargill's highly visible consumer products businesses in other South American countries, it is obvious that the company is also pursuing a regional strategy of visibility in the marketplace.

Cargill originates the durum wheat for its pasta in Canada and the US, transports it to Venezuela, then mills, manufactures, packages and advertises the product. It is now the biggest pasta company in the country. In addition, with a flour mill attached to each of its three pasta plants, Cargill is also the second largest flour miller in Venezuela. Besides its pasta, Cargill sells branded flour, rice and cooking oils in Venezuela, having acquired the oil refining, marketing and distribution business of Ormaechea Hermanos CA in Turmero, Venezuela, in 1991.

Cargill's strategy in Venezuela is to make or acquire 'products consumed daily by rich or poor, old or young,'[310] avoiding convenience foods because the poor cannot afford them and the rich don't need them because they have servants to prepare their food. The middle class, at 20 per cent of the population, is too small to constitute a market in a country with a population of only 20 million.

While Cargill's experience in Venezuela may be unique so far, there is no reason to think that they are not learning all the time how to best manage a vertically integrated line, from grain grower to retail shelf. They are also learning how to operate in the kind of class-structured economy that is becoming common around the world. One should therefore expect to see the company develop in similar ways in other countries outside Europe, North America and the Pacific Rim.

Mexico

In 1990, Mexico was the fourth largest customer of US farm products after Japan, Canada and South Korea. Mexico has about 57 million acres of arable land, compared with 464 million acres in the US.

Cargill established a beachhead in Mexico in 1964 with the opening of a molasses trading office in Mexico City called Carmela. Three years later it established the grain trading and agricultural brokerages Carmex and Carmay. In 1971 Cargill acquired C.C. Tennant Sons & Co. and began trading minerals under the name Tennant Mexico. When Cargill acquired Hohenberg Bros Co. in 1974 it became a cotton broker in Mexico as Empresas Hohenberg, Industria Hohenberg, and Empresas Algodonera Mexicana. Cargill de Mexico is one of 19 seed-producing members of the Mexican Seed Growers and Distributors Association.

Heinz Hutter, then president of Cargill, offered his recommendations on how Mexico could improve its agricultural production in a talk at the University of Illinois in 1990. Among his recommendations: increase farm size; convey land titles to communal farmers; make it possible for 'efficient farmers' to buy land freely.* Two years later, in mid-1992, the Mexican government amended the country's constitution (Article 27) to enable it to implement the policies recommended by Cargill, among others, and began allowing mills to apply for import licenses for wheat. Previously, all wheat imports were coordinated by CONASUPO, the government food distribution agency that had nearly complete control of the importing and internal marketing of wheat and corn.

As part of its privatization campaign, the government of Mexico put five corn tortilla flour mills up for tender in mid-1993. The mills were owned by Miconsa, a subsidiary of CONASUPO, and the second largest corn flour producer in the country, privately owned Masseca being the largest. Among the bidders for the five mills were Cargill and Archer Daniels Midland. The winning bid, however, went to a Guadalahara businessman.[311] Cargill will have to find another way in.

The Mexico City newspaper *El Financiero*[312] carried a substantial article on Cargill in Mexico in 1993. Describing Cargill as 'already a major supplier of corn to Mexico,' the article commented that, 'historically, the company has tended

---

* One of the most important changes in the constitution pertained to the *ejidos*, the communal farms that gave Mexican peasants security of tenure on the land they worked. This was one of the major achievements of the Mexican revolution, but it was also a major obstacle to the 'modernization' or 'rationalization' of Mexican agriculture. The *ejidos* prevented farm consolidation and industrialization. What Cargill and others were calling for was the removal of this obstacle to their freedom. The constitutional change that allowed peasants to gain title to the land simply cleared the way for the land to be acquired, one way or another, by others.

to dominate the markets it enters. Its presence in other countries raises questions over who will control Mexico's food supplies.' The article quoted Cargill spokesman Greg Lawser as saying that:

> The company's operating philosophy throughout the world is to begin with reasonably small capital investments in fields where we believe we can bring expertise and technology of use to the area, and to grow our business from that small beginning.

El Financiero pointed out that this corporate strategy conveniently dovetailed with the development policy of President Salinas de Gortari to encourage big investors to take over small enterprises, especially in agriculture. Commenting that 'information about Cargill's designs on Mexico is difficult to obtain,' *El Financiero* provided Lawser's response: 'The commodity business doesn't talk about its strategies.' He hinted, however, that Mexican exports of fruits and vegetables might be a new business area for Cargill. This is a very good possibility, given that Cargill acquired Richland Sales, a California produce distributor, in 1992.

The *Cargill Bulletin*, when it still spoke about Cargill's more 'personal' affairs, provided the rationale for its Mexican expansion:

> As the economy grows and incomes rise, more Mexican consumers will be able to satisfy their appetite for high-quality meats ... Demand for US poultry should remain strong if the Mexican economy continues to improve and the emerging middle class channels more money into upgrading its diet.[313]

The trade journal *Milling & Baking News* shares this point of view, pointing out that, on average, Mexican consumers spend more than a third of their incomes on food: 'As incomes rise in the rejuvenated economy, Mexican consumers will make upgrading their relatively low-quality diets a priority.' US feed grain producers, says the magazine, will reap the biggest rewards, as export sales rise to fuel larger meat and poultry production in Mexico.[314]

CHAPTER 11

Juices, Fruits and Vegetables

Handling large quantities of fresh fruits and vegetables is nothing like handling large amounts of stable (or staple) commodities, whether liquid or dry. Grain is essential, it will keep and its storage costs are low, which is why it has always been the first choice of traders and speculators. Milk, at the other end of the spectrum, spoils quickly and is costly to store even for a short time. So it is not hard to see why Cargill has stayed away from dairy products of all sorts, except, probably, skim milk powder – which, from a trader's perspective, is closer to grain than to the milk from which it comes.

It is also reasonably obvious why Cargill would get drawn into frozen orange juice concentrate before any other form of fruits and vegetables. Cargill actually entered this line of business with citrus pulp pellets which, as far as handling goes, are more like grain than orange juice, anyway. Moving from citrus pellets to oranges is not as big a jump as from citrus pellets into pears, for example, because oranges are at the stable end of the fruit spectrum and can be stored on the trees at a ripe stage for a matter of weeks, if not months.

From its start in citrus pellets in Brazil, Cargill has been moving around the world (from Pakistan to Florida to Japan) into citrus concentrate, other juices, and most recently, into fresh fruits and vegetables. An October 1994 ad in the trade paper of the North American produce industry for 'Richland Export Sales – a Cargill Company' in California, carried the heading 'Export Experts' and assured customers of consistent quality and year-round supply of peaches, grapes, nectarines, celery, asparagus, melons, apples, kiwifruit, onions, and many other fruits and vegetables.[315] It looked to me like a sort of birth announcement, indicating that Cargill has decided to enter the fresh produce business in a serious way after a trial marriage. Soon after that there was another little item reporting that Richland had opened an office in Wilmington, Delaware, a distribution hub for the east coast, indicating an even deeper commitment.[316]

Many produce companies seem to be as perishable as the goods they handle, looking beautiful one day and shriveled the next. Cargill is well aware of the advantages its financial resources and broad base offer:

> The juice business is as special for the capital investment required as it is for its cyclical, often volatile price swings. It's not a business for the fainthearted, uncommitted or undercapitalized. We have a distinct advantage in the

126

financial strength and support of our parent company during both the good and bad times.[317]

Cargill's entry into the European juice market arose out of its livestock feed business in Brazil, which was based on citrus pulp pellets purchased from Brazilian orange processors Cutrale and Citrosuco. In 1975, when orange juice prices were half of what they were a decade later, Cargill decided to invest $15 million in a small frozen orange juice concentrate ('FCOJ') plant in Bebedouro, Brazil. This plant had been built in 1962, but was idle when Cargill bought it due to the owner's lack of operating capital. Once again, Cargill entered a new line of business by acquiring an existing facility. Its timing couldn't have been better. A disastrous frost in Florida pushed prices up and created a demand for Cargill's Brazilian FCOJ.[318]

At the time (late 1970s) about 80 per cent of Brazil's citrus industry was controlled by Cutrale SA and Fischer SA (later purchased by Dreyfus)* and only about 5 per cent of its orange juice production was consumed domestically, the rest of it exported as frozen concentrate in 55-gallon drums (frozen after being put in the drums).[319]

Cargill continued to follow its proven strategy. It reinvested the plant's earnings in additional capacity and increased output by 15 per cent annually. In 1980 Cargill built a special juice terminal in Amsterdam to receive FCOJ in bulk and outfitted a container ship with a refrigeration system and a stainless steel hold to transport the frozen concentrated juice in bulk from Brazil to Amsterdam. A year later this same ship made its first delivery of 4.5 million litres of FCOJ from Brazil to the United States.

By 1984 Cargill was shipping 90,000 tonnes of frozen orange juice concentrate out of Brazil annually – 15 per cent of the country's total orange juice concentrate exports. Cargill shipped about one-third of this to tank warehouses in the port of Tampa, Florida, from where it was delivered to customers such as P&G, Kraft and Quaker. They, in turn, blended the Brazilian product with sweeter concentrate from US oranges. The rest of Cargill's exports went to Europe via Amsterdam, where it was sold straight because Europeans like the more acidic character of the juice. At that time, Cargill's plant at Bebedouro was bringing in almost $200 million per year and Cargill was planning a second plant to process fruit from its newly planted groves.[320]

About then Cargill developed a means of moving the concentrate at -7° to $-8^\circ C$, meaning that the concentrate was still viscous enough to be pumped from tank to tank. Previously the concentrate was transported at $-20^\circ C$. The new process made it possible for Cargill to concentrate the juice at its plants located at Bebedouro and Uchoa, pump it into a tanker truck, haul it to its terminal at Santos port, pump it directly into its waiting bulk tanker, ship it to Amsterdam

---

* The name of Fischer/Dreyfus no longer appears in references to Brazilian processors, and I have been unable to find out what happened to the company.

or New Jersey, pump it ashore again, and finally pump it again into tanker trucks for delivery to dairies, food processors and institutions for bottling, blending, and food manufacturing. This process can be called 'continuous flow'.

The next step for Cargill Agricola (the actual name of its Brazilian subsidiary) was to have Hyundai in Korea build the first vessel specifically designed to carry bulk orange-juice concentrate and peel oil. The 13,000-tonne ship, which carries 11,000 tonnes of concentrates, was christened the *Bebedouro* in 1986 and Cargill's first converted bulk FCOJ tanker was rechristened the *Uchoa*.[321]

As a company, Cargill has always been willing to seek new opportunities and when necessary, is quite willing to enter into joint ventures with companies that are otherwise its competitors. When faced with a common enemy, or in this case a potential new market opportunity, the enemies can suddenly become allies, if only for a special occasion.

Following this scenario, in 1987 Brazil's two largest orange juice processors, Citrosuco Paulista and Sucocitrico Cutrale, along with Cargill Agricola and Tetra Pak (the Swedish aseptic packaging giant), reached an agreement with the Russian government for a joint venture to process, package and distribute orange juice imported from Brazil. Cargill Agricola was, at the time, Brazil's third-largest orange juice processor. The agreement called for a plant to be built 500 km south of Moscow in Lipyceck. Soviet apple juice was to be bartered for Brazilian orange juice concentrate. The plant was to process locally grown apples into juice for sale in Europe and the US and the hard currency earned then used to pay for the Brazilian orange juice concentrate.[322]

At the time, Citrosuco Paulista, Sucocitrico Cutrale and Cargill Agricola controlled 80 per cent of Brazil's orange juice exports and the same three companies accounted for 53 per cent (800,000 tonnes) of the world's total orange juice production.[323] Brazil supplied about 40 per cent of the orange juice market in the US, which was worth $3 billion a year. Coca-Cola (Minute Maid), P&G (Citrus Hill) and Beatrice (Tropicana) were the three largest US distributors of this juice.[324] (Tropicana is now owned by Seagram Co. Ltd.)

Recent figures give the combined production of the top two companies, Citrosuco Paulista and Sucocitrico Cutrale, about 60 per cent of total Brazilian production and 30 per cent of global orange juice production. Sucocitrico Cutrale, the world's largest producer of orange juice, puts out 245,500 tonnes per year, while Cargill claims to produce 100,000 tonnes of concentrate annually.

Europe and the US were not, however, the only destinations for Brazilian orange juice. With the growing affluence of the Japanese consumer as an attraction, large transnational corporations like Cargill saw new opportunities and became determined to force their way into the Japanese market.

The California 'growers' co-operative' Sunkist got there first, exporting 134,500 tonnes of oranges and orange juice to Japan in 1987.[325] At the time, the production in Japan of orange juice from imported oranges was 10 per cent cheaper than from local Mikan oranges, and the cost of production of orange juice abroad was 23 per cent to 30 per cent cheaper than Japanese production.[326]

The Japanese farmers' cooperative ZEN-NOH has been the traditional supplier of orange juice from domestically grown mikan oranges. For a long time it supplied more than 70 per cent of the Japanese orange juice market and was protected from external suppliers by import quotas. In 1989, Japan's import quota for frozen orange juice concentrate was 23,000 tonnes, out of a total of 85,000 tonnes consumed by the nation, with imports allowed specifically for blending purposes.[327]

The volume of orange juice imported, however, was expected to rise to more than 60,000 kiloliters by 1992, while domestic production was estimated at 20,000 kiloliters for the year, thus reversing the import–domestic ratio.* Of the imports, about 94 per cent was concentrate, and 75 per cent of this was from Brazil and 19 per cent from the US.[328]

For more than a year before the April 1992, opening of orange juice imports, leading Japanese trading houses were looking for partners among overseas producers. At the same time, Citrosuco Paulista SA and Sucocitrico Cutrale SA of Brazil built storage for imported frozen concentrate in Toyohashi City, Aichi Prefecture. The facility is able to store 20,000 tonnes of concentrated juice, one-quarter of Japan's annual orange juice consumption.

Nippon Fruit Juice Co. (Mitsui) made a deal to import and market the juice for Citrosuco, while Sucocitrico Cutrale's concentrate is imported by Pacific Juice Co. and sold by Mitsubishi Corp. and Itochu Corp. (formerly C. Itoh).[329] Mitsui also arranged to import orange juice concentrate from Berry Citrus Products in Florida, Alimentos de Veracruz in Mexico, and Cambuhy Citrus in Brazil.

Itochu hoped to import about 10,000 tonnes a year from Sucocitrico Cutrale SA, but to ensure year-round supplies, Itochu also acquired sales rights from Caulkins Citrus Co. Ltd of Florida and planned to import 30–40,000 tonnes of fresh juice a year from that company.[330]

Being uncharacteristically late in entering the fray, Cargill was said to be characteristically interested in bypassing the trading houses and supplying juice directly to Japanese bottlers. The company even got as far as choosing Funabashi, Chiba Prefecture, as the site for storage tanks, but that site ended up being used for its short-lived beef processing project. Instead, in 1993 Cargill Japan began importing frozen orange juice concentrate from Brazil in 55-gallon drums for processing and blending with other juices, such as apple and pear, at its new 3500-tonne capacity plant in Kashima, southern Japan. Cargill plans to expand this plant when the market permits. For the present, Cargill claims 30 per cent of the imported orange juice market in Japan (a figure which seems unreasonably high).[331]

The advent of imported orange juice has had a big effect on the Japanese demand for native mikan mandarin oranges, which has dropped from 23 kg per person

---

* I apologize for the differing systems of measurement, which are unfortunately unavoidable since it is is difficult to translate accurately between measures by weight and by volume. Figures are given for comparison purposes.

in 1973 to 7 kg per person in 1993 as 'too many other snacks competed for their appetites.' While total orange juice consumption has remained stable at around 80,000 tonnes a year, now much of the demand is met by imported frozen concentrate, 80 per cent of which comes from Brazil and 20 per cent from the US.

Mikan oranges are a wonderful fruit when eaten fresh, but when dehydrated, stored and reconstituted, make terrible juice. To make the end product palatable, there was, until the liberalization of imports, a legal blending requirement for processors that provided local farmers with a market for their 'juicers'.

There are still about 110,000 growers of mikan oranges in Japan with some orchards up to 300 years old,[332] but the future for them in an open market is not promising. In mid-1994 I found that the price of domestically produced co-op brand mandarin orange juice at the retail level was nearly twice that of juice from Brazilian concentrate. The same ratio was true for apple juice, with juice from New Zealand concentrate about two-thirds the cost of domestic juice.

Cargill currently claims an advantage over its bigger competitors who have built bulk tanks because the Japanese market is a maximum of 80,000 tonnes, and a single bulk tanker load is 15,000 tonnes or more. To indicate the kind of problems that very large suppliers can encounter, I was told that one Brazilian company shipped a tanker load to its Japanese partner, but the partner would not buy the juice and the shipper had to sell (dump?) it in Korea. Such accounts, and official trade figures, may be misleading, however, because juice can be imported into Japanese port storage facilities, such as those of the Brazilian companies, and then re-exported to another destination in the region without appearing in the trade statistics and without being dutiable, as long as it was never 'landed' in Japan. This may explain the apparent over-capacity in Toyohashi City. It may also explain Cargill's determination to take a more flexible route.

As both a producer and a global marketer and trader, Cargill enjoys a distinct advantage over companies operating as only one or the other. Cargill is well equipped to speculate in the commodity which it is also producing, and what it might lose as a speculator it can make up as a producer and vice versa – if it hedges its bets well. FCOJ is traded on the cotton exchange (it had to be put somewhere!), and the volatile FCOJ market is just what speculators love. The following newspaper accounts of the commodities trade illustrate this volatility:

1992: Frozen orange juice concentrate for November delivery fell to $1.086 a pound on the NY Cotton Exchange. The price continued to drop to .966, the lowest price since May, 1986, because of USDA projections of a very large 1992–93 Florida orange crop. Celeste Georgakis of Cargill Investor Services reported that Brazilian processors had dropped their prices to $1.156 a pound to preferred customers, 'a move that took the industry by surprise.'[333] (It is hard to believe that there was any 'surprise' when 'the industry' includes Cargill and the commentator is a Cargill employee.)

1993: Expectations of near-record orange harvests have sent Florida prices to their lowest levels since the 1950s. Orange growers in Florida received .45 a pound for juice solids this week, down from $1.48 a year ago. The industry says the break-even price for orange production is $1 a pound.[334]

Futures prices dropped to .6795 a pound in the face of production forecasts up 23 per cent from 1992. Growers are getting about .42 a pound.[335]

Frozen concentrated orange juice sank to $1.75 a pound on the NY futures market.'[336]

Certainly not a company to put all of its eggs into one basket, Cargill began looking around for alternative sources of orange juice as soon as it knew its Brazilian operation was a success. It ended up in Pakistan where it built the country's first fruit juice concentrate plant in 1990 after four years of negotiating. Cargill is the sole owner of the plant located in Sargodha, Pakistan's main citrus area northwest of Lahore in the Punjab. The Pakistan Government provided incentives such as an eight-year tax holiday and duty-free import of all the machinery installed in the plant. The project was modelled on Cargill's plants in Brazil, and with the help of the US Government, Cargill took a group of farmers from Sargodha to Brazil to learn how to improve growing techniques. The Cargill factory was to produce 5000 tonnes of concentrate a year initially, but Cargill hoped to double this quickly by reinvesting profits and increasing yield and season.[337]

'Cargill had actually established its presence in Pakistan in the early 1980s through its purchase of the British company Ralli Bros which was involved in cotton trading. It is now one of the largest cotton traders in SE Asia for cotton out of Pakistan.'[338] The rationale for Cargill's move, besides broadening its supply base, is that Pakistan is the world's major producer of kinno, a satsuma-type orange developed at the University of California in the 1930s. The most important characteristics of the kinno are its taste, high Vitamin C content and its color. The frozen kinno concentrate is exported to Amsterdam and used for blending and colouring because it has the rich orange colour of Fanta orange drink which until now has generally been produced artificially. Cargill believes the West and Japan are willing to pay the extra cost to have natural rather than synthetic coloring agents.

In 1989 Cargill also acquired apple and pear processing facilities in Argentina and Chile. The two facilities combined can produce 16 million liters of apple and pear juice concentrate per year, and this puts Cargill at the head of the list as South America's largest apple juice exporter. The company also processes passionfruit and pineapple juices into frozen concentrate at its plant in Fiera de Santana, Brazil. Cargill ships apple juice concentrate in 55-gallon drums or 300-gallon bins to blenders and bottlers around the world.[339] The company also has a plant in Ferrara, Italy, for processing apples into concentrate. The consequence is that the consumer who buys apple juice from concentrate anywhere in the world may well be buying a Cargill product, though it is not Cargill that does the reconstituting.

Apple juice concentrate offers a big financial advantage over orange juice concentrate in that it can be stored safely at chilled temperatures and even at room temperature for a period of time, though it would then have to be sent back through the line to be purified and/or reconcentrated before sale.

In order to accomodate the continuing growth of its juice and fruit lines of business, in 1989 Cargill created its Worldwide Juice, Fruit and Vegetable division, even though at that point it did not appear to own any vegetable operations. The division's major operation at the time was Citro America, with its four juice processing plants in South America and Pakistan (two in Brazil, one in Argentina for apples and pears, and one in Pakistan).

But there are limits to how much orange juice anyone is going to drink, and consequently there are also limits to how much of any single commodity one can sell in a single market. But if you have gained experience with oranges and orange juice, why not try pears (when you already have experience in juicing them) and grapes?

In August, 1991, after three years of scouting, Cargill took another step in filling out its Worldwide Juice, Fruit and Vegetable division with the purchase of tree fruit shipper Richland Sales Co. of Reedley, California. Following the Cargill purchase, Richland president Mark Lewis figured that his company was the largest peach shipper in the US, packing 5.5 million boxes of peaches, plums, nectarines, pears, kiwifruit and grapes from California and Chile.

Less than a year later, Cargill decided it was safe to take a small expansionist step, and in May 1992 Richland purchased Delano, California, grape grower Prosper Dulcich & Sons.[340] Cargill officers described this as only the beginning of their produce ventures: 'We wanted to start with something small to medium in size with the idea we could develop the business and get bigger,' division president Doug Linder said.[341]

Linder said Cargill will probably make innovative contributions to the industry, perhaps in areas such as packaging and transportation. Other shippers said the company's financial strength and its ties to Washington would help give the industry a clearer legislative voice.[342]

With Cargill backing, Richland almost immediately spent $1 million to install a 'superline' to double its daily packing capacity and accommodate different pack styles and brand labeling, thereby increasing its annual volume in 1992 by 10 per cent and its sales to about $60 million.

When asked about their autonomy, Cargill location managers are quick to emphasize that they are running essentially 'free-standing' businesses. When pushed, as recounted elsewhere, they will acknowledge the limits of their autonomy. Doug Linder, as president of Cargill's Worldwide Juice, Fruit and Vegetable Division, 'now sits as Richland's chairman and makes all final decisions from Cargill headquarters in Minnetonka,' reported *The Packer*. 'While Richland managers are given room to exercise their own judgement and style, all roads at Richland now lead to Cargill,' said Linder.[343]

Since being purchased by Cargill, acquiring Prosper Dulcich, and then making a marketing deal with Morgan Johnson of Madera, California, Richland has doubled the volume of grapes imported from Chile, giving the company nearly year-round coverage of the market. (California supplies grapes from mid-July to November, Chile supplies from December to April.)

Richland's operating concept, according to *The Packer*, is 'to function with the efficiency of a small company under the umbrella of a large firm.'[344] Richland's next move was to get back into the apple and Asian pear business after a five-year hiatus. When this was reported,[345] no mention was made of Richland's parent, Cargill.

The next step for Cargill's Worldwide Juice, Fruit and Vegetable division was its biggest one yet by far. In fall 1992 Cargill purchased from Procter & Gamble a large fruit-juice processing plant in Frostproof, Florida, and immediately expanded plant capacity from 13 million to 14.5 million boxes of oranges annually (three times Richland's volume). The plant's extensive cold storage capacity was particularly attractive to Cargill and, in conjunction with its Brazilian plants, provides the company with the ability to supply orange juice concentrate throughout North America on a year-round basis.*

This was certainly not a risky move for Cargill since for years it had been a supplier of Brazilian juice concentrate to P&G, and Cargill-originated juice can be found in brands such as Tropicana, Minute Maid and Sunkist, as well as in private labels. In addition, much of Cargill's concentrate, like that of its Brazilian competitors, never reaches the consumer at the retail level as straight orange juice at all, going instead to bottlers and blenders to produce a great variety of soft drinks.

In its first year of operating the Frostproof plant, Cargill processed about 7 per cent of the Florida orange harvest, including oranges from its own groves.[346] (About 90 per cent of Florida's orange crop is processed for juice, while most California oranges are eaten.)

In conjunction with its phosphate mining operations just down the road from Frostproof, which require holding large areas of land both as mining reserves and as reclaimed land, Cargill owns more than 3000 acres (1200 hectares) of orange groves in central Florida. In fact, Cargill is doing some creative experimentation with orange production on reclaimed land (see Chapter 16).

Cargill appears to take the same thoughtful approach to waste management and ecology in the Frostproof operations as it does in its nearby phosphate mining operations. It purifies and utilizes the processing water – including much of the 80 per cent water in the orange itself – by piping it six miles to where it can be used to irrigate forage grass which absorbs the nutrients in the water. The grass is then harvested several times a year and fed to cattle, while the water that percolates through the ground is collected in drainage pipes and used to irrigate a 223-acre (90-hectare) citrus grove.[347]

Coming full circle back to Cargill's beginnings in the citrus business, the citrus peel from the Frostproof plant is itself ground, dried and pelletized, then shipped

---

* In 1993, FCOJ imports from Brazil were down to about 12 per cent of US supplies from more than 30 per cent several years earlier.

to Cargill's port facility in Tampa, Florida, from where it is exported to Europe for sale as livestock feed through Cargill's distribution system.

In reading the trade papers, in light of the above, I have to wonder what lies behind an item such as this:

> The Cuban government and a group of Brazilian business people have agreed in principle on 10 investment projects, including citrus processing plants in Cuba.[348]

Cuba could be a very attractive source of citrus for the US, and it would seem to me quite possible that some of these 'Brazilian business people' might be representing Cargill. To do business with Cuba, Cargill would have to go through one of its subsidiaries, such as Cargill Agricola, since the US embargo prohibits US companies from doing business with Cuba.

Or what is one to make of this story? US Sugar Corp, the parent company of leading Florida vegetable grower-shipper South Bay Growers Inc., is becoming a citrus processor, but has no plans to ship fresh oranges. South Bay subsidiary Southern Gardens Citrus Processing Corp. has planted 3 million citrus trees on 29,000 acres (12,000 hectares) in southwest Florida in the past eight years. In January it opened a 132,100 sq. ft. facility in Clewiston, Florida.[349] In September 1994, South Bay Growers Inc. went out of business, reporting a $10 million loss last season as a result of low market prices.[350]

CHAPTER 12

The Pacific Rim I:
The Region and Taiwan

Creating a Market: the Region

We do it all the time, changing people's eating habits. It's good for them to
have a bigger choice.

Charles Alexander, Director, US Agricultural
Trade Office, Seoul, August 1994.

After the end of World War II in 1945, Japan was displaced, at least for a time,
by the US as the dominant power in the Pacific region. Japan, along with Korea
and Taiwan, were, during that period, the victims of a new form of imperialism, US food aggression, as the countries were occupied by both North American
troops and food. The food was sometimes in the form of direct relief to keep
people from starving; sometimes it was aid for reconstruction, buying allies in
the struggle against the 'communist menace'; and often, and more enduringly,
it was creating a market for surplus American food. The net effect was the same:
change the eating habits and create dependency on American supplies of wheat
and white flour for direct human consumption primarily in the form of white
bread, and create an intensive livestock industry based on imported feedstuffs,
namely corn and soybeans from the US.

Once reconstruction and the industrialization process was underway, the US
programs were carried out under the 1954 'Food For Peace' banner of Public
Law 480 (PL 480), which was essentially a market expansion program wrapped
in the American flag of anticommunism. More recently, even as the threat of
'communism' was dissolving, US food imperialism was renewed and extended
with the 1985 Farm Bill and the accompanying Export Enhancement Program
(EEP). This program was designed by US agribusiness interests to maintain US
corporate domination of global food trade at any cost, particularly in the face of
subsidized exports from the European Community/Union.

The most obvious victim of this food imperialism has been, and will continue
to be, the domestic agriculture and rural society of the recipient countries, That
has, however, never been an issue of concern to US-based transnational cor-

135

porations like Cargill which regard Japan, Taiwan and Korea primarily as markets for food and feed. As one of the major suppliers of food and feedstuffs, Cargill has been both agent and beneficiary of this form of imperialism.

The 'geography' of the Pacific Rim and its 'emerging markets' is increasingly important to corporations faced with the saturation of the North American and European markets, so I spent some time there trying to understand how Cargill views the region and what its strategies have been. Fortunately I was able to talk with many Cargill people, some of their TNC competition, government researchers and policy people, and many local opponents of what Cargill is doing and advocating.

Taiwan

Taiwan has long occupied a special place in the heart of American cold warriors as the last bastion of freedom confronting the Red Menace of China. As such, illusions about Taiwan's independence have been maintained even while the economic independence of the country has been undermined by the imperialism of development aid and the market demands of American agribusiness. In recent years the magnetism of the real China, with its billion potential consumers, has undermined the political significance of Taiwan. As a regional hub and staging point for the great China market, however, Taiwan retains a particular strategic significance.

The land area of Taiwan is 36,000 square kilometers, but the interior is mountainous and stunningly beautiful, as its name 'Formosa' attests. Only about 29 per cent of total area, around the perimeter of the island, is suitable for agriculture. Four million of the island's population of about 21 million is defined as 'agricultural', but there are fewer than 800,000 'farm families', each with an average holding of 1.1 hectares. The total cultivated area of about 876,000 hectares is fairly evenly split between irrigated and dry land farming. Agricultural land currently sells for $300,000 to $2.5 million per hectare, which makes agricultural production very expensive.[351]

'There are still too many people engaged in agriculture,' states the booklet cited above, representing the policy of the Council of Agriculture, or agricultural ministry, and also reflecting the fact that agricultural production has grown faster than the population and domestic demand.

Taiwan has also been the fastest-growing market in the Pacific Rim for US agricultural exports, according to *Milling & Baking News*. It states that:

as in the case of South Korea, the modern wheat foods industry of Taiwan dates from shipments of food aid wheat and flour from the United States during the 1950s. Taiwan was a major beneficiary of the PL 480 program until 1965. Since 1973, Taiwan has signed consecutive five-year wheat agreements with a group of participating US grain exporting companies.

The result has been that the US has accounted for about 88 per cent of Taiwan's wheat imports for the past ten years.[352] Taiwan imports almost all of its soybean, wheat, sorghum and cotton requirements.

Until 1993, the Taiwan Flour Mills Asssociation, representing all of Taiwan's 35 flour millers, was the sole wheat purchasing agency, and 'it was encouraged by the government to purchase mainly from the US.'[353] Quite naturally, then, it dealt with US Wheat Associates as the representative of the US exporters, among them Cargill.

Since 1952 meat output in Taiwan has increased tenfold, and now accounts for more than one-third of the total value of agricultual production, with hogs replacing rice as the top value agricultural product of the island, with poultry in third place. The intensity of hog production has created a manure problem, as it did in Denmark, and the government is now helping the industry to install waste treatment facilities.

Even though consumption of beef and veal stood at a very low 2.1 kg per person annually in 1990, domestic production was able to satisfy only about 8 per cent of consumption, the balance being imported primarily from Australia and New Zealand.[354] *

Cargill began trading in both Taiwan and Korea in 1956, the year Tradax was founded by Cargill as its global trading subsidiary. In 1968 Cargill received permission from the Taiwan government to build a feed mill, which opened in

---

* The trend in Taiwan agriculture is obvious from the changing livestock inventory:

	beef cattle	hogs	dairy cows	chicken	eggs (millions)
1955	412,000	2,800,000	839	6,513,000	128
1960	420,570	3,164,570	1,916	7,650,000	193
1970	294,680	2,900,000	4,430	14,822,000	575
1980	133,800	4,820,000	11,045	41,400,000	2,023
1985	143,200	6,673,000	22,750	59,313,000	3,345
1990	154,240	8,565,000	46,340	76,979,000	4,032
1993	165,600	9,845,000	57,650	92,329,000	4,916

(Source: *Taiwan Statistical Data Book*, 1994)

	Exports: pork/swine (currently 99% to Japan)	Imports: corn (feed) (96% from US)	soybeans (feed) (100% from US)
1985	$234,400,000	$422,237,000	$390,769,000
1986	392,150,000	354,502,000	398,685,000
1987	652,107,000	353,626,000	429,988,000
1988	617,475,000	548,207,000	551,800,000
1989	507,476,000	610,235,000	543,864,000
1990	661,502,000	702,776,000	511,313,000
1991	984,766,000	732,959,000	492,725,000
1992	1,009,931,000	714,977,000	548,978,000
1993	1,059,274,000	685,451,000	618,723,000

(Source: *Agricultural Trade Statistics of Republic of China*, 1993)

1971 in Kaohsiung. Cargill's second mill, in Taichung, opened in 1975. The company's 1991 booklet about its Taiwan operations reports that when the Kaohsiung mill started operating, it 'provided high quality feed for Taiwan at low price and declared the end of monopoly [sic] of Taiwan feed market.'

Each of Cargill's two mills in Taiwan has a capacity of 30,000 tonnes per month. The Da-Tu mill produces 13,000 tonnes per month of layer feed, 5000 tonnes of pig feed, 4000 tonnes of duck feed and 3000 tonnes of broiler feed. Plant superintendent Lin volunteered the interesting bit of information that duck feed does not have to be medicated because Peking ducks have naturally high levels of antibodies. Chicken feed, on the other hand, has to be highly medicated. Most of the feed produced by Da-Tu goes out in bulk by truck either directly to larger farms or to dealers who bag it for retail sale.

As for the sources of feed ingredients, corn is imported from the US via Seattle, the fish meal comes from Canada and the soybean meal is purchased locally because the major product of soybeans is the oil and the meal is priced as a by-product. Broken rice which has been in storage for more than a year can also be purchased from the government. (Rice is an excellent binder, making pellets very hard.) Cargill Taiwan's head office in Taipei does all the purchasing according to the mill's requirements and specifications.

While taking us through the mill, superintendent Lin asked if we had noticed the amount of manual labor, a lot of it bagging feed and handling it by the bag. He said that headquarters in Minneapolis would like the plant to automate and get rid of all the manual labour, but the plant management has resisted and has tried to explain to Cargill that labor relations are too important to be treated that way. Lin said it is their own policy to automate slowly as people leave or retire. A lot of the employees have worked there since the plant opened 19 years ago, and the managers clearly feel some responsibility to these people.

Cargill might treat its regular workers well, including being concerned about their safety in the mill, but before entering I saw a peasant woman, barefoot, wearing only simple clothing, carrying a backpack sprayer to the mill building. When we came out, there she was, spraying the grass around the mill. It was apparent that there was little regard for her health and safety.

Andy Chu, director of Cargill's Da-Tu mill in Taichung, does not quite share all the views of more central players in the Cargill hierarchy. Speaking as a Taiwanese, he was quick to say that the GATT was not good, that it would be bad for Taiwan farmers. With high land prices and high labor costs, Taiwan will become another Singapore, not a positive development from Chu's perspective. Chu also commented that with its excellent management skills and the volume of its purchased ingredients, Cargill's mills in Taiwan will continue to be successful, even as other companies leave for China.[355]

The mill management is not only resisting abrupt automation in the plant. It is also resisting head-office pressure to computerize all bookkeeping and bring it into line with the company's global system for all of its feedmills. The managers said they have very good staff who maintain close relations with their customers, and they do not want to jeopardize these good relations by automating them. It is important to talk with the customers, they said, and to know how they are doing. (As mentioned in Chapter 8, I heard exactly the same thing from the employees of a Cargill subsidiary in Nebraska, who did not like Cargill's centralized system because it would drive away their customers.)

Late in 1990 Cargill announced it would build a pork-processing plant in the Kojo region of Taiwan, 100 km north of Kaohsiung at Da Cheng, as a joint venture between Cargill Taiwan Ltd and Taiwan Sugar Corp. The plant was to slaughter 3000 hogs a day (equivalent to the capacity of Japan's largest processing plant) when completed in late 1992, and export 30,000 tonnes of pork a year to Japan. Cargill figured that Japan imported about 360,000 tonnes of pork a year and if its plant operated at full capacity, it could supply just under 10 per cent of this quantity.[356]

The plant did open in 1992, with its hog supply coming largely from its partner, Taiwan Sugar Corp., which produces about 600,000 hogs a year in its own intensive hog production facilities. The processing plant, originally a 50–50 partnership, is now owned 60 per cent by Cargill, 40 per cent by Taiwan Sugar, more in keeping with Cargill's standard policy regarding control. At the same time, it is clearly to Cargill's advantage to have a large minority shareholder with the kind of near-liquid resources and political power that Taiwan Sugar has.

Since the plant opened, it has been slaughtering 2000 hogs per day on a single shift. Although it could kill more, the plant is doing very well, with very high quality, and 85 per cent of its production is going to Japan as deboned chilled or frozen pork, according to Gary Applegate, president of Cargill Taiwan Corporation. The plant has a very good reputation in Japan for being free of any drug residues, such as sulfa, which is a problem for most other producers wanting to export to Japan. While there are 27 other hog processors in Taiwan, only seven of those are allowed to sell to Japan, Applegate told me. Besides which, Applegate said, Cargill's Taiwan-produced pork tastes better, has better texture, and a longer shelf-life than other pork.[357] (I had walked into his modest office on the third floor of a nondescript building first thing in the morning the day after a typhoon had knocked out most the communications facilities, so there was not the usual stack of faxes from the day and night before to deal with and our conversation was leisurely.)

Applegate told me that the complementarity between Cargill's feed production and Taiwan Sugar's pork production is less than Cargill expected it would be, but if Cargill is the supplier of the main feed ingredients, imported corn and soybeans, it is a good bet that Cargill makes a fair bit of money even without doing the feed manufacturing itself. By the same token, if the margin on hog slaughtering and processing is a bit slim at times, Cargill has still made money on the feed they have sold to Taiwan Sugar. As for their partner, Applegate credited Taiwan Sugar with being the best-run government company in the world – a very high level of praise, given Cargill's competence (and experience).

Applegate also said that Cargill is less active in Taiwan than in other areas of Southeast Asia such as Indonesia, Malaysia, and particularly China. In Taiwan, as in Korea, he said, feed was their way into the country, inferring that it would also be used in pursuing their traditional strategy of establishing a beachhead in a new location with a familiar product line in other countries in the region.

Cargill already has a joint-venture feed mill in China, which it regards as a learning experience, according to Applegate, and now it is building two more mills. It intends to have five feed mills in operation in China by 1997. Most of the feedstuffs are expected to be of Chinese origin. This will be just the opposite of the situation in Taiwan, where 95 per cent of the feed ingredients used in its two mills are imported, mostly from the US, although some groundnut (peanut) and rapeseed meal is imported from India.

Applegate expressed his pleasure with his staff who are so good at buying soybean meal and other commodities that they can buy in the US midwest for delivery in Taiwan and match the cost of meal purchased in Taiwan from much closer sources in China. 'They know where all the soybean meal is, how much there is and where it is going, all around the world.'

Applegate was also pleased that a branch of Cargill Investor Services (CIS) had been established in Taipei in May 1994. 'It lowers the cost of doing business by providing low-cost money [low-interest financing].' This is an interesting revelation because Cargill advertises CIS as handling only its customers' accounts (as described in Chapter 4).

Cargill's directory also lists 'M.A. Cargill Trading Co' in Taipei. Applegate described this as a molasses trading company that also handles other feed components, such as tallow, as well as hides and other low-value raw materials. M.A. Cargill also operates Sea Continental, a shipping company that owns no ships, but arranges cargoes for Cargill and others throughout the region.

Cargill's biggest competitor in Taiwan, as in many other places, is Continental Grain.

In looking to the future, Applegate says Cargill Taiwan has reached a limit with feed and pork processing unless Taiwan becomes a regional hub for 'further processing' and distribution of meat produced elsewhere, such as beef from Australia, the US and Canada, and chicken from Cargill's plant in Thailand. In this scenario, the white meat would be shipped to the US where it is preferred, and the dark meat to markets in Southeast Asia where it is preferred. Taiwan itself is too small to be an attractive market, compared, for example, to Korea which has twice the population of Taiwan (three times if North Korea is included). All that Taiwan has to offer is its geographical location and its skilled but high-priced labor.

Two days later, to my surprise, I heard this very same outlook expressed by three policy researchers at the Institute for National Policy Research (INPR), which is funded by a wealthy Taiwanese financier specifically to create policy for the President of Taiwan. When I met with the researchers, I asked them what role the corporate sector in general, and companies like Cargill in particular, had in policy formation. Their very polite response was that they had never thought about it. Not only had they never given a thought to the role of agribusiness in shaping agricultural policy, they knew absolutely nothing about Cargill and what it was doing. Then they told me what they thought about Taiwan's role: there is a core, a semi-periphery, and periphery. We see Taiwan as the core, a shipping point, using our capital to reach the peripheral markets. We have no land and there is a shortage of labor, so we have to intensify our agricultural production and industry using our capital. We can work in partnership with companies like Cargill to secure our own economy.

This response left me wondering about the innocence, if not the sincerity, of the researchers, and about mechanisms of thought transfer and subliminal policy formation. Given Cargill's extensive experience in shaping public policy, there is no reason to think that they have played their cards differently in Taiwan.

On the other hand, it has not all been smooth sailing for Cargill in Taiwan. At one point, the company complained that it was being shut out of soybean tenders by the BSPA ('The Breakfast Club'), Taiwan's leading purchasing group, which buys about two Panamax cargoes a month of US soybeans by open tender. ('Panamax' refers to the maximum size ship that can navigate the Panama Canal.) Cargill's general manager in Taiwan at the time, Jason Lin, described the Taiwanese market as 'an oligopoly with only 15 major crushers.' Cargill usually got one-third to one-quarter of the business, but that changed when a key BSPA member company reported that a 54,000-tonne cargo sold by Cargill was significantly short weight when it was delivered and the club demanded that Cargill and the carrier, Maersk Line, take the cargo back or offer compensation. Since they refused, the group continued to boycott Cargill until the dispute was settled.[358]

Referring to his experience of the US in trade negotiations, and reflecting the attitude of representatives of smaller countries, a senior Taiwan GATT negotiator said to me:

> So many companies, so many senators ... We do not distinguish between the US government and the companies. We can make no difference. We don't have the resources to counter the lobbying of the US Wheat Associates ... The rice millers force the US government to subsidize rice and force an extension of the market for it. So the US will impose policy on other countries like Taiwan. The US imposes its policy on Japan first, then Taiwan. If Japan yields to US pressure, we must follow.

Curious about Cargill's partner, Taiwan Sugar Corporation, I interviewed three of their senior executives. While they were cautious and guarded, what they did say, coupled with what is printed in their corporate literature, painted a clear picture of a company radically different from, yet able to do business with, Cargill.

The Taiwan Sugar Corporation was formed at the end of World War II out of four Japanese-managed companies that were originally established by the Dutch East India Company in the seventeenth century. When Japan occupied Taiwan in 1895, they recognized the importance of the companies and kept them going, using the sugar they produced to make alcohol for fuel during the war. In the late 1940s the Chinese came from the mainland and took over the company, incorporating it into the Kuomintang (KMT), the governing party of ruler Chiang Kai-shek. This resource made the KMT the richest political party in the world, according to one Taiwanese opposition member.

Since 1949, Taiwan has been a major sugar-exporting country, though its exports peaked in 1953. Over the years the Taiwan Sugar Corporation has diversified to some extent, but it still owns 58,000 hectares of land in Taiwan and sugar remains its primary business activity, even if it is a money loser. The annual deficit can be made up by selling a few hectares of land! Today the company has about $1 billion in annual sales, half of that in sugar for domestic consumption, 15 per cent in hogs, about 11 per cent in sugar by-products and food, and another 11 per cent in land development.

Taiwan Sugar Corporation has been in hog production since 1953 and today produces 600,000 hogs a year on 29 farms, the largest one producing 60,000 pigs per year. Pollution is now under control, they say, thanks to the utilization of the latest waste management technology and government support.

In the era of privatization, selling off Taiwan Sugar is apparently not on the books because of the size of its landholdings, and there is now a debate as to whether the land belongs to the people of Taiwan, that is, the government directly, or to the corporation. In the past Taiwan Sugar has simply acted as a private landowner, doing as it pleased with its landholdings. This is now being contested by those who say that Taiwan Sugar is not acting in the interests of the people, particularly since it wants to maximize the financial return on its land by selling it for housing and Disneyland-like projects. The opponents of this kind of profiteering and land use claim that Taiwan Sugar has *land use* rights only and is not free to sell or lease the land for other purposes.

Having accepted a limited future for itself on the island, Taiwan Sugar is moving abroad, building a 6000-tonne-per-day sugar mill in Vietnam and exploring opportunities in Indonesia as well. It is also moving its bagesse pulp mill to Australia while importing cows from Australia to develop its domestic cattle operations as a kind of holding operation on its unprofitable sugar lands.

President Enterprises is Taiwan's largest integrated food processing and retailing group, and in mid-1994 it expanded operations into the US with the purchase of the fifth-largest US baking company. In the first half of 1994 it also had an extraordinary financial gain resulting from the sale of a Taiwan pig farm for conversion into a condominium development. And it probably all started with PL 480 white flour from the US.

CHAPTER 13

The Pacific Rim II: Korea

The stage was set for the present economic structure of Korea by a series of unfortunate historical experiences: the 35-year Japanese occupation; the forcible division of the country by the US and USSR in 1945, leading to the extremely destructive Korean War (1950–53); the corrupt rule of Rhee Syngman, which neglected land reform and opened the south to the beginnings of economic domination by the US; and finally the 1961 military coup by Park Chung-Hee who took it upon himself to modernize the nation. It is the Park model – rapid industrialization based on exports – which set the pattern of economic development practiced throughout the past three decades. The Park plan demanded a massive, low-wage factory labor force, which was obtained by a cynical neglect of the agricultural sector and a low-grain-price policy coupled with imports of foreign agricultural goods, resulting in the exodus of huge numbers of rural people who could no longer survive by farming. In 1990, 5 per cent of the Korean population held 65 per cent of the total private land, or 47 per cent of all land, and the majority of those owners were said to be *chaebol* [conglomerates], the top five of which are Samsung, Hyundai, Daewoo, Lucky-Goldstar and Hanjin. These big export corporations also benefitted from massive loans at favorable rates, obtained with government backing from the US and Japan.[359]

It is not enough, apparently, that Korea is already the third-largest importer of US agricultural products. The frequently seen advertisement for Marlboro cigarettes – the American cowboy image – seems to be representative not only of the attitude toward Korea of the tobacco pushers, but of Cargill, Continental, Archer Daniels Midland, and the US Government itself. It was particularly noticeable in the attitude of the Korea director of the US Meat Export Federation and the director of the Agricultural Trade Office of the US Embassy, both of whom I met in Seoul.

The offices of the Agricultural Trade Office (ATO) of the USDA in Seoul are in a nondescript building behind the fortified US Embassy. Behind the double armored doors, metal detection devices and armed guards of the ATO are also the offices of the US Meat Export Federation, US Wheat Associates, and other publicly supported lobbies of US agribusiness. Besides standing on the American flag, these groups receive half their funding directly from the US Government and the other half from the industries they represent.

The US is not well-liked in Korea, though Japan is disliked even more for its decades of domination of Korea which only ended with Japan's defeat in 1945. The US is disliked for its long-time support of repressive governments, its aggressive attitude toward Korea as a market, and its hostility toward reunification of Korea. The US has, in fact, gone so far as to act as an *agent provocateur*, creating continuing conflicts between the North and South. The most recent large-scale escapade was the alarmism generated over the so-called nuclear threat from the North in the summer of 1994, which ended only when President Clinton did an about-face.

Cargill in Korea

Even with the correct address and a knowledgeable guide it took quite a while to find the Cargill office in Seoul. One of the first questions Yoon Ik-Sang, director of Cargill Trading Ltd, Korea Branch, asked was, 'How did you manage to find this office?' I smiled and gave him an evasive response, and he smiled, acknowledging, with Asian courtesy, that I did not need to and was not going to inform him. I had similar experiences in other locations, reflecting the success of Cargill's corporate policy of invisibility.

I was later told by Korean farmers about Cargill's advertisement in the farm papers: a large blank space with no words, only the Cargill teardrop-in-a-circle logo in one corner, without the customary 'Cargill' inside. It seems there is a certain hostility towards Cargill, so they keep their name out of sight, while still trying to familiarize the farmers with their logo. (It's apparently the same situation Cargill faces in Nebraska, as already described, and in India, see Chapters 15 and 16.)

Three-quarters covered by mountains, inhabited by 43.7 million people, and now highly industrialized as a result of deliberate state policy since 1960, South Korea is increasingly attractive not as a supplier but as a market for imported food and agricultural products. From what I was told, Cargill shares this perception of Korea's opportunities.

South Korea's two million farm families comprise 10 to 12 per cent of the country's population. The average farm size is 1.2 hectares, and even this holding is often broken up into several small fields. My strongest image of the Korean 'rural' landscape is of these small, intense rice paddies abutting huge new apartment complexes housing up to 20,000 people each.

Cargill proclaims the benefits of agricultural 'modernization', but the reality is that Cargill, in Korea and elsewhere, has to engage in a balancing act between serving the interests of huge conglomerates like the Korean *chaebol*, the demands and sensitivities of a still numerous rural, if not farming, population, and its need to shape the business climate to suit its own corporate interests. These three agendas seldom coincide, regardless of any visions of globalization generated by the GATT.

Nevertheless, the fact is that Cargill, as a commodity buyer, trader and distributor, can serve the interests of both the *chaebol* and itself. As a processor it can maximize returns by processing commodities, such as livestock feed, and compete with the *chaebol*, as long as it does not threaten them. In the case of beef and pork, Cargill can play a more direct and uncomplicated role in the market place since it has sources the *chaebol* can neither reach nor control. Cargill's overall advantage lies in its integrated functions, interests and flexibility. These factors enable it to get what it can where it can without being so aggressive as to antagonize its opposition into hostile action.

Cargill Trading was established in Korea in 1986, at a time when the company was expanding rapidly into new regions. Prior to that, Cargill acted only through local agents. Now there appear to be two divisions: the feed division and the trading division. While 'Excel' is on the office door, I was told that it is a separate company with no connection, and when I asked where I could get information about it, I was referred to Brad Park of the US Meat Export Federation as the person to see about beef imports.

Cargill, according to Yoon Ik-Sang, is involved in the cotton trade in Korea through its subsidiaries Hohenberg and Ralli Bros. It is not involved in rice trading because in global trade it is too small and because the US Rice Millers Association has the market sewn up with the Korean government. (Cargill became a rice miller in 1992 with the purchase of the largest rice mill in the state of Mississippi, but apparently has not yet made its presence felt in the Rice Millers' Association.)

So far Cargill has only a small role in the fruit juice market because Cutrale and Dreyfus, the major exporters of Brazilian orange juice to Korea, got into the market first. In addition, Sunkist of California is the major supplier to Korean distributor Haitai, while Del Monte has a deal with Lotte, the major Korean department/food store chain.

Although one might expect Cargill to be in the seed business in Korea, according to Yoon it has not bothered because the market is too small. Livestock feed grain importing, feed milling, and oilseeds are the most public aspects of Cargill's involvement in Korea.

Cargill first got permission to enter the livestock feed business in Korea in 1986 when a process of modernization and consolidation was taking place in the industry. The domestic players agreed that Cargill should not be allowed to build a new mill and made their views known to the government. Cargill got around them by agreeing to buy an old mill, Young Hung Mulsan Co., in southern Korea. It then proceded to dismantle the mill and move it to Chungnam in west-central Korea were it was rebuilt. The mill now has a 300-tonne-per-day single-shift capacity.

In spite of its presence as a miller, however, Cargill is not doing as well as Continental and A.C. Toepfer (50 per cent owned by ADM), according to the Korea Feed Association. The four largest feed millers are Cheil (part of Samsung, with two feed mills), Woo Sung (two mills), Purina (four mills) and Miwon (three mills), and each of these operations are big enough that they can purchase

Panamax-capacity boatloads of feed ingredients on their own accounts for their own use. One of the responsibilities of the Korea Feed Association is to purchase Panamax-capacity shipments of feed grains on behalf of its smaller millers. While Cargill's milling capacity makes it too small to use Panamax-size loads for its mill alone, as a buyer for other companies it can consolidate loads and reap the benefits in its own milling operation.

The rapid increase in livestock accompanying the expansion of the milling industry has brought its own particular ecological consequence, namely pollution from manure concentration. In its descriptive brochure, the Korea Feed Association points out that due to their high dependence on imported feedstuffs and the associated imbalance between feed production and manure production, Korean feed millers and livestock raisers are creating a major environmental problem. In 1970 Korea manufactured only .51 million tonnes of compound feed ('mixed with a shovel'), utilizing only .31 million tonnes of imported feed ingredients. In 1991, by contrast, 11.5 million tonnes of compound feed was produced, utilizing 8.5 million tonnes of imported feedstuffs. This dramatic increase reflects both the increase in livestock numbers, and an increase in the use of manufactured feeds requiring imported feedstuffs.

Table 13.1: Livestock numbers[360]

	1981	1993
Beef cattle	1,283,194	2,260,472
Dairy cattle	194,205	553,343
Pigs	1,831,518	5,927,504
Chickens	42,999,172	72,945,362

Cargill is a significant supplier to the milling industry, importing rapeseed meal from China and corn from wherever the price is best. In recent years this has also been China, though in 1994 US corn became more 'competitive' due to the increase in the price of Chinese corn and the drop in US corn prices. US corn (from Nebraska) is shipped out of Pier 86 in Seattle or a Gulf of Mexico port. Feed-grade barley is not allowed into Korea, though feed-grade wheat is and there is a steady demand for it.*

While the Korea Feed Association describes itself as a major force in public policy, they also say that Cargill is the major influence on US trade policy in Korea. Whichever way Korean livestock and meat policy goes, however, Cargill cannot lose. If domestic beef production declines, and with it the market for

---

* Cargill is the largest exporter to Korea from Canada, the commodities being feedstuffs (mostly milling and grain handling by-products like screenings) and wheat for milling. This trading is done entirely and independently from Vancouver. Cargill also ships soybeans, but not canola, to Korea, according to Lachlan Coburn, Branch Manager, Cargill Ltd, Vancouver.

livestock feed, Cargill may lose as a feed importer and miller, but it will gain as a beef importer. Or vice versa.

To my surprise I was told that, unlike the Japanese, Korean farmers prefer foreign-label feeds like Purina and Cargill to local feeds, thinking that they are better, even though, according to the Feed Association, the quality is the same.

The Korea Wheat Flour Milling Industry Association represents the three big 'tycoons' of Korean industry (Hyundai, Daewoo and Samsung) who were reborn after the liberation from Japan at the end of World War II. They were able to import very cheaply the raw materials for the 'three whites' – sugar, wheat flour and cotton – under US Food For Peace and aid programs, and process and sell them dearly in Korea. The 'tycoons' had supply contracts with companies like Cargill, according to Yoon, and the outcome was that the suppliers and the processors did very well at the expense of the Korean and American people. Samsung, in particular, made windfall profits as an importer and processor of US PL 480 wheat with Cargill as its agent. The US government provided concessional wheat sales to Korea under PL 480 until 1981.

Today it is the big Japanese trading companies that control 90 per cent of Korean food grain imports (about 2 million tonnes of wheat per year) both for the *chaebol* and for the many small flour mills. Of course, it helps that the GSM 102/103 program of the US government (see Chapter 9) provides financing, which neither Canada nor Australia provide. And while the Japanese trading companies may control the trade, they still have to buy the grain, and it is companies like Cargill which have the originating capability (country elevators, etc.).*

The same pattern can be found in soybeans, a major Korean food source, even though of the 1.2 million tonnes consumed, 1 million tonnes are imported, 90 per cent from the US and 10 per cent from Brazil, Argentina and Paraguay. The three major soybean processors, Samyang Foods, Dongbang Yuryang and Cheil Chedang (Samsung) are all associated with one or another of the *chaebol*, the Korean equivalent of the Japanese *zaibatsu*. The major processors buy from the major importers – Mitsubishi USA, Marubeni USA, Tomen America (all Japanese companies), Kimpaco and Global International Trading of Hong Kong, and Central States Enterprise of Florida.

Cargill first sought permission in 1988 to build a soybean processing plant to produce edible oil in Korea, a perfectly logical development for its worldwide integrated oilseed sourcing and supply system. A year later the Korean Finance Ministry gave Cargill permission to process 300,000 tons of soybeans annually after both US Commerce Secretary Mosbacher and Trade Commissioner Carla Hills had pressed the Korean government to accept Cargill's proposal. Korea's Agriculture Minister, however, said he would not approve the investment by

---

* In the early 1980s the largest Japanese companies, including ZEN-NOH, became insecure about their dependence on companies like Cargill and Continental, so they started to buy into the US grain handling system, acquiring their own export facilities. They discovered they were in hostile territory and have largely withdrawn in recent years, though it is virtually impossible to get any details.

Cargill because he feared that it would devastate the nation's soybean-related industries and soybean farming:[361]

> If Cargill expands here, it won't be just a matter of the sale of a few more bags of fodder or tanks of oil. That is because we can see in this move the terrible plan to export raw materials as well as to process them here for profit, then ultimately to force the small Korean businesses into bankruptcy and take over the whole market.[362]

Behind the scenes there is a slightly different (but unsubstantiated) account of the reason for Cargill's failure to gain permission. In February 1988, Rho Tae Woo became president of Korea. His son-in-law was president of Dongbang Yuryang and, according to the Korea Feed Association and others, Rho could not allow Cargill to threaten a family interest. With 90 per cent of Korea's essential soybean imports coming from the US at the time, the big three companies announced that they would not continue to buy from the US if Cargill was allowed in.

While this story may not be true, it is certainly a true picture of the kind of power relations that Cargill both enjoys and has to deal with. It does not always get its way – at least not immediately.

At the end of 1992, after continuing pressure from the US Government, the Korean Government finally gave in to Cargill in spite of the strong opposition of Korean soybean growers, processors and farmers' organizations. According to the Korean Soybean Processors Association, once Cargill got approval, it discovered that there was already 25 per cent overcapacity in the processing industry, making any additional capacity an unwise investment. Recognizing Korea as a 'mature' market, with little room for expansion, Cargill is now looking elsewhere, particularly to Malaysia and China.*

One of the 'irrationalities' of the Korean situation is that the price of domestic beans is set by the government at a level five to six times the cost of imported beans. The Korean processors say they feel obliged to support Korean farmers and purchase the domestic production even at those prices, though for the past three years the price has been held steady in order to bring soybean prices closer in line with other commodities whose prices have been allowed to rise.

The fact is, however, that the processors are obliged by the government to buy Korean soybeans but are compensated for the difference in cost between domestic and imported, and that goes for yellow corn as well (three to four times the cost of imported). The beans and corn are allocated by the government to the companies according to the size of their milling operations and they are then

---

* When Cargill first filed its application to build a soybean mill, it called for an investment of $12.9 million to produce 30,000 tons of soybean oils and 144,000 tons of soybean meal annually. When its application was finally approved at the end of 1992, the investment figure had been raised to $21 million with an increase in production to 54,000 tons of oil and 240,000 tons of meal in five years. Korea's domestic production of soybeans is no more than 20 per cent of its total demand of 700,000 tons of soybean meal and 170,000 tons of oil. (*Korea Times*, 13 January 93)

compensated accordingly. Cargill has tried to get this subsidy as well, even though the subsidy was introduced against the wishes of the government as compensation to the farmers for market liberalization.

Beef

Korean cuisine is moderately heavy in beef, and Korea is the world's fifth largest beef importer and the third largest importer of American beef, just behind Japan and the European Community. In fact, 60 per cent of the beef consumed in Korea is imported from the US with IBP supplying about half of it. Monfort (a ConAgra subsidiary) and Excel, Cargill's US beef subsidiary, supply most of the remainder. Australia and New Zealand supply the other 40 per cent of Korea's imported beef.

As the export promotion arm of US beef packers, the US Meat Export Federation is responsible for boosting US beef exports, anywhere and everywhere, though in recent years the major task of the Federation has shifted from promotion to forcing open various markets for US beef. It does this by pressuring members of the US Congress which pressure the US government which then pressures the Korean or other governments.

The *Korea Times* commented in 1988 that US Trade Representative Clayton Yeutter 'demanded that Korea import US beef not only for tourist hotels but also for restaurants after the general elections ... [He] also demanded that Korea simultaneously lift its import ban on frozen potatoes used by McDonald's fast-food chain.'[363]

Brad Park, a Korean American, is the Federation's representative in Korea. He described for me the background to the present Korean debate about food imports, reflecting in his description the policy position of Cargill and others:

Korea was considered to be an agricultural country until about 1960. From the beginning of the Korean War in 1950, when almost everything got destroyed, until around 1960 everyone was kind of struggling to get something to eat and about 70 per cent to 75 per cent of the population was considered to be farmers, or of farm background. Then during the 1960s Korea started to industrialize and by 1990 the population in the farming sector had declined to 11 or 12 per cent. A lot of farmers' children had moved to the city, but remained farmers at heart. At election time, all these people become farmers again.

Now farm production comes to about 5 per cent of the GNP, so economically it does not make sense for government to put money into agriculture. But politically, it does, because 50 per cent of the population will vote as farmers in election time. About 2000, or 2010, this will change, when the good old memories of farming are gone. There are a lot more important issues than agriculture.

In 1982 to 1985, Korea needed a lot of beef. The economy was growing rapidly and as income goes up so does demand for high quality foods like beef. But the supply of beef was inadequate and, up to that time, the only beef imported was what is referred to as high quality beef for the tourist hotels. The price of cattle went up along with the price of beef at that time, so Korea began to import both beef and cattle. So much was imported that there was oversupply and the prices plummeted. This was during President Chun Do Hwan's administration, and it was his younger brother who got involved in this, made a lot of money and a big mess, and was eventually jailed. At that point the government halted all beef imports.[364]

Beef was first imported into Korea in 1981 and thereafter imports both of beef and breeding cattle increased so rapidly that in late 1984 and early 1985 the government halted all imports of beef in order to curb the decline in prices.

Table 13.2: Beef production 1981–93

	Number of raising households	*Head of beef cattle*
1981	851,418	1,283,194
1985	1,047,573	2,533,449
1989	654,040	1,536,060
1993	569,957	2,260,472

In 1988, using as an excuse the need to feed the American tourists flocking to the Seoul Olympic Games, the US brought a lot of pressure to bear on the Korean Government to reopen the market. If they had to do it, however, the Korean Government wanted to do it rationally, so they established the Livestock Products Marketing Organization (LPMO) to import beef for 'general' restaurants and manage the total until full liberalization of the beef market in 2001. The LPMO will continue to be the primary importer, purchasing by tender, though its percentage of the market will drop, while the Simultaneous-Buy-Sell (SBS) system, set up in 1993, will handle an increasing share of imports on the basis of negotiations between buyers and sellers. This is a verbal system, meaning that it is open to manipulation without leaving a paper trail. In 1993 the SBS system had 10 per cent of the import quota and its percentage will gradually increase as the total amount of imported beef increases, while the LPMO percentage declines.

Even though domestic production has increased, it has not been fast enough, acccording to people like Brad Park. The result is a growing gap between demand and imports (through the LPMO), creating a very promising market in both amount and quality. From the farmers' perspective, however, a rapid increase in supply means an equally rapid decline in prices for slaughter cattle, so now the Government of Korea is caught between the political reality of farmers facing diminishing returns for their labour and pressure from the US meat exporters via the US Government for free trade.

Park describes the role of the Meat Export Federation as that of 'adviser' to the US Government:

But [he continues] it is entirely up to the US Government what position they take. We are strictly a voice from industry. We – Wheat Associates, Feed Grains Council, Meat Export Federation, Soybean Association and so on – are called cooperators with the ATO. We do not have to be here, but the ATO encourages us to because we are operating as a group. It is more convenient and economical for us to be here in this situation [sharing the same offices]. Funding is one-half membership, one-half government. We have about 300 members, and about 100 of them are packers. A lot of times we are invited to trade negotiations as observers. Our main function is as a liaison office, for the convenience of our members who want to do business here, and for Koreans who want to buy.

Park said that there is a very symbolic saying in Korean, written in Chinese characters, 'explaining' imported food products: 'Body and Land are not two different things,' that is, what you eat is what you are. It is a good idea, he said.

One thing we would have to say is that there are no Korean cattle in this country because virtually all the feed grain is imported. The way I like to interpret this is that when you are eating good quality food, you keep your good health and build good situation, regardless of where it comes from. I think we have to see it that way. Now we have much more choice, we can pay a lower price and get good quality products because of this more open market system. The government should try to get the most high value, most economical food for the people.

Agribusiness and Government

As director of the Agricultural Trade Office (ATO), in the corner office down the hall from Park, Charles Alexander is responsible for 'market development'. Dennis Voboril, who refers to Alexander as his 'boss', is US Agricultural Attaché.
Alexander explained that his job is to help Korean importers of US products and US exporters.

We try to solve the problems that industry encounters – such as 37 containers – $1.3 million worth – of hot dogs held up at the container port because, they said, they discovered a regulation that they had not been enforcing; these are frozen cooked sausages and there is no category in the food code for this product, therefore they have to have a 30-day shelf-life. With a 30-day shelf-life they are perfectly importable, 30 days from date of manufacture. But it takes about 30 days to get them here.[365]

Two months after I heard that story from Alexander, the US National Pork Producers Association, the National Cattlemen's Association and the American Meat Institute filed a petition calling on the US government to impose trade sanctions on Korea in retaliation for halting trade in frozen cooked US sausages. The associations complained that Korea imposed short shelf-life requirements and long inspection procedures to prevent American meat from entering the country.[366] The working relationship between the publicly funded US Meat Export Federation, the US Agricultural Attaché, and the commodity associations is very cosy:

Here at the working level we don't very often stand back and look at policy, [said Alexander] We're dealing on a day to day basis – we want access, we need access, our people want access, we should have it – Korea is free to export all its products to the US, we ought to be able to export our products here. That's what it boils down to for us.

You have to understand, there are almost as many farmers here as there are in the US. This industry has to adjust. The farm population is about 2.2 million, which includes husband and wife as farm family. In the US the figure would be about 2.1 million. This number has been going down [in Korea] because this is where all their workers came from, and they are fortunate they had factories to work in.

Prices here are artificially high. If they want cheap rice, all they have to do is import it. Price stability is now number one priority here. Two things are happening: they are tightening up money supply, but drought is pushing up food prices, and this directly affects industrial wages. So they will import more than their quota for beef this year. They are bringing in 50,000 tonnes of garlic and 35,000 tonnes of onions, they are bringing in pork – a lot of stuff to keep prices down ... Garlic and onions are a good example: they hate to import, but they hate to see the prices go up. So they wait until prices go up and then rush out to buy the first onions they find. So they bought some really poor onions from China, instead of letting the market work and suppliers import before there is a crisis. And they buy on tender for the lowest price – so they get what they pay for. They refuse to let the market work.

The role of *chaebol*? The only thing farmers hate more than the government are the *chaebol*. They are involved in bulk commodity trading, but you will not see their name on finished products for fear of backlash and farmer and/or consumer boycott. [Like the Cargill logo without the name? BK.] They are all lined up to go into corporate agriculture, but they are probably more interested in land control and speculation than in food production. They are all set to be the new landlords.

In Korea, Japan, and Europe, there is policy which says we want *x* number of people on the land. In the US the push for the past 50 years has been for efficiency in crop production. And you have seen the farm population drop to 1.9 per cent of the population, with 150,000 farmers producing 50 per cent of the production in the US. You can't get much more efficient than that. So when we approach the Korean market, our natural mindset is that they need to get bigger, there are too many Korean farmers. They have to be more efficient. It doesn't matter how good a farmer you are, you cannot make a living on 1.2 ha of land. You can't sell enough product to make a living. You're not going to get any sympathy for Korea from me!

Government functionaries listen to the people who pay their salaries – just about everywhere in the world except Korea and Japan. I've never met a more officious bunch than these damned Koreans I meet seem to be. They are bright, they are smart, but they are convinced that they are right.[367] *

---

* Korea's food trade deficit rose in the first half of 1994 to $2.79 billion. Exports to China were a mere $29 million while imports were $635 million. The growing deficit was attributed to an influx of foreign products after trade liberalization opened the agricultural market, particularly in imports of feedstuffs and beef. (*Korean Times*: 9 August 94)

CHAPTER 14

The Pacific Rim III:
Japan and Hong Kong

Japan

When William Wallace Cargill bought a small grain elevator in Iowa in 1865, Commodore Matthew Perry had already succeeded in inducing Japan to open its ports to US merchant vessels ... When Commodore Perry brought his black ships, the menacing symbol of advanced Western technology, to Tokyo Bay, the Japanese had no habit of eating beef. They did not need feed grains.[368]

Japan now imports 88 per cent of its wheat, 96 per cent of its soybeans, 40 per cent of its fruits and 10 per cent of its vegetables.[369]

Prior to and during World War II, Japan was primarily a nation of rice-eaters ... Decisions made during the US occupation following the war led Japan to begin large-scale imports of wheat and to encourage demand for bread and other grain-based foods. A school lunch program was started, providing children with bread or rolls every day. The success of this effort is one of the great tales of modern-day milling and baking ... Another legacy of World War II, though, is a domestic support program for rice that was originally put in place by General Douglas MacArthur to spur people to remain in farming in the hope of building a base of pro-democracy farmers.[370]

While the forceful conversion of the Japanese to wheat-eating may be viewed as a smashing success by the US industry that has benefited from it, the Japanese themselves have other opinions. My host in Tokyo told me of her memories, as a schoolgirl, of being quite literally forced to eat the horrible white bread that was provided under the school lunch program. They were told to hold their noses when they were forced to drink the 'milk' made from skim milk powder that had so generously been provided by the US.

Japan was officially occupied by the United States, with the administration of its government under the command of General Douglas MacArthur as Supreme Commander of the Allied Powers, until 1952. Although it had ordered the great Japanese business combines, the *zaibatsu*, to be broken up, as the Cold War took over the US realized that it would be prudent to overlook the reemergence of

154

the *zaibatsu* in the interests of strengthening Japan's economic recovery. Such apparent concern for Japan's economy was a thin veil for the more powerful passion of anticommunism. The US preferred an anticommunist ally to a reformed society, and the *zaibatsu* to a socialist economy.

For example, although Mitsui was supposedly dissolved in 1945, by 1960 it had emerged as the world's largest trading company. Itochu (formerly C Itoh) has more recently surpassed it.* By 1994, the top five *zaibatsu* dominated the corporate world:[371]

Table 14.1: Biggest corporations in the world by sales (billions of US $):†

Itochu	$184.2	Japan
Mitsui & Co.	168.6	"
Mitsubishi Corp.	165.1	"
Sumitomo Corp.	162.4	"
Marubeni	149.0	"
General Motors	119.7	USA
Ford Motor	108.5	"
Exxon	99.2	"
Nissho Iwai	98.4	Japan
Toyota	97.6	"

Cargill in Japan

Cargill's life in Japan is an interesting story of Great Power relationships, and if Cargill has found its way hindered, if not blocked outright, by the *zaibatsu* of Japan, it is in striking contrast to its experience in India, where it was not the established powers but the powerless peasants who threatened its progress. (see Chapters 15 and 16). These different forms of resistance to a corporate intruder stand at opposite ends of the spectrum of power.

---

* Known as C Itoh, after the name of its founder, until quite recently (and still so identified in many of its subsidiaries), Itochu Corp was established in 1858, though its present incorporation dates only to 1949, that is, about the end of the era of post-war reconstruction under General MacArthur when such giant conglomerates were ordered to be broken up. Today, one corporate directory describes Itochu as the 'most vigorous' of the trading companies. Its sales in 1992 were approximately $200 billion, with foodstuffs (including its meat packing and cattle interests) making up only 11 per cent (about $22 billion) of that total, while machinery and construction were 34 per cent, metals were 24 per cent, and energy and chemicals were 17 per cent. 1993 sales were down at $185 billion, with foodstuffs making up about 10 per cent of the total.

† Everyone who makes a list has their own criteria. *Fortune* lists companies by groups, one category being 'industrial corporations'. Of course these lists never mention that the private companies are absent. In *Fortune*'s 1994 list Cargill would rank 18th with its sales of $48 billion if it were considered an industrial corporation and if it were publicly traded. The lists are helpful, however, in getting some sense of magnitude and relationship.

As Cargill has experienced, the five giant Japanese trading companies today exercise significant control over the economy of Japan, if not the government itself. Cargill has had to find its allowed, or tolerated, place in their social order. The company continues to hope that the Japanese market will be forced open by a combination of US Government and corporate pressure, but it may be that the *zaibatsu* are more powerful, or more clever, than both the foreign TNCs and the US Government.

Cargill has been doing business *with* Japan since 1950 when the Foreign Trade and Exchange Law was put into effect in Japan. Cargill was able to act as an agent or buyer for Japanese interests, supplying grain from Kerr Gifford in Oregon. In 1956 Cargill started actually doing business *in* Japan when its subsidiary Tradax (then based in Montreal) acquired Andrew Weir (Far East) Ltd, an importer and supplier of foodstuffs that had been set up just after the war.

An informal history of Cargill in Japan, written by a retired employee, describes how, in the late 1950s, feedgrains were 'low key' but foodgrain imports expanded rapidly and contributed to a transformation of Japanese lifestyle from traditional diet to western habits [white bread]. The same writer describes how a 'friendly crusher' built a new oilseeds crushing plant that could accommodate Panamax vessels. 'Friendly crusher' turned out to be Fuji Oil Co. Ltd, an affiliate of Itochu, and their supplier was Cargill, the only company at the time that could afford to trade in whole shiploads of oilseeds. Cargill was able to guarantee supply in return for having a guaranteed buyer. At times this meant that Cargill was even able to buy from competitors and sell to 'friendly crusher' at a handsome profit. (Itochu also has 'friendly relations' with another oilseed processor, Ajinomoto, and Ajinomoto and Cargill are business associates in Iowa, as mentioned in Chapter 3.)

Oilseed meal was another product Cargill was able to purchase and deliver by the shipload and consequently at low prices in the late 1960s and early 1970s, giving it control of more than 90 per cent of Japan's imports of oilseed meal, a key livestock feed ingredient. In 1973 Tradax made an after-tax profit of $100 million on its soybean trading alone, with Tradax Japan contributing more than 10 per cent of that. Later, when Tradax Japan nearly lost its shirt in the process of some fancy dealing to supply Itochu, its 'friendly JTC' (Japanese Trading Company) came to its rescue.[372]

The company did business as Tradax Japan until 1985 when the name was changed to Cargill North Asia Ltd (CNAL). In 1992 the name was changed again, this time to its current Cargill Japan Ltd.

The company's business in Japan expanded in 1972 when Cargill Inc. acquired C.Tenant Sons & Co. of the US, which had already established a Tokyo branch in 1963 through its subsidiary Tenant Far East Corp. of Hong Kong. This branch carried on an export–import business in non-ferrous metals, which Cargill has continued to do while adding other lines of activity. J. Norwall Coquillard, president of Cargill Japan, said in a recent interview:

At first, the company merely carried its products to Japanese ports, where they were turned over to Japanese companies for domestic distribution and sale. Cargill was doing business 'to' Japan, in other words, not 'in' Japan. The company would be much better off today if it had built its own facilities back in the late 1960s, but at the time ... our prime interest was in trading grains.[373]

As the value of the Japanese yen (unit of currency) began to climb in the mid 1980s, Cargill changed its approach and began to establish real beachheads. Its first effort followed its traditional practice of acquiring established businesses in which it already had expertise: it bought the grain business of Honda Motors in 1983.

In 1985 it followed its alternative strategy of establishing a new business building on one of its 'core competencies': Cargill's seed division established an experimental farm in South Kyushu. A year later a second experimental farm was established by Cargill Seeds in Tokachi region of Hokkaido. Now Cargill Japan's seed department, located in Sapporo, distributes hybrid corn and sorghum seed, 95 per cent of which is imported from Cargill subsidiaries ('principals') in the US and France since it has no Japanese seed lines. Cargill claims that the Japanese seed companies (Sakata is number one and Takii is number two in Japan) also import most of their seed from affiliated companies in the US and simply repackage it and sell it as domestic seed in Japan. Cargill's role in this, however, may be somewhat ambiguous: 'Cargill wants to sell the grain seed directly to Japanese farmers. In fact, Cargill has been selling seed to Japanese farmers for more than ten years, but always through Japanese agents,' according to a 1988 article on Cargill in a Japanese business journal.[374] The seed corn market is only 3500 tonnes for all of Japan, which is very small, but the margin is very high, I was told. Sakata and Takii both have hybrid fruit and vegetable seed lines which they sell extensively in the US.

There is no record of what happened to the grain business Cargill bought from Honda, but it was probably absorbed into its larger grain operations without giving Cargill a real beachhead in Japan. As for its second beachhead, the seed business, it remains a small operation, certainly not the kind of dominant player Cargill expects to be in its chosen lines of business. Perhaps the Japanese companies have simply been successful in containing it.

Japan is an affluent and growing market, however, and Cargill was obviously not content with simply being a trader and supplier to others nor happy with a marginal role in one of its chosen lines of business. It still wanted to establish a beachhead in a major industry, such as livestock feed, where it could run its own business, establish its own customer base and grow. With Japanese imports of feed ingredients running at 16 million tonnes, it was a natural for Cargill.

Self-sufficiency, however, has been basic policy for Japanese agriculture since World War II, and since 1953 it had been Japanese policy to encourage the expansion of livestock production while favoring Japanese companies.

Thus, while anyone could build a feed plant as long as they met the building and milling standards, they had to obtain authorization from the Customs Office to import the feed ingredients duty free. This authorization was a ministerial function based on evaluation of supply-demand conditions in the area where the mill was to be built. Without being able to import feed ingredients duty free, no plant could compete in the Japanese market; permission to import feed ingredients for use in the manufacturing of feeds still does not permit importation of grains or oilseeds for any other purpose, and imports are limited to keep any single company from gaining a dominant position.

Japan's self-sufficiency ratio for livestock feed, expressed in terms of domestically sourced feedstuffs as a percentage of total feed demand, provides a simple picture of the failure of its policy and with it, Japan's increasing dependency on imported feedstuffs:[375]

Table 14.2: Japanese self-sufficiency ratios 1960–92

1960	1970	1980	1990	1992
62.9%	37.8%	28.2%	26.3%	22.8%

This increasing dependency is all the more striking when combined with the general decline in livestock numbers in recent years. For example, the number of dairy cows in Japan peaked in 1985 at 2.1 million head and had dropped to 2.0 million in 1994. The pig population peaked in 1989 at 11.82 million and has declined to 10.62 in 1994. Broiler chickens peaked in 1986 at 155.64 million and have declined to 127.39 million. While laying hens have been increasing in number, they appear to have reached their peak at 146.97 million in 1994. Beef cattle are the one category probably still growing, but the increase has not been dramatic: from 2.57 million in 1984 to 2.92 million in 1994.[376]

When Cargill decided to act, in 1985, it first announced that it would focus on beef production and packing on Hokkaido, in the north, but rapidly dropped that strategy and settled on Kyushu, in the south, to establish a beachhead feed mill at Shibushi, Kagoshima Prefecture. There it met local resistance from the prefectural assembly.

At that point, Cargill turned to the US Government to make 'a representation' to the Japanese Government to allow it to build the plant under the required ruling by the Japanese Customs Office that the company could import feed ingredients without paying import duties. It was not long before the Kagoshima Prefectural Government, in 1986, decided to sell Cargill the land it required for the feed mill, overriding the fears of other feed millers and farmers who feared that this would lead to integrated livestock production under Cargill's control.[377]

The official account is that Cargill got permission because the livestock industry in Kyushu was expanding at the time and it was judged that another mill would not cause harm to existing feed mills.

The Korean Feed Association provided me with what is probably a more accurate account. They say that when Cargill tried to get into feed milling in Japan, the government would only permit them to buy an existing plant, not build a new one. But when Cargill tried to buy a plant, all the mills in Japan agreed not to sell. Then the US Government intervened on Cargill's behalf and the Japanese government finally relented, giving Cargill permission to build a new plant. The tradeoff was that unlike other importers of feedstuffs, Cargill was required to pay duty on what it imported.

A candid insider's account of the process was provided by a news story in 1992 about Juels Carlson, president of Cargill North Asia Ltd from 1985 to 1990. Apparently Carlson was sent to Tokyo with the task of 'breaking through the investment barriers the Japanese government and agricultural industry had established to prevent internal competition.'

According to the story, Carlson was successful in getting permission for Cargill to build its feed mill:

> Despite the opposition of that country's powerful agricultural industry ... As Carlson explains it, Cargill had right, politics and common sense on its side. His strategy, in simple terms, was to refuse to take no for an answer, even the many versions of yes in Japanese that, in effect, mean no ... Cargill v.p. Wm. Pearce said Carlson was able to enlist the support of key Japanese politicians at the local level and in the Diet, the Japanese parliament. Eventually, the US trade representative in Japan weighed in on Cargill's behalf, and the license was granted. In all, it took about five years and most of Carlson's time in Tokyo.[378]

In 1989 the requirement for ministerial authorization to import feed ingredients was lifted and today there are about 100 feed mills in the business, though there are only 19 members in the Japanese Feed Trade Association, among them Cargill. (In 1994, the Association had five directors, one each from Tomen, Itochu, Marubeni, Mitsubishi and Mitsui.)

Cargill has not expanded, preferring, apparently, to sell ingredients to other companies. On the other hand, perhaps the *zaibatsu* have forcefully indicated to Cargill the position it is to occupy. Cargill Japan's feed division is now just another feed company, with the exception of its function as an intelligence unit for its corporate parent, according to key industry people, who figure that Cargill does a lot of business with the Japanese trading companies.

I was told by one Cargill executive – in another country, to be sure – that Cargill built its feed mill in Japan with half the capital of other plants in Japan, and that when the feed plant opened, it did so with a policy of no credit to farmers. He claimed that this was the reason it took only two years to get the plant to operating capacity.

On the other hand, what Cargill discovered, I was told in the Ministry of Agriculture and elsewhere, is that Japanese farmers are not just like those in North

America. They are very demanding and expect their feed supplier to meet very precise specifications, whereas in North America feed is feed, and individual farmers add their own supplements. Japanese farmers, I was told by the Feed Trade Association, are also conservative and do not like switching suppliers, from whom they can get credit. So Cargill has found it preferable to import in volume and supply other millers in bulk, letting them have the headaches of dealing with the individual farmers. This sounds very much like the seed business, where Cargill and others prefer to import in quantity rather than develop seeds in and for a small regional market.

The domestic feed industry produces about 26 million tonnes annually, and Cargill probably produces only about 0.1 million tonnes of that, according to Feed Trade Association figures. The situation will probably change to Cargill's advantage, they say, as imported beef forces down the price of domestic beef and farmers have to buy feed on price more than on specifications. According to a Ministry of Agriculture official, imports of processed beef are likely to increase due to the very high labor costs in Japan for domestic processing. McDonald's, for example, uses all imported beef.

Having tried seed and feed, it is hardly surprising that Cargill also tried fertilizer, where it ran into familiar opposition. When it proposed to build a fertilizer plant in Kumamoto Prefecture, the prefectural government rejected its proposal because of its possible impact on Chisso Corp., a local fertilizer plant.[379] Cargill had to go to southern Kyushu to establish its fertilizer bulk blending plant, in 1988, at Miike Harbour, Ohmuta (west of Shibushi), as a joint venture with Mitsui Chemical Company. All ingredients are imported. Cargill claims that when the plant opened, as with its feed plant, its prices were 25 per cent below those of its Japanese competitors, forcing them to lower their prices. Other people would describe this as buying market share. Cargill does not say what happened to prices once they got established.

Having less than stunning success with agricultural inputs, Cargill decided to move upscale (more 'value-added' in current jargon) to try to capture higher returns in one of its major product lines. Instead of just importing boxed beef from their plants in the US and selling it to Japanese processors and distributors, it decided to do the processing and distribution itself in Japan.

The first steps were to establish an office in Osaka in 1990 and make a deal with Daiei, Japan's largest supermarket operator, to carry Excel beef imported from the US and Canada under the brand name 'Kansas Beef'. The third step, announced in early 1991, was to build a beef 'further-processing' plant in Japan to 'enable Cargill to serve the expanding appetite of Japanese consumers for red-meat products as Japan liberalizes its meat-import laws.'[380]

Consistent with its policy of holding a controlling interest in any joint venture, Cargill North Asia Ltd held two-thirds and Showa Sangyo Co. one-third of the new company, the first foreign-owned meat processing plant in Japan. Showa

Sangyo's contribution to the partnership was in the form of a newly built seven-storey refrigerated warehouse in Funabashi, just east of Tokyo. Cargill's contribution was a portion-control processing plant built alongside. Together they were to build up their distribution network. Cargill expected Japan's imported beef market to increase steadily and it looked forward to controlling 30 per cent of the market.

Barely two and a half years later, in October 1993, Cargill halted its Japanese subsidiary's beef processing and distribution operation and sold the processing plant to Nippon Meat Packers Inc., one of Japan's biggest meat packers, at a loss, it is said, of $10 million. (Cargill has had a joint venture with Nippon Meat to produce broiler chickens in Thailand and market them in Japan since 1989. Cargill runs the plant and Nippon sells the chicken.)

Although Cargill had increased its sales to 15 per cent of the beef imported from the US or 27,000 tonnes, its primary competitor, IBP, had increased its share of beef imported from the US to 40 per cent or 74,000 tonnes. Unlike Cargill, IBP has been content to be a supplier to the Japanese processors and distributors.[381]

Industry people say that part of the problem with Cargill's enterprise was Showa Sangyo's lack of experience, and possibly interest, in distribution. They say that while the processing plant was very good, Showa Sangyo was really only interested in receiving rental from Cargill for its refrigerated storage. But they also say that a major problem was Cargill's own manager, who had no under-standing of the Japanese system and seemed to think that what worked in the US could simply be duplicated in Japan. Cargill has now fallen in line with its arch-competitor IBP and plans to settle for selling imported beef to Japanese dealers.

Apparently Cargill was unable to meet the requirements of the Japanese distribution system, where food service industries and supermarkets demand extremely frequent small-lot deliveries. Nippon Meat Packers, dominant in the domestic distribution network for imported beef, has a system that gets customized beef orders to restaurants and supermarkets across most of Japan within 24 hours of clearing customs.[382]

In spite of the apparent efficiency of Cargill's joint chicken venture in Thailand with Nippon Meat Packers, the market for imported frozen chicken is limited because the production of fresh (which is much preferred to frozen) poultry meat in Japan is very big. But, as with most of Cargill's businesses, thanks to its integration, if one goes down another goes up. This means that even if the prospects for exporting processed chicken to Japan are limited, there is a good future for chicken feed.

Cargill does have an advantage with the chilled pork it imports from its plant in Taiwan (as opposed to frozen from most other sources), but the Japanese market for pork has been limited by competition from beef as the prices of beef have fallen due to increased imports.*

It is not just Cargill and IBP that are flooding the Japanese market with beef, however. By 1992, 20 Japanese companies were running cattle ranches in Australia, including Itochu, Marubeni and Nippon Meat Packers. Itochu also had a beef packing and freezing plant in Australia and a 20,000-head feedlot in partnership with Teys Feed Lots Pty. of Australia. Nippon Meat Packers had 30,000 head of cattle on its farm in Queensland in mid-1992 and anticipated raising that to 45,000. Marubeni invested $30 million in 1988, including $10 million for the Rangers Valley Cattle Station. A ZEN-NOH executive said that these Japanese beef operations in Australia were not a success, however, because while the Japanese companies could sell high-end cuts in Japan, they had trouble selling the rest of the animal due to the lack of experience and distribution contacts, which are precisely Cargill's advantages.

If, or when, the Japanese distribution system breaks down – or is broken down under pressure from GATT/WTO or bilaterally from the US – Cargill will probably make a success of its marketing efforts in Japan, according to its friendly competitor, Itochu. (Itochu would not reveal its own strategy. When I asked, I got merely that familiar smile that says, 'Good question, no answer.')

It has, however, always been Cargill's strategy to cover its flank by maintaining friendly relations with its major competitors, such as the Japanese trading companies, by being a reliable supplier. As reported earlier, for years Itochu

---

* When Japan ended beef import quotas 1 April 1991, the import tariff rose from 25 per cent to 70 per cent to cushion Japanese producers, then dropped to 60 per cent in 1992 and 50 per cent in 1993.

Beef imports	1991–2	1992–3	1993–4
tonnes:	326,919	423,429	566,911

In 1993–4, Australia supplied 53.2 per cent of Japan's beef imports and the United States supplied 42.9 per cent.

Average annual per capita consumption in Japan:

	1970	1993
beef	2.0 kg	6.7 kg
pork	5.3	11.5
chicken	3.7	10.6
eggs	14.5	17.7 (Only Israelis eat more eggs!)

Average annual per capita beef consumption in:

Canada, 36 kg
Australia, 38 kg
US, 45 kg

Comparative prices for beef in Japan:
    Japanese Wagyu striploin beef: 1107 yen per 100 grams
    Imported Australian beef: 361 yen
    Imported US beef: 420 yen

Source: Ministry of Agriculture Forestry and Fisheries; LPIC Japan.

contracted with Cargill as a supplier of grains and oilseeds, and as one Cargill spokesman put it, 'They buy from us every time – they give us first crack.'

Itochu ended its contractural relationship with Cargill as a grain supplier in 1988 when, together with the Japanese National Federation of Agricultural Co-operative Associations (ZEN-NOH), it bought Consolidated Grain and Barge Co. in the United States. This gave the ZEN-NOH/Itochu partnership an integrated grain supply and distribution system, with four or five grain terminals on the Mississippi River at New Orleans and 40 or so country elevators. Even though ZEN-NOH is the dominant player in the feed business in Japan, responsible for 33 per cent of imported feed grains (down from 40 per cent due to shrinking herds and fewer farmers), the partnership with Itochu continues to make sense to both parties, apparently. It may simply be a matter of two Japanese companies working together to make sure Cargill takes no more of their business.

Itochu and ZEN-NOH have not been the only ones to enter the grain business in the US. Mitsui acquired facilities in the US when it bought a grain terminal in New Orleans from Cook Industries (which it has subsequently bought out in its entirety) in the late 1970s. Then Marubeni purchased facilities from Columbia Grain in Portland, Oregon, and Mitsubishi leased terminal facilities in Long Beach, California. US grain exports peaked in 1981, however, and the Japanese companies found themselves squeezed – by Cargill and Continental and others – in a shrinking market. They have since largely withdrawn, with the exception of Itochu/ZEN-NOH.[383] In addition to its grain interests in the US, Itochu has tie-up in oil seeds crushing with Oil Seeds International and a joint venture brown-rice mill in Arkansas.

Other Japanese companies, however, have successfully gotten around the 'grain majors' control of US grain by taking their businesses right into the US.[*] Pasco, a subsidiary of Shikishima Baking Co., the second largest baking company in Japan, decided in 1994 to build a $20 million frozen dough plant in Portland, Oregon, utilizing Oregon-grown wheat. The company expects to export 300 refrigerated containers of frozen bread dough each year from the plant.[384] (Taiwan's President Enterprises, as noted earlier in this chapter, has played the same game.)

Given the size and affluence of the Japanese market, fresh fruits and vegetables are another attractive line of business for Cargill. Having, perhaps, learned a lesson in the beef business, Cargill is currently carrying out a feasibility study on global sources for fruits and vegetables and looking at the possibilities of working with one or more of the very large Japanese supermarkets. Daiei, number one in Japan with sales of about $20 billion annually, would be one possible partner. (Ito-Yokado, owner of the worldwide 7-11 chain, has sales of $14.6 billion.) 'We

---

[*] 'Our president here prefers that Cargill be called a food company rather than a grain major', I was told in Japan. Which is how Whitney MacMillan said he prefers to describe Cargill.

would prefer to skip the Japanese trading houses,' a Cargill employee told me. So far, its only active enterprise in this line is the juice plant (described in the previous chapter) built in 1993 to handle imported concentrate, mostly orange juice, from its Brazilian subsidiary.

Cargill is shut out of the Japanese rice trade, I was told, because the US Rice Millers Association, representing the big California growers, is strong enough to deal directly with the US Government which brokers relations with the Japanese trading companies that do all the rice importing. In addition, all domestically produced rice has to be sold to the Japanese Food Agency. However, under GATT-required trade liberalization, Japan must allow 400,000 tonnes of rice to be imported in 1995 and this will rise in six years to 800,000 tonnes. The imported rice will probably be largely used for industrial purposes, as in sake and rice cracker production, while short-grain domestic rice will be used for direct home consumption because the Japanese are very fussy about their staple food. While US rice is closer to what the Japanese like than rice from Thailand, it still does not meet the standards they insist on. All rice imported into Japan from the US is medium grain from California.

Cargill claims that it engages in no direct political action in Japan – at least not through the front door. Itochu, however, regards Cargill's feed mill at Shibushi not as a successful business but as a political phenomenon signifying the ability of Cargill to use the US Government to create economic opportunities, in this case to pressure the Japanese Government and overcome local as well as corporate resistance. Others cite agencies such as the US Feed Grains Council as the ones who put pressure on the US Government and the Japanese Government through the Agricultural Attachés in the US Embassy.

The Feed Trade Association, of which it is a member, says that Cargill is so secretive that no one really knows what they are up to, though they think that Cargill has learned that the Japanese market is neither as profitable nor as receptive as it thought it would be. So while Cargill tells me it cannot push too hard and must be patient, Itochu's advice is that if Cargill wants to enter the Japanese market, whether in meat or fresh fruits and vegetables, it would be better to work with the big traders rather than trying to get around them.*

---

* Among the grain majors, Cargill describes itself as number one, Continental as number two, Dreyfus as number three, followed by Bunge and André Garnac. In Japan, Cargill now has 185 employees, Conti has 6 people, Dreyfus has 5, André Garnac has 3, and Bunge is just an agency. Cargill estimates its market share in Japan for its most visible activities to be:

Imported orange juice: 30 per cent;
Fertilizer: Maybe 1 per cent;
Feed: Less than 1 per cent, but still profitable;
Grain importing: 'It's hard to say, because the Japanese companies now buy FOB in New Orleans or wherever, but they may sell that grain to someone else, or import it for themselves. So Cargill's share of corn imports may be 20 per cent more or less, and soybeans a bit more, with very low margins. The margin that Minneapolis gives Cargill Japan has not changed in the past 8–10 years, with no compensation for the change in exchange rates or anything else.' (Shinichi Kume, public relations, Cargill Japan, personal interview, 24 August 94)

Hong Kong

Cargill Hong Kong *is* Cargill's China office, at least until they open an office in the Republic of China in the near future, according to Mike Hsu, manager of Cargill's grain department in Hong Kong.[385]

A lot of multinational companies don't feel comfortable dealing with China and don't speak the language, says Hsu, but most of the people in the Cargill Hong Kong office speak Mandarin (the official language of China, as opposed to Cantonese, spoken in Hong Kong), and Cargill has been active in China for the past ten years.

In spite of that, Hsu describes Cargill as 'a bit conservative' compared to Toepfer (a long-established German trading company 50 per cent owned and controlled by ADM) and Continental Grain, which Hsu describes as the most aggressive traders in the region.

In their Hong Kong office Cargill has a sugar department, which sells sugar to China; an oilseed department, which sells vegetable oils to China and buys oilseed meal (soybean, cottonseed and rapeseed); a charter department, chartering vessels for the corn and other commodities in which Cargill is an active trader; a steel department, which sells steel bar and cold rolled steel from Cargill's North Star Steel subsidiary to China; a fertilizer department; and, in preparation for future activity in China, Cargill Investor Services (CIS).

Hsu explained to me that Chinese people love to speculate, much more than western people, so Cargill thinks that eventually, when the Chinese are rich and once they understand how to trade on the futures market, the Chinese will be very big speculators or hedgers. Cargill is getting ready, with the hopes of being able to be one of their brokers. 'Once China gets rich, they are going to be very big speculators. They don't have money, but they love to have money, to risk their lives,' says Hsu.

Cargill also has an investment team which is responsible for planning future projects for Cargill in China. 'We try to sell most of our product line to China,' says Hsu. 'Our major focus will be on selling to China, not buying from China. It is so huge that eventually they will have to buy. The China market is important for the whole world.'

China in the next ten years will offer a very big opportunity to those people who are not afraid to speak Mandarin – like the people of Singapore, Malaysia and Indonesia – and who know how to deal with the Chinese, in part because they have a lot of overseas Chinese among their populations. A lot of people, said Hsu, think that within ten years the purchasing power of China will be as much as half that of the US and that it will be a very big economic power, particularly when one compares it with Japan, Korea and Taiwan, whose economies are not growing so much anymore. However, Hsu suggested, to be successful in China, western countries will have to change their trading strategies and companies will have to overcome the barriers of politics and language that stand in the way of their doing business in China. So what if it takes $5 million or $10 million and five years? The question is, what can we learn in that time for that money?

In the past three years Cargill has bought a lot of Chinese corn for delivery in the region because China has been exporting 8 million to 12 million tonnes of corn per year, Hsu told me. Before corn the major commodity for China was soybean meal and oilseeds. But China only produces about 95 million tonnes of corn per year, which is not very much when compared to the US which produces 200 million tonnes, and now Chinese corn is more expensive than US due to a change in Chinese government policy. When the government decontrolled the prices it paid for agricultural commodities and removed subsidies on food, the gap between city and country started to grow, resulting in a massive farmer migration to the rich areas, to the cities in the South – 200 million people some people say. So the government has somewhat frantically tried to push up farm prices in the past two years to counteract this and restore some social stability. Farmers annual income may have risen slightly as a result, but with a population that is 80 per cent farmers, who know how others are living thanks to TV and radio, that is not enough and the gap continues to grow.

On the whole, on average, China is a very poor country, Hsu said, but foreigners who don't want to go to the interior, who only want to see Peking and Shanghai, get the wrong impression. In the cities there are many people who are very rich and can buy anything.

Hsu articulated a common and crucial theme in current discussions about China: internal transportation in China is very poor, with the railroads in terrible condition, and the country is very large. As a consequence, it is cheaper to export food from the north and import food into the south than it is to transport it overland from the agricultural regions of the northeast to the industrial regions of the south. But this means that the food entering the south could come from anywhere in the world, and that food exported from the north has to compete with it. In other words, under its current pattern of development, China is very rapidly being integrated into the global food system of companies like Cargill. According to Cargill's Hsu, the south of China will be a very big market for Canada, the US and others.

For example, one per cent beer is the common drink in China and beer consumption is rising as rapidly as peoples' incomes. As the world's largest producer of barley malt, Cargill naturally has its eye on China. In 1991, before it purchased a majority interest in Ladish Malting Co., the largest malting company in the US, Cargill was already a major producer of barley malt in Europe with malting operations in France, Holland, Belgium and Spain. The purchase of Ladish moved Cargill into first place with 8 per cent of the world market, surpassing Canada Malting Co. Ltd which had been the world leader. (In the US, Fleishman-Kurth, a subsidiary of Archer Daniels Midland, is the second largest maltster, Froedert Malt Corp. is third and Great Western fourth.)

China currently buys only one to two million tonnes of malting barley annually, but everyone expects the Chinese government to decontrol the import of malting barley very soon. In the meantime, the western malting companies are trying to get a foot in the door through joint ventures, as suppliers of technology, suppliers of barley and suppliers of malt. It will be interesting to see where Ladish ends up.

CHAPTER 15

Cotton and Peanuts

Although neither a grower nor major processor, Cargill is nevertheless a major presence in world cotton trading through its subsidiaries Hohenberg and Ralli Bros & Coney. Cargill's involvement in cotton goes back at least to 1910 when the company established relations with Cotton Ginner Ltd in what is now Malawi. Someone within Cargill certainly knows the full story, but in his 900-page history of Cargill, W.G. Broehl says nothing about Cargill's involvement in cotton and neither of its cotton-trading subsidiaries are mentioned.

Given that typically about 40 per cent of the US cotton crop is exported, with a value of $2.5 billion, and accounts for some 30 per cent of the total world export trade in cotton, it is hardly surprising to find the five major global cotton traders based in the US are:

- Allenberg Cotton Co. of Cordova, Tennessee, a subsidiary of Dreyfus;
- Dunavant Enterprises Inc. of Memphis, Tennessee, a family-owned company;
- ContiCotton of Fresno, California, a subsidiary of Continental Grain Company;
- Ralli Brothers & Coney, a division of Cargill PLC (UK)
- Hohenberg Bros Co. of Memphis, Tennessee, a Cargill subsidiary with 10 offices in the US and offices in Central and South America.

Hohenberg trades American cotton on both domestic and foreign markets from its Memphis base and operates offices in places like El Salvador, Guatemala and Mexico. Ralli Bros & Coney trades non-US origin raw cotton worldwide from its UK base. 'Hohenberg manages risk and manages supply for customers who want just-in-time delivery of very specific qualities,' said Hohenberg manager Craig Clemmensen in Memphis.[386]

The US cotton harvest averages 14.5 million bales or 6.7 billion pounds of cotton (one bale weighs 500 pounds, or 226.5 kg) from some 12 million acres (5 million hectares) of land. US cotton mills utilize some 4 billion pounds (1.8 billion kg) of cotton fiber annually. In addition to the cotton fiber, the cotton harvest yields whole cottonseed and cottonseed meal which are used in livestock feeds and cottonseed oil which is used in food products. Being a manufacturer of livestock and poultry feed, Cargill can take advantage of its trading activities to supply its feed business.

An unexpected treat while visiting the Hohenberg office in Memphis was a look at their cotton grading 'station'. This is essentially a large room with very special lighting that faithfully reproduces the conditions of natural daylight. Every bale of cotton that office buys and sells is sampled and the fiber graded for staple, color, size and overall quality. Every bale is identified as to grower and growing location. Buyers are thus able to specify exactly what kind of cotton they want and Cargill can deliver according to very precise specifications. The grading is still done by hand by highly skilled graders, hence the need for 'natural' light. Only the tensile strength is electronically tested. In the midst of globalization, electronic communications and corporate oligopolies, this reliance on human skill to maintain a quality basis of trade seems strangely old-fashioned, yet somehow comforting. Trading coffee on the basis of actual sample tasting is the only other example I know of such trading in real commodities.

It is ironic that cotton, the darling of current 'natural' fashions, is one of the most chemically intensive crops grown in the world. In the US it requires annually the purchase of more than $4 billion worth of supplies and services; more than $350 million in fertilizers; $600 million in agricultural chemicals; $100 million in planting seed; $700 million in fuel and equipment; and $530 million in farm labour. This is interpreted as a good thing by the National Cotton Council of America which claims that cotton stimulates more in US business revenue – estimated at some $50 billion – than any other US crop.[387]

The Soviet Union was also a major cotton producer, and its collapse brought out the vultures. Cargill has certainly not been alone in assiduously evaluating the rapidly changing situation and positioning itself to invade and take over the enterprises that seem most promising. Since Uzbekistan produced 65 per cent, or 1.6 million tonnes, of the total Soviet cotton crop, it was perfectly logical for Cargill's Ralli Bros division to open a cotton trading office in Tashkent, Uzbekistan, in late 1991.[388]

'We have to remember that the Soviet Union has been, over the past 27 years, the most important single trading partner of Cargill,' Cargill International chairman Leonard Alderson told Cargill employees at the end of 1990.[389] Talking about Cargill's strategy for the FSU (Former Soviet Union), Cargill vice president Dan Huber said, 'We're going to focus our efforts on what we know ... We will start with projects in our core competencies – projects like seed, oilseed crushing, fertilizer production application and distribution, feed manufacturing and grain warehousing ... We will also focus on the key agricultural areas or zones ... We will insist on having management control of any ventures.'[390]

One has to wonder how Cargill is making out in this enterprise. A syndicated newspaper story in late 1994 reported that Uzbekistan is 'a state in which criminality and corruption have become effectively institutionalized. Cartels financed by the drug industry and privatized cotton monopolies dominate the country.'[391]

In mid-1993 Cargill formed a joint venture company called Den in the former Soviet Republic of Kazakhstan. The plan was for Cargill to hold 47 per cent of the company while the Kazakh trade company would hold the majority share. While this is contrary to Cargill's strict policy of holding majority interest in its joint ventures, in this case it means that Cargill 'has an early toehold in one of the most agriculturally rich CIS republics.' The Kazakh government approved a resolution that allows Den to buy surplus commodities – left over after all state orders have been filled – from the republic's farmers. The government also ordered the state grain-purchasing agency to turn over to Den grain elevators with a total storage capacity of 600,000 tonnes.[392] This should give Cargill a pretty good start.

Cargill partially explained the reasoning behind its commitment to such an enterprise in its *Bulletin*: 'Kazakstan is attracting foreign investment ... partly because the old centralized government structure remained in place.'[393] The *Bulletin* article is self-congratulatory, as well, in saying, without mentioning Cargill, that Kazakstan 'has benefited from the expertise of Western companies in maintaining grain exports.' (Later in October it was reported that Kazakhstan has enough grain, despite an expected 6 million tonne drop in production that year, to export grain to other former Soviet republics. Cargill probably knew this months earlier thanks to its infra-red satellite imaging facilities.)

Cargill has always been able admit to some of its mistakes and make a tactical retreat when conditions seemed appropriate, as with catfish and the Japanese beef business. So in spite of long-time involvement, in 1993 Cargill decided that its Africa Division ought to sell its 40 per cent interest in the largest cotton-ginning business in Nigeria, Cotton and Agricultural Processors. The company's market share had dropped from 80 per cent to 47 per cent in the previous three years and its poor financial condition had been aggravated by a large loan from the state that Cargill headquarters did not approve of. The managing director of Cargill Ventures Nigeria said there were lessons to be learned, including:

> Stay away from minority businesses which Cargill does not manage; do not burn any bridges when divesting; and, be selective when choosing partners and try to avoid parastatals, which are bureaucratic.[394]

Besides which, there are other cotton interests to pursue, like China's. Cargill ships cotton by the container load to China from Galveston, Texas, among other places, and according to one of its managers, handles 25 per cent of China's cotton trade. In 1994 China had to import 283,000 tonnes of cotton from the United States* (nearly 30 times 1993's imports) because of poor yield in its own crop due to boll-worm infestation.[395]

---

* Because it is a major buyer of China's cotton goods, the US is expected to receive 80 per cent of the orders for cotton that China will have to import in the face of a severe domestic shortage. The crisis has its roots in China's record harvest in 1984, which produced 6.3 million tonnes of cotton, much of which Chinese farmers could not sell. Many communities rushed to open new mills to handle the surplus cotton and take advantage of strong foreign and local demand. Since then, however, erratic supply has created an unstable market, and the harvest in 1993 was only 3.8 million tonnes. The textile industry employs about 15 million workers. Mid-1994 world prices were high at 86 cents per pound. A normal price is about 60–64 cents. Chinese farmers are angry at the combination of low state prices for cotton and the soaring prices of fertilizer and pesticides. (MC:12 May 94)

Cargill is pleased that its cotton trading subsidiary Hohenberg has overcome tradition and convinced some buyers to purchase large amounts of cotton on an 'undifferentiated basis' within a given range, rather than by specifications bale by bale as described above. This is like buying grain in the US on the basis of an average quality, rather than from the Canadian Wheat Board on the basis of a specific uniform grade. Of course it is to the trader's advantage, not that of either the buyer or the seller, to work on an 'average' basis. Floor sweepings, gravel, and dirt in general can gain commodity status if what they contaminate, or dilute, is of high enough quality to average it out.

Among its cotton-related holdings Cargill had a cottonseed company, which it sold in 1994 to Delta and Pine Land Company of Scott, Mississipi, in order to be able to focus its efforts on corn, sorghum, sunflowers, canola and alfalfa.[396] Cargill may have chosen to abandon cotton seed breeding to Calgene Inc., which owns Stoneville Pedigreed Seed Company in Mississippi, and instead take on crushing seed for Calgene. Cargill subsidiary Stevens Industries, which processes peanuts, had already agreed in 1992 to process specialty canola oils for Calgene. Cargill may mave decided that it was better to cooperate than compete, given that Stoneville's sales of cotton seed were up substantially in 1994. Early that year Calgene had received USDA approval for its genetically engineered 'BXN' bromoxynil (herbicide) tolerant cotton varieties. (Bromoxynil is manufactured by Rhône-Poulenc.) Calgene had also reached an agreement in early 1994 with Plant Genetic Systems (PGS) of Belgium to exchange genetic engineering technology, whereby Calgene gained the use of PGS's Bacillus thuringiensis (Bt) insect resistence technology in its cotton breeding.[397]

Further evidence that Cargill made a strategic decision in selling its cottonseed business comes from its concurrent purchase of Goertzen Seed Co. of Haven, Kansas. This firm specializes in wheat and other food grains. Cargill appears interested in developing specialty wheats and other potential 'identity-preserved' food crops that are more closely alligned with its 'core competencies' in flour milling.

Peanuts

The lowly peanut (groundnut) does not attract much public attention, but Cargill's involvement in the US peanut trading and processing industry is not really surprising when one considers the size of the industry.

The US has ranked third behind India and China in peanut production for many years, though in seven out of ten years from 1981 to 1990 it was the leading peanut exporting country. Per capita consumption of peanuts in the US is among the world's highest, and over half of US production goes into domestic edible uses. A quarter goes into export edible markets, accounting for more than one-third of world peanut trade. The remaining quarter is crushed for oil and meal, or used for seed and animal feed.

Cargill's position in US peanuts is nevertheless highly ambiguous. The company is a bit shrill in its advocacy of the free market and its condemnation of government interference and regulation, yet peanuts are among the most controlled food products grown in the US. The apparent contradiction is probably best explained by a combination of opportunism and pragmatism. Being curious, I sought out Cargill in southeast Georgia.

'Sylvania Peanut Co. – Cargill Inc.' the sign on the front of the little office building said. Across the road was a no-longer-inhabited traditional share-cropper's house – the long front roof covering a full-width front porch. Sylvania Peanut Company has been around a long time, buying, grading and selling peanuts, and was Cargill's 'beachhead' in the peanut business. Following its customary strategy, once Cargill had learned something about the business it made a decision about whether to get in deeper or to make a strategic retreat. Apparently Cargill liked what it found and decided to advance, so it bought Stevens Industries in Dawson, Georgia, and rolled the Sylvania company into it. Stevens is a much larger company that processes peanuts and makes peanut butter, though it does not have a refinery for producing peanut oil – yet. Stevens is currently going after the peanut butter contract for the US school lunch program. (Nothing like a government contract to give free enterprise a boost!) A lot of Stevens/Cargill peanut butter is sold to Procter & Gamble and marketed under one of its names, another one of Cargill's 'invisible' presences at the retail level.

In recent years, exports of 'Canadian' peanut butter and peanut paste to the US have jumped from 148 tonnes in 1988 to 14,547 tonnes in 1993, making up 80 per cent of all peanut butter imported into the US, which would lead one to think that Canada was becoming a major peanut grower. Canada's peanut production, however, remains very low and confined to a very small area in the southern corner of the province of Ontario.

What is actually happening is that peanut processors in Canada are importing low-cost peanuts from Argentina and China, turning them into peanut paste, which is just short of being peanut butter, and exporting the product to the US, where a corporate ally can finish the processing and sell the peanut butter on the local market as 'made in the USA'.

This is possible because peanuts are a controlled crop in the US and grown under a quota and two-price system. 'Quota' peanuts are sold on the domestic market at about $700 per ton, with 'additional' peanuts sold into export at about half the domestic price. The industry has been protected for years and continues to be under Section 13 of NAFTA. The peanut paste is being imported from Canada through a loophole in the regulations, very similar to the US export of dairy products into Canada, where dairy production is regulated similarly to peanuts in the US.

As a result of this large volume of 'Canadian' peanut paste going into the US, American peanut growers asked for a 'dumping' investigation and the US International Trade Commission obliged. Several user groups, including the Independent Bakers Association, opposed any import restrictions. On the advice of US President Clinton, however, the ITC halted its investigation prior to a rescheduled public hearing in June 1994. It seems that the American growers, who had asked for the investigation in the first place, were the ones to ask that it be called off, apparently because they did not want to draw public attention to the subsidies they were receiving under the current two-price peanut program. The current world price for peanuts is about half the US domestic support price for quota peanuts.[398]

When I returned home after my trip which included the visit to the Sylvania office, I wrote the company for further information:

Gentlemen:

A couple of weeks ago I was passing through Sylvania on my way north and I stopped by your office to learn a bit about peanuts. I wish to thank you for your courtesy and helpfulness.

I made a few notes at the time, and looking back over them I realized I had not asked when Sylvania Peanut Co. was established, or when Stevens purchased it. I would appreciate it if you could send me that information. Obviously the company has been around a long time and it would be interesting to know a bit of the company's history. I think you also told me that it was Cargill's entry point into peanuts, is that correct?

Thanks again. I hope you all have a good year.

Brewster Kneen

To which I received the following reply:

Dear Mr. Kneen,

In regards to your visit, I have some concern as to the purpose of your visit and the additional information you request.

Prior to the release of any additional information from this office I would ask that you give us more detailed information as to:

1.　Who is Brewster Kneen?
2.　Why the interest?
3.　Who will this information be available to and for what reason?

I am sure you understand that there are certain procedures that must be followed.

Sincerely, Jim Martin, Manager

To which I replied:

Dear Mr. Martin,

What a strange reply.

I know Cargill has a reputation for secrecy, but I do not understand what is so confidential about the information I requested.

I am a freelance writer living in Toronto and writing primarily on the food system. I have a special interest in biotechnology, which is not relevant in this case.

I am interested in all aspects of agriculture and the food system, in part based on 15 years as a livestock farmer and the organizer of two co-operatives.

The information I gather is not copyrighted or privatized in any way. Therefore I cannot answer your question as to who might see or use it. My database is available to anyone wishing to purchase it. Please see the enclosed card.

What are the procedures that you must follow?

Sincerely, Brewster Kneen

I am still waiting for a reply.

CHAPTER 16

Fertilizers

In fertilizer, as in other sectors, Cargill has successfully implemented its basic business strategy: buy into a line of business at fire sale prices, obtain unrestricted access to cheap raw materials, handle huge volumes in bulk, 'add value' through processing along the way if possible, and trade the end product around the world.

The three major components of commercial fertilizer are N, P and K; nitrogen, phosphorous and potassium. The nitrogen is produced from natural gas, the potassium comes from potash, and the phosphorous comes from rock phosphate. Cargill is involved primarily in the first two.

Phosphate

Most of the world's phosphate rock is mined for processing into phosphate fertilizer to be exported for agricultural purposes to markets around the world. In 1993, 60 per cent of global phosphate fertilizer production was exported from its country of origin. Due to global economic recession, however, phosphate rock production around the world declined from approximately 153.6 million tonnes in 1990 to 117.3 million tonnes in 1993.

Morocco in northern Africa contains at least 50 per cent of the world's phosphate rock reserves and is the world's largest unprocessed phosphate rock exporter, though in recent years it has built up a considerable capacity for conversion of rock into fertilizer and chemicals. Morocco's total phosphate rock sales were 18.2 million tonnes in 1993, with the Moroccan Office Cherifien des Phosphates (OCP) holding 31 per cent of the global market.[399]

The conversion of phosphate rock into a soluble form for use as fertilizer requires sulphur and large amounts of ammonia to produce its most common form, diammonium phosphate (18–46–0) generally known as DAP. The United States produces 60 to 65 per cent of the total global production of 21.6 million tonnes of DAP. US domestic sales of DAP in 1990 amounted to $1 billion out of a total of $7 billion spent on all fertilizers.

India is also a large DAP producer, but it relies on imports of the key materials (phosphate rock, sulphur and ammonia) or the intermediate product (phosphoric acid) and utilizes all of the output in its domestic market. India also accounts for about 15 per cent of total world DAP imports, while China accounts for about 25 per cent and Western Europe for 20 per cent. Total global trade in DAP is about 14 million tons per year, with the US accounting for 65 per cent of this and Morocco 15 per cent.[401]

Table 16.1: Phosphate Rock Production, major producers[400]

	('000 tonnes)			
	1990	*1991*	*1992 (est.)*	*1993*
China	15,845	17,627	17,956	18,600
Morocco	21,189	17,988	19,447	18,193
US	46,041	48,096	46,171	35,138
USSR/CIS	35,082	28,573	19,447	16,003
Total, all producers	153,664	145,155	135,473	117,307

One-quarter of the world's phosphate is to be found in central Florida under five to fifty feet of sandy soil in two locations, referred to as the Northern District and Bone Valley. The two sites provide about 80 per cent of US phosphate production. The 40-square-mile Bone Valley deposit was discovered in 1881 by the US Army Corps of Engineers, but it was created something like 15 million years earlier when seas covered the area and deposited the remains of billions of tiny sea organisms in the beds of sand and clay. To get at the phosphate rock, the overburden is first scraped aside and piled for future use in site restoration; the actual phosphate ore is removed by means of giant draglines. It is then washed, spun, crushed and vibrated, yielding fine clay suspended in water, coarse phosphate rock, and a mixture of sand and fine phosphate which is then processed further. The slurry is piped to settling ponds, the sand is stockpiled for future mine restoration, and the phosphate is hauled by rail and truck to the processing plants. Because phosphate rock is not water-soluble, treatment with sulphuric acid is essential to convert the rock into fertilizer and other products.

When Cargill purchased the Gardinier fertilizer plant on Tampa Bay in 1985 from the Gardinier family of France, it had already been mining phosphate at Fort Meade in Bone Valley and shipping the ore to the Gardinier fertilizer plant for processing. The plant, built in 1924 by the US Export Chemical Company with the most advanced technology at the time, was in bankruptcy proceedings in 1985. (These were the same conditions under which Cargill purchased its first FCOJ plant in Brazil.) One of Cargill's first acts was to lower wages. As one employee put it, 'Cargill made us pay a bit for the generosity of the Gardinier family, which treated us very well – perhaps too well.'

The plant was run-down, and in 1988 40,000 gallons of phosphoric acid spilled, killing the fish in the Alafia River. Cargill was fined $2.2 million and ordered to upgrade the facility.[402] Cargill, in a characteristic manner, paid the bills, did the cleanup and upgrading at a cost, it says, of $125 million, and has since gained public recognition for its environmental conscientiousness:

> In terms of environmental awareness, many within Cargill cite the accidental spill ... as a turning point ... [that] brought environmental issues to the forefront and accelerated Cargill's environmental efforts.[403]

From the 3.6 million tonnes of phosphate rock it mines each year in Bone Valley, Cargill produces 7 per cent of the total US phosphate fertilizer supply, primarily in the form of DAP. Only 15 to 20 per cent of the plant's production goes to the US or Canada, and 85 per cent of what is exported leaves the Port of Tampa by water, loaded directly onto ships from storage at the Gardinier plant.

Cargill figures it has 15 years of phosphate ore reserves on hand underground at all times, while a constant swapping of land goes on so that companies can mine contiguous parcels. Some land is owned, some leased. The full cycle from removal of overburden and mining through complete reclamation is three years, as required now by state law.

As has already been mentioned, sulphur, in the form of sulphuric acid, is a key ingredient in the production of phosphate fertilizers. Cargill uses about 600,000 tonnes of sulphur annually, which it brings in molten form from Mexico, Texas, Louisiana and Caribbean ports. Drawing on its skill and experience in bulk transport by water, the company designed a special barge/tug unit and had it custom built for this purpose. The 433-foot S/B *Alafia* was christened in January 1991.

Phosphate mining, like all open-pit mining, leaves horrendous scars on mother earth. In recent years public pressure has led to legislation requiring the restoration of mine sites. In Florida, as mentioned above, companies are now allowed three years from commencement of mining to full restoration of the site.

Still, what one sees while traveling the backroads of central Florida is very depressing. Bone Valley, south of highway 60 east out of Tampa, in the centre of the state, is a moonscape of overburden piles and gaping scars. In the midst of this forlorn landscape, however, as I tracked down Cargill's Fort Mead mine site, I came upon the lands the company had restored. I was not expecting to see citrus groves and dryland cattle feeding on verdant pastures on restored mine sites. Discussing this with the mine manager on a Sunday morning when no-one else was around, I learned – and I could see it with my own eyes – that Cargill is experimenting with various restoration schemes, dependent on the character of the overburden being restored. It looked to me as if Cargill is being genuinely creative about it.

Cargill's strategy is to match potential uses of the land with the water and overburden available. Some land is being turned into wetlands, some into citrus groves (2000 acres), some into blueberries (40 to 50 acres I was told), and some into alfalfa if, for example, it has more clay that can benefit from the long taproots of the alfalfa. I saw a beautiful herd of mixed cattle on some of this alfalfa land. In 1994, for the first time, the oranges harvested from Cargill's 2000 acres of groves on reclaimed land will be processed by Cargill's new Frostproof juice plant, which is very close to Bone Valley at Frostproof.[404]

In May 1993, typically taking advantage of a severe depression in fertilizer prices, Cargill moved into the position of second-largest phosphate fertilizer producer in the world with the $150 million purchase of Seminole Fertilizer, a division of Tosco Corporation of Greenwich, Conn. The plant had earlier been owned by W.R. Grace & Co. The Seminole operations produce 760,000 tonnes of phosphoric acid per year, while Cargill produces 840,000 tonnes at its Tampa plant. The acquisition also gives Cargill an additional mine in Fort Meade and another at Hookers Prairie along with fertilizer plants in Riverview and Bartow, right on Highway 30. Being inland plants, they have to be served by truck and rail transport. Cargill reports that nearly 100 railcars of sulphur are required each month at the Bartow plant, while 1800 railcars leave the plant with fertilizer every month. Cargill's total phosphate production now gives it about 14 per cent of the US market.[405]

When I was looking for the Cargill mine at Fort Meade, I stopped to ask directions from a telephone line crew. They gave me directions all right, but also volunteered that when Cargill bought the Seminole plant they made all the employees sign resignation slips and submit their resumé. They then hired back those they wanted, at lower wages and with only two weeks' vacation, no matter how much they had accumulated, which for some long-term employees was as much as five weeks. 'What they want is control, so they can make more money,' is the way one of the men put it. 'They want to drive everyone else out, just like Agrico and IMC!' Then they wanted me to tell them who Cargill really is!

IMC-Agrico and Vigoro Corporation are other partners in the phosphate oligopoly.* Prior to 1992, IMC Fertilizer Inc. owned 39 per cent of the US phosphate rock capacity and produced 15 per cent of its phosphate fertilizers, while the Agrico division of Freeport-McMoRan Resource Partners of New Orleans was the second largest phosphate fertilizer producer.[406] Since then, IMC and Agrico have merged their US phosphate operations into IMC-Agrico.

Nitrogen Fertilizer, Canada

Cargill's moves into fertilizer production and distribution in Canada provide a good case study of how the company establishes a beachhead and expands, reflecting not an impulsive decision, but a well-planned long-term strategy. One can see

---

* In addition to producing phosphate fertilizer in Florida, the Chicago-based Vigoro Corporation is also a North American producer and distributor of potash, nitrogen-based fertilizers and related products. Vigoro's Kalium Canada Ltd mine in Belle Plaine, Saskatchewan, supplies about 4.5 per cent of world potash production and 13 per cent of North American production (company announcement, G&M:11 March 94). Late in 1994 Vigoro added to its potash holding with the acquisition of Central Canada Potash from Noranda Inc. for $140 million. The highly efficient mine is located in Colonsey, Saskatchewan, and has 200 years' worth of reserves. (G&M:15 November 94)

many parallel actions around the world by Cargill over the years, and there is no reason to think that it will suddenly change a highly successful strategy. On the contrary, as the company's resources continue to grow, so will the application of this strategy.

In 1992–3, 4.1 million tonnes of ammonia and 3 million tonnes of urea were produced in Canada, aided by Cargill's new Saskferco Plant. At the same time, Canada was down to three operating phosphate fertilizer plants, with production of 763,000 tonnes of ammonium phosphates. (Canada's total fertilizer imports in 1992–3 were 218,000 tonnes of urea to eastern Canada and 552,000 tonnes of ammonium phosphates, split between eastern and western Canada.)[407]

Cargill used its familiar strategy of buying existing facilities rather than building new ones when entering a new territory or sector to establish its beachhead in Canadian fertilizer. Just as it had bought a significant position at the 'retail' grain-handling level with the purchase of National Grain in 1974, so in 1989 Cargill Ltd purchased the retail fertilizer distribution network of Cyanamid Canada Ltd in Ontario and Quebec and overnight established a visible presence throughout the region.

Cargill Ltd president Kerry Hawkins described the purchase as the completion of a chapter in the development of their eastern Canadian agricultural business: 'We have now met our objective of providing a diverse and efficient range of services to the farmer.'[408]

Cargill's manner, or lack of manners, in such transactions was reflected in the experience of Cyanamid employees at the time of Cargill's takeover. When I visited the Cyanamid fertilizer outlet near Alliston, a woman in the office told me that while nothing had changed, the only information they had about the deal was what they read in the newspaper. The assistant manager in another Cyanamid facility said that when Cargill bought Cyanamid's fertilizer business nothing was said to the staff and they were not even asked if they wanted to work for Cargill.

Five months later, in May 1989 Cargill announced that it would build one of the world's largest fertilizer plants at Belle Plaine, Saskatchewan, in partnership with the provincial government. The $350 million nitrogen fertilizer plant was expected to be operating by the spring of 1992. The province and Cargill formed Saferco Products Inc. to own and build the plant. According to one of the first news stories about the project:

> The province's investment is temporary: it intends by this October to re-sell its interest to private investors. Said to be a last-resort option is a sale of the province's shares, privatization-style, to the general public ... Cargill will have exclusive marketing rights to the plant's production.[409]

The nature of Cargill's relationship to the government of Saskatchewan is a curious one for an advocate of the free market. It is public knowledge that Cargill received assurances of provincial government support which were more substantial than even those sought by the Saskatchewan Wheat Pool for a similar proposal. The government not only turned its back on the Saskatchewan Wheat Pool, but also on a small Alberta company, Canadian 88 Energy Corp., which had put forward a proposal for a series of small nitrogen fertilizer plants in Saskatchewan. Canadian 88 only asked the provincial government for a low-interest loan of some $10 million out of a total cost of $60 million to build the first plant at Rosetown, Saskatchewan. The project was probably considered too small for the government to bother with.

In announcing its project, Cargill said that the Belle Plaine plant would supply the prairies, Ontario and Quebec. There is no way, however, that Canadian farmers could ever use the amount of nitrogen fertilizer the proposed plant would produce: 125,000 tonnes annually of anhydrous ammonia and 660,000 tonnes of granular urea. On the other hand, the Mississippi River is closer than Vancouver (and it's 'downhill' with no mountains), making it feasible for the plant to be a 'world-class operation', as Cargill spokesperson Barbara Isman described it to me. As I discovered when I found a map of the railways, Belle Plaine is about 40 miles west of Regina, and just west of Belle Plaine a mainline railway branches off in a south-easterly direction through Weyburn and Estevan, Saskatchewan, and on down to Minneapolis-St Paul at the head of the Mississippi River, where Cargill Port is situated.

As for the public financial support, Isman indicated that Cargill was going for a joint venture at Belle Plaine because then the public support could not be defined as a subsidy in the context of the Canada–US trade agreement.

Two major factors determined the plant site: transportation, as described above, and natural gas, the feedstock for nitrogenous fertilizers. Natural gas is readily available at Belle Pleine from the pipeline that runs by the door. The supplier is SaskPower, a provincially owned Crown Corporation, established in 1949 to provide electricity and natural gas to the residents of Saskatchewan.

In announcing and defending the project, the provincial government stated that negotiations had been going on for some time. Apparently, then, while SaskPower was making changes in its structure to accommodate the deregulation of natural gas, it was also negotiating with Cargill concerning the disposition of a very large volume of that gas. In fact, the plant is the largest consumer of natural gas in the province: 18 billion cubic feet per year.

Another process favorable to Cargill's interests was occurring at the same time: natural gas distribution was deregulated in 1987, making it possible for customers to buy gas directly from producers and negotiate prices. SaskPower's responsibilities became limited to operating the pipeline. This meant that Cargill, or Saferco, could negotiate freely with the producers of natural gas over volumes, rates and conditions – just as Cargill would like to be able to do with grains.

Late in 1989 the conservative provincial government backed away from its plans to privatize SaskPower altogether due to overwhelming public opposition.

Public concern over unlimited sales of gas and other natural resources to the US makes a fertilizer plant an efficient way for a private corporation to export natural gas, but in the form of liquid and granular fertilizer. Public criticism can be stifled by saying that these are 'value added' commodities.

Both anhydrous ammonia and granular urea can easily be transported in bulk, by rail, to Cargill Port in Minneapolis for further shipment by water anywhere in the world, and as urea is also a source of protein for livestock feed it could be well utilized by Cargill's Nutrena feed division. This also gives Cargill some additional leverage in the soybean market, soybeans being the primary source of protein for livestock feed.

Construction of the $435 million project began in the spring of 1990, and plans called for Cargill to own 50 per cent of the operating company, Saferco Products Inc., the Saskatchewan government would hold 49 per cent, and the remaining 1 per cent would go to a financial institution. This arrangement gave Cargill effective control.

While claiming that the project would not require any public subsidies, the provincial government agreed to provide a loan guarantee for the $305 million required for construction, with the remaining $130 million to come from equity shareholders. Thus for $65 million – and only $65 million worth of risk exposure – Cargill got a $435 million fertilizer plant, with the public holding the remainder and the risk. The third party to the deal was Citibank Canada.[410] Cargill also obtained the right of first refusal if the province ever decided to sell any portion of its share.*

In 1991 Saferco Products Inc. changed its name to Saskferco Products Inc. and announced that the plant would be capable of producing at least 2000 tonnes a day of granular urea and 350 tonnes of anhydrous ammonia, twice the capacity of the average 'world-scale' plant. Company president Don Pottinger said the plant would bring 'a new, reliable and important source of nitrogen fertilizers to northern US farmers' and that 'the plant's central location and proximity to major transportation routes provides easier access to these much-needed products.'[411]

In response to the plant's opening, Cargill's only regional competitor in nitrogen fertilizer, Simplot Canada, announced that it would delay a planned $200 million renovation and expansion of its Brandon, Manitoba, nitrogen fertilizer plant.

Two months later, Simplot announced it would go ahead with a $25 million expansion of the plant by moving a mothballed nitric acid plant from a munitions factory in Joliet, Illinois. The company did not plan to increase ammonia production capability, preferring to take advantage of surplus market supplies

---

* In November 1994, the president of Crown Investments Corp., the holding company for the Province of Saskatchewan, reported that the Saskatchewan government could be forced by Cargill to sell its 49 per cent share of Saskferco to the company at fair market value, but that the government could not force Cargill to sell its 50 per cent share. Even if Cargill does decide to buy out the province when it has the legal opportunity between 1997 and 2002, the province will still be responsible for about $305 million in loan guarantees. (WP: 10 November 94)

when necessary. 'There are at least a million tonnes of surplus ammonia that have to be exported somewhere,' said a Simplot executive.[412]

In the spring of 1994 a Simplot manager in Manitoba told me that Cargill's timing was good. There is room for Saskferco, he said, and they have kept us on our toes. It has not hurt us, he said, but it may have held prices down. They say there is still room for one more plant in North America – it's a strong market, though some of it, like the corn belt, is mature or over-mature, though on the Canadian prairies it is still an immature market. Saskferco is exporting to the midwest and east, he said, as well as offshore. He also said he thought Cargill had a contract with China.[413]

The Saskferco plant made a profit of $300,000 in its first full year of operation, running slightly above its designed capacity of 125,000 tonnes of ammonia and 660,000 tonnes of urea annually.[414]

Potash Fertilizer, Canada

Though it would appear that Cargill has no stake in the potash industry, it is quite likely that with the connivance of the government of Saskatchewan, Cargill will end up with a significant ownership stake in Saskatchewan, and hence world, potash supplies.

The term 'potash' is usually used to describe potassium salts, mainly potassium chloride and potassium sulphate, which are extracted from mineral salts and brine. Potash salts are produced in 13 countries, with almost two-thirds of production traded internationally.

Canada and the former Soviet Union account respectively for one-third and one-quarter of total world production of potash, and Canada is the world's largest exporter. Potash is found deep under a large area of southern Saskatchewan, and Saskatchewan's 10 mines account for about 40 per cent of the world trade in potash with annual sales to foreign countries worth about Can$1 billion.

The Potash Corporation of Saskatchewan controls half of the potash industry in Saskatchewan, has a total annual production capacity of 9.2 million tonnes, and enough recoverable potash reserves in its four mines to continue to produce at current capacity for more than 100 years. By late 1994, with potash demand increasing for the first time in five years, particularly in China, Brazil and India, the Potash Corporation mines were operating at full capacity, accounting for 20 per cent of world potash supply.[415]

Exports of muriate of potash (potassium chloride) accounted for 94.5 per cent of potash sales in 1992, the 13.9 million tonnes having a net value of $1.7 billion. The largest importer of potash is the US which imported, in 1990, 6.7 million tonnes, 6 million of this coming overland from Canada.

About half the potassium chloride exported by Canada is transported by sea, meaning that it is either railed to the Neptune Terminal in Vancouver (the terminal is owned by Canpotex, the export sales company for all six Saskatchewan potash firms) or to Minneapolis-St Paul and then loaded on barges for the trip down the Mississippi River. The bulk materials handling industry as a whole receives as much, if not more, revenue from transporting potash than the actual producers themselves do.[416] Cargill is well positioned to make money coming and going.

In the fall of 1989 the Conservative government of Saskatchewan took a series of steps to privatize the Potash Corp. of Saskatchewan, which had made a profit of $106 million for the province in 1988, and announced to the people of Saskatchewan (who already owned the company as a crown corporation), that 'you too can participate with the Province of Saskatchewan and other investors in strengthening the future of this world-class industry leader ... How? By purchasing Potash Corporation of Saskatchewan Inc. Ownership Bonds.'[417]

Given the record of the Saskatchewan government at the time, there is good reason to suspect that while it was ostensibly negotiating the Saskferco deal with Cargill, conversations were also going on as to how Cargill might gain effective control over the province's potash resources.

While the provincial government was promoting the Ownership Bonds to its citizens, it was also selling, across Canada, the US and Europe, more than $200 million worth of common shares in the new company. Whether Cargill was the buyer of any of these was not mentioned, though individual groups, companies or people were supposed to be limited to no more than 5 per cent of the shares and foreign ownership was to be limited to 45 per cent.

By mid-1990, the privatized Potash Corp. had 38.7 million shares outstanding, with the provincial government holding 11 million of them. Another 11 million were effectively held by Saskatchewan citizens who had bought government bonds convertible into common shares. It was not revealed who owned the other 16.7 million shares, a potential controlling interest.

In the spring of 1994 the Potash Corp. of Saskatchewan announced that the provincial government had introduced legislation to remove all restrictions on the holding of shares in the company, except that the privatized crown corporation would have to retain its head office in Saskatchewan. The door has been opened to Cargill.

CHAPTER 17

Seeds

Cargill keeps very quiet about its seeds business generally, yet within the trade it claims to be the largest seed company in the world outside the US.* (Pioneer Hi-Bred is the undisputed global leader – see the end of this chapter.) Cargill has also used seed, as the Trojans used their famous horse, to establish a 'beachhead' in a new 'geography'.

Cargill seldom mentions its global seed business except in its seed industry publications and its promotional materials aimed at farmers. Seed used in crop production is unlike the rest of Cargill's lines of business, and unlike the crop it produces, in that it is not a high volume bulk commodity, and not even Cargill can make money out of transporting or storing it. Nor is it traded on the futures markets (no money can be made speculating in it), and there is no processing required to speak of. Nevertheless, there is good money in hybrid seed, which routinely sells for five times as much as open-pollinated seed, and more recently, patented seed. The biggest return, however, comes from the addiction and dependency that can be created by means of hybrid seed: addiction to chemical fertilizers (a Cargill specialty) and agro-toxins (which Cargill sells but does not manufacture); and, dependency on the seed company for new seed every season. For Cargill in particular, the greatest value in the seed business may be in its utility as a strategic weapon in entering new territory.

Will Cargill apparently started experimenting with seed breeding in the last century, and his company has been in the seed business since 1907. When 'modern' hybrid corn was invented in the mid 1930s, Cargill was not long getting into it, marketing hybrid seed under the Crystal Brand name and utilizing the breeding stock developed originally at the public (land grant) Universities of Minnesota and Wisconsin.[418]

Years later, in 1953, the company was charged with adulteration of seed, that is, selling seeds that were not what the label said. It had been adulterated with inferior seed, weed seed or even simply dirt. Cargill settled out of court when it became apparent that at least some of the charges were true. It also left the seed business except for its hybrid corn operation because its reputation had been

---

* The November 1994 issue of the industry journal *Seed World* has a directory of 'Seed Industry Giants'. Cargill Hybrid Seeds is listed as a division of Cargill Inc. and the only information about it is that it sells 'domestic and international' corn, sorghum, sunflower, alfalfa and canola, and that it sells 'international only' wheat, rice, safflower and soybeans.

so badly tarnished that the company recognized that business would be bad for some time.[419]

From Cargill's perspective, hybrid seed is attractive as a means to establishing beachheads in new regions and geographies because it requires virtually no capital investment. Practically all the company has to do is send a salesman with a few bags of seed, an airplane ticket, and enough money to buy a motorbike.

Hybrid seeds are also extremely attractive as a means of creating dependency among farmers on Cargill's 'crop inputs' of fertilizer and advice and as indebted suppliers of commodities either for trade or processing.

Cargill strategist Jim Wilson has described Argentina in the 1960s as Cargill's 'first major beachhead' where the product-line used was hybrid corn seed. Tanzania and Turkey are also good expressions of this strategy. In Tanzania the manager works with a staff of 24, most of whom are involved in seed production. Four or five of the staff 'bounce around the country on dirt bikes setting up a dealer network' and selling and delivering seed in small quantities of one to 10 kg. The managers work with 'contract seed growers who run much bigger farms than most of their customers.'[420]

In 1991 Cargill expanded the corn and sunflower seed business that it had established in Turkey in 1987 by building a $1 million seed-conditioning facility in the south of the country. Until the mid-1980s, according to Cargill, Turkish farmers planted traditional open-pollinated varieties. Then changes in government policy encouraged companies like Cargill to introduce hybrid seed. The addition of their new Turkish plant brought the number of countries in which Cargill had hybrid seed operations to 27.[421]

Cargill in India

Gandhi would not have liked it, but, then, he was never much of a shopper. Indians in the 1990s are.[422]

Cargill had decided in 1983 to establish a beachhead in India via seed, but it was not until 1992 that it was able to actually implement this strategy, using hybrid corn and sunflower as the advanced troops.

As in other areas where Cargill has pursued this strategy, its long-term goals far exceed the simple marketing of seed. Argentina and Turkey, like India, have the potential to become major grain and oilseed growing regions for Cargill's global system of processing and marketing. In the case of India, it is Rajasthan and Punjab in the north* that, with the benefit of irrigation, could become global sources of grains, while the south central region, including the states of Karnataka

---

* No mention is ever made of the much larger area of Punjab that lies within Pakistan. It is a political taboo, in dealing officially with India, to recognize that portion of Punjab lying within the current borders of Pakistan as a legitimate political territory of Pakistan. At least for now, Cargill has to operate on one side of the border or another, and it has opted for the Indian side.

and Maharashtra, could become major sources of corn and oilseeds. These regions now produce a wide variety of foods for the people of India, and women play a vital role in food production, from selecting and conserving seed to caring for and harvesting the crop. What happens to women, and what the people would eat under the regime of Cargill is another question altogether. Market economies, and market corporations like Cargill, regard farmers as male and cater to people with money. The equitable distribution of money/wealth that would enable people to participate in the market is not their problem.

To understand Cargill's moves in India, however, it is necessary to understand something of recent Indian policy changes regarding foreign enterprise, trade and ownership rights, whether of seed, land or business itself.

In July 1991, the Government of India fell into the arms of the World Bank/IMF and ushered in a new economic and industrial policy with a marked devaluation of the rupee. At the time the economy was in a crisis of sorts: there had been a steady increase in the fiscal deficit for more than a decade and the country was on the verge of default on external payments. The devaluation of the rupee was quickly followed by massive external loans and an IMF-guided policy of economic change through structural adjustment.

Now the industrial sector appears to be in recession, partly due to the collapse of numerous small- and medium-scale enterprises as the result of liberalized imports. Nearly half of the Indian corporate sector is now said to be 'sick'.

> Indian society is getting more and more expenditure-oriented and heading for consumerism with liberalised imports favoring ostentatious consumption of the rich and privileged ... Multinational financial institutions as well as trans-national corporations are gaining the upper hand while indigenous financial institutions and the central and state governments are playing a docile and sub-servient role of meekly accepting the consequences of foreign economic aggression.[423]

Under the new economic policy, foreign equity in Indian companies can be increased from 40 per cent to 51 per cent without government permission or even prior consent of the shareholders. Further liberalization will make 100 per cent foreign ownership possible while providing for the transmission of profits and royalties abroad. For example, Indian-owned Tata Oil Mills Company (Tomco) merged with Hindustan Lever, while Godrej Soaps merged with Procter & Gamble, and PepsiCola raised its equity position to 51 per cent of the Voltas company.[424]

In regard to seed in particular, India's 'New Policy on Seed Development' in 1988 encouraged increased collaboration between domestic and foreign companies in order to increase the import of technology and genetic material and to encourage private seed companies with the objective of providing Indian farmers 'with the best seeds and planting materials available in the world to increase productivity.'[425] The new policy reduced the duty on imported seeds from 95 per cent to 15 per cent, but stipulated that importers had to submit adequate quantities of seed to the Indian Council of Agricultural Research to be used for trials at 12 to 15 different locations and to be stored in genebanks. The policy opened new opportunities to TNCs with its emphasis on the importation of High Yielding Varieties (HYV) of seed (more accurately referred to as High Response Varieties).[426] It was obviously no mere coincidence that when approval was finally received from the Indian Government in 1988, Cargill began to implement its 1983 decision to enter the seed business in India. The question to be asked is: What was Cargill's role in shaping India's 'New Policy on Seed Development'?

Cargill Seeds India is a joint venture in which Cargill Inc. holds 51 per cent and Tedco, a Tata company, holds 49 per cent. (Cargill also has a marketing agreement with seeds distributor Rallis, another member of the Tata Group.) In 1988 John Hamilton, managing director of Cargill Seeds India, set up an office in Bangalore and 'research' operations began the following year with the marketing of hybrid sunflower and corn seeds starting in late 1992, according to Hamilton. The 'research' Cargill carried out in India consisted of limited seed trials and selection of varieties of imported germplasm it deemed to be suitable. A company press release trumpeted that: 'All Cargill hybrids sold in India are derived from imported germplasm as part of the Cargill strategy of providing the best genetics of the world to the Indian farmer.'[427]

Such a statement expresses a deeply colonial attitude as well as a highly unscientific approach to genetics. Germplasm is the expression of the relationship between an organism and its environment at a particular moment. In practice, Cargill acts as if the organism exists apart from any particular space or time. Not only is this bad science, it also expresses contempt for indigenous knowledge in general and traditional plant selection and genetic conservation in particular.

Hamilton told me of his frustration with the Indian Government and the pace of liberalization, saying that a lot of the announced government policies had not been put in place.

We have a number of areas where we're trying to do business with government, saying, look, you've announced this policy in the papers, but the reality is that nothing has changed. But we get a pretty good hearing ... As the people have become generally more enlightened and aware of what the world has to offer India and what India has to offer the world, some of the political figures are becoming possessed of a very open-arms attitude.[428]

The emergence of Cargill in India as a seed company, coupled with the push to conclude the Uruguay Round of the GATT negotiations (with its strong emphasis on intellectual property rights, including the patenting of seeds), ignited a campaign against the GATT and Cargill in December 1992.

Over 500 farmers, belonging to Karnataka Rajya Ryota Sangha (KRRS), stormed the office of the American multi-national, Cargill Seeds India Private-Limited, on the third floor of a building on St Mark's road and threw out all the papers and files onto the road and burnt them here today ... They also threw out the seed-samples kept in the office.[429]

While it was reported in the press that no company official was attacked in line with the Sangha's policy of non-violence, and the office personnel never claimed that they were in any way harmed, John Hamilton commented to the effect that the KRRS needed to be reined in and said to the public: 'Let them do anything within the law, but let them not smash Cargill.'

Undeterred, in early 1993 Cargill started to build a seed processing factory on a 32-acre site at Bellary, 300 km north of Bangalore. The facilities were to include an administration and seed technology training centre 'to develop modern agriculture,' according to Hamilton. (This is the same strategy Cargill employed in Brazil, as described in Chapter 10.) The plant was scheduled to begin production in October 1993, but early in the morning of July 13, the farmers of the KRRS gathered at the site and with poles and their bare hands demolished the partially completed facility. In January 1994, I saw for myself that Cargill was rebuilding, but progress was delayed because it first constructed a fortress around the premises, complete with high granite walls and guard towers, to protect the plant from the farmers.

The leaders of the KRRS took me to villages and towns to talk to farmers and seed dealers and everywhere the story was the same: the hybrid sunflower seed that Cargill had sold for commercial production in the last two years produced only a fraction of the advertised yield, no matter how strictly the suggestions for growing were followed, and no matter how costly the fertilizers and chemicals. Now the Rallis seed dealers, the distributors Cargill had contracted for distribution, refuse to carry Cargill sunflower seed.

Cargill claims that it has been working with over 3000 farmers in Karanataka, Tamil Nadu and Andhra Pradesh, buying the seed they have grown from Cargill stock. It also claimed that as of mid-1993 it had consolidated its position in the sunflower and maize seed markets, with a market share in different regions ranging from 7 per cent to 15 per cent. Hamilton has said that the company also expects to export seeds, and will go ahead with plans to engage whole villages (2000–5000 people) in seed production.[430]

Following the July 12 attacks by the KRRS on the Cargill facilities at Bellary, police began to provide full security to all Cargill structures. But as the bill rose, Cargill refused to pay it, in spite of the statements of Mr Hamilton that Cargill did not wish to impose a burden on the police.

But now Hamilton has gone back on his words and is saying that providing security is the State's job and that the company would not make its own security arrangements. The bill has bounced and the police are hapless as the multinational is applying pressure tactics through the US Embassy.[431]

Mangala Rai, of the Indian Council of Agricultural Research, told me in an interview[432] that India is a big potential market for sunflower seed. For example, five years earlier no sunflowers were grown in Punjab, but by 1993 there were 100,000 hectares. The seed for this expansion was all supplied by private sector companies, even though until recently India had a largely state-owned seed industry providing around 38 per cent of the seed needed by Indian farmers.

Rai described how sunflowers have a unique role to play in Indian farming because of their photosynthetic tolerances, enabling them to grow in very different conditions. According to him, the varieties that Cargill was making available in India were not the best on the market. While Cargill may have better varieties, Rai explained, they did not want to bring them here because India has not had varietal protection. Instead, Cargill wants to push and talk up their inferior varieties. Cargill will have to do research in India, he said, as they cannot just bring in seed and apply it to the whole country. India is a continent and there is just too much variety. Rai has found that they just do not listen to Indian advice. 'We do not recommend any single variety for the whole country, only by zones, but there is no restriction on sales, regardless of what we recommend,' said Rai. 'Cargill is only hurting itself by selling the seed it has, and Rallis has a good reputation which Cargill can destroy. That is probably why Rallis dealers won't sell Cargill seeds now.'

Cargill has been marketing its seeds under India's 'truth in label' system rather than selling certified seed, but Cargill claims all its seed is tested by the Indian Council for Agricultural Research (ICAR). This is only partially true, because while Cargill may have put sunflower varieties into the ICAR trials, what they have sold is not what ICAR recommended on the basis of its trials. Cargill says it objects to the Indian certification program because it requires that seed samples be deposited in the government seed bank. Rai, however, explained to me that this was a bogus excuse because no-one other than the depositor of the seed can have access to it without the consent of the depositor.

Prof. M.D. Nanjundaswamy, a Karnataka state legislator and the leader of the farmers' movement (KRRS) in Karnataka state, told me[433] that he has been working with farmers for 26 years:

> Building on this, it took us 12 long months to bring the farmers to this point of resistance on the seeds issue and to organize and educate them on intellec-tual property rights and the Dunkel Draft. By and large the Indian farmers are illiterate, but they could understand this issue because they live with the plants every day and they live with the seeds every day. That is one of the reasons they could understand it. Because of their relationship with plants and seeds they could even understand genetics much faster than the Indian intellectuals.
>
> Since the mid-1960s, more than 25 years of direct experience of the Green Revolution and its culture helped in making the farmers understand how GATT is working out to become the second chapter in the enslavement of farmers, following the so-called Green Revolution.
>
> Even now farmers are experiencing the Green Revolution, and when we link this up with GATT, they understand it much faster. That is why such a

big number is participating in the movement. It runs into millions. At the demonstrations it is $\frac{1}{2}$ to 1 million. At the October 2nd demonstration, according to the police report, it was more than 800,000. But of course we could not count them.

In Karnataka we have 35 million farmers, and our membership is still only 10 million, not even one third, so I am not yet satisfied. We have a decentralized system of membership, with villages recruiting members, so whole villages are members. We have 27,000 villages in my state and we count membership in terms of villages. So we go from village to village, and we send audio tapes to the villages.

We had our first seminar on the Dunkel Draft of the GATT in February 1992, in Bangalore. That was the beginning of our movement against GATT. It was only after the Dunkel Draft was submitted that I opened the phone book and looked up Cargill and discovered they were already in Bangalore. Cargill has two objectives in India. First, take control of the seed and second, take control of the food market. They want to damage the food security system in India by introducing sunflower and maize. They will not even allow Indian people to use maize as food because they will use it for other purposes, such as animal feed. By increasing the growing areas for maize and sunflower, they will be making India dependent on imported food.

Cargill is getting in touch with farmers, but not directly. They use a coordinator. The farmers have no legal contract with Cargill, but Cargill has a contractual relationship with its coordinators, who are usually larger farmers, and the coordinators have contact with farmers and the farmers sign a contract with the coordinators. The farmers do not read it, [most of them being illiterate, as already pointed out] or have a copy of it.

Last year, according to the contract, Cargill was to pay 42 rupees per kg but the farmers were paid actually less than half of that, and at that, they were paid very late. Cargill could get away with it because of their grading system, rejecting part of the seeds as substandard. The seeds they reject as substandard they recombine with the good seed and sell as commercial seed. They promised 16 quintals [1 quintal = 100 kg] per acre, but our farmers got as low as one quintal or even as low as 50 kg per acre, after following Cargill's recommendations for chemicals and fertilizers. The maximum one of our leaders and best farmers got was 6 quintals per acre, though he followed Cargill's recommendations meticulously. Cargill keeps denying this, but they give no guarantee.

Farmers were apologetic to their neighbors who followed them in growing sunflowers for Cargill. Now Cargill has stopped talking about sunflowers and are talking only about maize. The farmers are comparatively satisfied with Cargill's maize, but we don't know where it goes.

While Cargill claims they do field trials and research here, our information is that they have not done any here. They have not even submitted samples of the seeds they have brought in to our National Bureau of Plant Genetic Resources in Delhi. They are supposed to under law and they are violating that law continuously. They have said it is a question of intellectual property rights. We exposed it, but now they claim they have submitted samples and are conducting trials. I asked for sites and scientists and they refused to provide that information.

Cargill's John Hamilton described Cargill's relations with the farmers rather differently than either Nanjundaswamy or Rai. He told me:

We have roughly 3000 farmers working for us at the moment, working with us in the context of a cooperative contract for the production of seed. Cooperative is my word, I guess, inasmuch as we cooperate with the farmer. It's his land, and as such it is his water. But unlike the other seed companies, our guys are present for preplant preparation, for planting, and we visit the farmer three to five times a month during the season. Some of our farmers may see a Cargill technologist twice a week.

What the farmers who had grown for Cargill told me, however, was that they never did see a Cargill technician, even when they were having trouble. Hamilton was reasonably specific about Cargill's intentions in India:

The possibility of shifting production in India is significant and we know that where we pick up farmers who, shall we say, are focused on development, and we give them good genetic material and we give them good training and we hold their hand through the growing system – you give these farmers two seasons, and boy, their productivity changes by factors of like 100 per cent.

The Indian farmer knows what hybrid technology is, he knows that if he does this he will get a better yield and if he does that he will get a better yield, and that sort of thing. He's very quick to pick up on change. This has already developed over a period of years and the agricultural output of this country is going to grow, in specific crop areas, substantially.

Hamilton's assumption that farmers are male, reflected in his consistent use of the male pronoun, of course flies in the face of reality, unless one is talking of high-input industrial farmers, who are predominately male. Around the world it is almost universally women who are responsible for feeding the family, from selecting and saving the seed to planting and cultivating and through to preparing the food, and perhaps because of this responsibility, women have been much less inclined to heed the call of the Green Revolution or of TNCs like Cargill than the men.

What Hamilton and Cargill clearly have in mind is large-scale production of corn and oilseeds – sunflowers and rapeseed/canola – in the south of India and small grains in the north, which is already much more mechanized than the south. 'I think India can become a wheat exporter. If we can harness population growth in India, then wheat exports are a real possibility. Industrial use of corn is on the increase, and if we grew more corn there would be more industrial use.'

The growing area in the south is accessible and quite close to the coast, making it a potential source of commodities for export. In the north, the growing area is inland and presents a larger problem of access to the global market, as discussed in Chapter 6 (and see also Chapter 18).

In discussing the very touchy issue of intellectual property rights, Hamilton made Cargill's strategy quite clear: proceed without them while lobbying hard for them. On the one hand Hamilton says, 'What India does about intellectual property rights won't make any difference to us. We made a conscious decision to operate in India many years ago,' while in almost the next sentence he told me that:

> through the Seed Association of India, we have been lobbying the government already – well, I've been here for six years and we have been lobbying for six years ... We are very happy that India has agreed to be a participant with the rest of the world in GATT. The Dunkel Text as originally written was consistent with what we would want as a seed company in India. Farmers' rights will be protected. The seed industry doesn't want to impact on farmers because you can't control the farmers, and it is immoral and impractical.*

As for other agricultural ventures, Hamilton said that Cargill was already importing a significant volume of fertilizer into India and that it supplies a number of Indian companies, including Rallis India and SPIC in Madras.

Hamilton, being something of a one-man show, does some of his own PR work. He gave me a copy of *Our Link*, 'a Cargill Seeds India Publication, October, 1993, published by John Hamilton on behalf of Cargill Seeds India Pvt. Ltd for Private Circulation Only.' This issue (possibly the only issue), is an attempt to discredit the farmers criticizing Cargill: 'A group associated with KRRS has been involved in a campaign of misinformation and two specific instances of violence against Cargill. The allegations leveled by the group and its leader have already been contested and refuted by intellectuals, farmers, the media and Cargill itself.' It's fine for Hamilton to say that and hope he is believed, but judging by the newspaper clippings I have and Hamilton's failure to identify his supporters,

---

* According to C.P. Chandrasekhar, writing in *Frontline* (14 January 93), 'Until 1989, India refused to discuss the issue of IPRs in trade talks, and then it abruptly changed its position. Under the current agrement, the India Patent Act of 1970 will have to be amended to introduce product patents for food, chemicals and pharmaceuticals. Under the current patent regime, Indian manufacturers have been free to produce drugs patented abroad by using a different manufacturing process. The India Patent Act will now have to revert to its pre-1970 status, allowing patenting of products and processes. The GATT agreement also requires India to provide patent protection for new plant varieties ...

'The patent regime envisaged seeks to reverse the burden of proof, putting the onus on the defendant of proving that he has not violated a patent. This reverses one of the fundamental tenets of Indian jurisprudence, which puts the burden of proof on the plaintiff rather than on the defendant. Under the Dunkel Text, a product would be assumed to be made by a patented process, unless proven otherwise. This is the sense in which the 'product by process patent' of the Dunkel Text marks a drastic shift from the concept of 'process patent' which is a fundamental tenet of the India Patents Act.'

it is clear that Cargill had few friends to come to its aid. Nevertheless Hamilton writes that,

> Cargill Seeds India acknowledges the important role played by the Indian farmers who still produce up to 85 per cent of all Indian seeds. At the same time, the company is convinced that it can make a significant contribution to the nation's agricultural productivity. The yield from quality seeds is far superior to that obtained from seeds simply saved from one crop to the next year or by an unscientific sharing of seed stock. Moreover, hybrids such as those from Cargill offer improved resistance to drought, pests and diseases.

Pioneer Hi-Bred

Cargill may be a major seed company outside of North America, but Pioneer Hi-Bred International is the undisputed global leader in the hybrid seed business, and it's all built on corn. (1993 net sales of Pioneer Hi-Bred: $1.3 billion, with 45 per cent of the US seed corn market.) Pioneer Hi-Bred's chairman and president, Thomas N. Urban, outlined his views on the future of agriculture in a speech in September 1990, and in so doing gave an articulate presentation of a perspective Cargill obviously shares.

He started by explaining his partiality to the term 'industrialization' as 'the process by which production was restructured under pressure of increasing levels of capital and technology' and by which, ultimately, consumers' wants and needs were fed back into a production and distribution system in order to improve desired quality, availability and price.

Equally important, according to Urban, is that industrialization (as he defines it) provided for a management system which allowed each step in the economic process to be integrated, resulting in increasing efficiencies in the use of capital, labor and technology:

> In my opinion, production agriculture in the western world is now entering the last phase of industrialization, the integration of each step in the food production system ... Identity-preserved products are 'production' clones of 'brand name' products in marketing parlance and, in fact, may often be the same thing. Such products are 'prescription products' produced outside of a traditional commodity system
>
> As an example, processors have pointed out that those characteristics which have been added to the harvestability and storability of corn grain are contrary to the kernel characteristics that improve the efficiency of processing operations. As breeders we have moved toward harder textured products. The processor wants soft-textured, thin-pericap kernels. These products will have to be produced on a contract basis since such grain deteriorates passing through the traditional commodity distribution system.

Urban foresees the design of crop genetics, affecting protein, digestibility and oils, 'linking meat, milk, and egg production to specialized grain and oil seed producers.' Management of such a system would require an industrial structure such as is found in today's integrated broiler industry. 'Uniformity and predictability are keys to efficient operations. The industrialization process lends itself to maximizing both.'

Capital, labour, and technology are much more efficiently exploited by an industrial management system than by cottage industry or the agricultural efforts of individual, financially autonomous units ... Capital will prefer the manufacturing enterprise to the autonomous producer.

Urban even thinks that the industrialization of agricultural production might draw young people back into agriculture 'as they see the cost of entry come down and increased opportunities for personal advancement beyond the farm within a system and across systems.'[434]

Cargill Seed in China

Two brief accounts of commercial relations regarding seed between Cargill and the government of China give some insight into the importance attached by companies like Cargill to secrecy and the ownership of information of all sorts, including genetic. The two accounts, paraphrased below, differ in detail and I have not been able to find any further information.

First: Some years ago China developed a commercially attractive rice hybrid, capable of increasing harvests by up to 25 per cent. In 1981 China granted exclusive rights for seed development, production and marketing in specified countries to two US seed companies: Cargill Seeds and Ring Around Products Inc., a subsidiary of Occidental Petroleum. The agreement between China and the two companies forbids the sharing of information and materials concerning hybrid rice with other governments or with the International Rice Research Institute (IRRI), which is backed by Rockefeller and Ford money.[435]

Second: A hybrid rice variety, capable of boosting harvests by up to 25 per cent, now covers more than a third of China's 33 million hectares of rice paddy. But the rice variety that allows its production – a so-called male-sterile line of rice that will not self-seed, and so may be easily crossed with another variety – is not being made available to the rest of Asia. Instead, Cargill Seeds and Ring Around Products Inc. are known to have exclusive license agreements with the Chinese government for seed development, production and marketing in specified countries. The IRRI found out about the agreement in 1987 when it discovered that something forbade the sharing of information and materials concerning hybrid rice with other governments or with IRRI.[436]

CHAPTER 18

Salt

North America

Salt attracts little attention, being everywhere and nowhere. It is so cheap, it seems, that we probably never really notice the price or read the label, much less wonder where the few cents really goes. But as with all bulk commodities, it's all a matter of volume. If you can handle enough of it, you don't need to make much on this pound or that kilogram. This is a type of business Cargill knows very well, so it should not really come as a surprise that Cargill is involved in the salt business. In fact, Cargill estimates that it has 10 per cent of the world salt business, including both food grade and industrial/road salt.

Four companies – Morton, Akzo, North American Salt Company and Cargill – dominate the salt business in North America. Morton International Inc. is reported to be the largest, with 22 locations around the country producing about $500 million in sales per year,[437] but this ranking is contested by Akzo-Nobel.

North American Salt, a private subsidiary of Harris Chemical Group of Kansas, was formed in 1990 out of Sifto Salt, American Salt, Carey Salt and Great Salt Lake Mineral companies.* It has mines in Cote Blanche, Louisiana and Goderich, Ontario. North American Salt, which claims to be the third largest in North America, says the Goderich mine is probably the largest salt mine in North America.[438]

Akzo-Nobel, a Dutch company, says it is the 'largest and finest salt company in the US today' in its corporate publicity. It operates rock salt (for road de-icing) mines in Louisiana, Ohio and New York State and solar salt plants in Utah and in the Netherlands Antilles. Akzo also operates a large refinery (formerly International Salt which it acquired in 1988 and merged with its Diamond Crystal Salt Company) on Lake Seneca near Watkins Glen, New York. This plant produces 300,000 tonnes of food-grade salt per year as well as salt for the chemical and pharmaceutical industries. At Seneca, salt is extracted by pumping fresh water from the lake through bored wells into the rock salt deposits about 2000 feet

---

* Carey Salt Holdings, Inc., of Mission, Kansas, had acquired Sifto Salt from Domtar Inc. of Montreal in 1989. Sifto/Domtar had owned the Ontario and Louisiana mines. (M&B:17 October 89)

below the surface. The dissolved salt returns to the surface as brine for refining through an evaporation process.

A few miles from the Akzo plant, and right in the middle of the town of Watkins Glen, is a similar refinery owned by Cargill, acquired in 1978. The plant was expanded in 1994 to produce 1000 tonnes per day to match, or surpass, the Akzo capacity.

Not far to the east of Watkins Glen in Lansing, New York, just up the shore from Ithaca on Lake Cayuga, Cargill operates its only underground salt mine in the US, which it acquired in 1969. Here rock salt is mined, much like coal, from a depth of 2000 to 2300 feet. The mine produces about 1 million tonnes of rock salt per year for road de-icing throughout the northeast US.

The salt deposits which these three mines are exploiting were formed some 300 million years ago by evaporating sea-water pools and form a large basin underlying much of Pennsylvania and parts of Ohio, New York and Ontario. In addition to the mines mentioned above, there are several other mines and companies exploiting this same large salt basin.

Cargill also had a mine in Belle Isle, Louisiana, which it closed in 1984, and in 1991 all Cargill Salt Division operations in the US were unified under the Cargill name following the merger of the Leslie Salt Co. into Cargill. Cargill continues to market consumer salt products under the Leslie brand name, while most commercial and industrial salt products are marketed under the Cargill brand name.[439]

It seems to be fashionable, or 'natural', to advertise that only 'solar salt' or 'sea salt' is used on premium potato chips and the like. This is a trifle misleading, given that a great deal of the salt consumed worldwide comes from the natural evaporation of sea water. So the 'sea salt' on your organic potato chips from California probably comes from Cargill's major solar salt facilities in Newark, California (30,000 acres (12,000 hectares) near the southern end of San Francisco Bay), or from Port Hedland, Australia. 'Sea salt' may be considered more ecological or healthy, but it would appear to be primarily a matter of image.

In California, salt making by solar evaporation begins during the late spring and early summer when water from San Francisco Bay is taken into a pond system where the sun and wind evaporate the water and produce a brine, which is then transferred to ponds for crystallization. The whole process takes five years to produce a batch of salt.[440]

What happens to old salt ponds? In 1994 Cargill sold an area one third the size of the city of San Franciso to the California Wildlife Conservation Board for $10 million, one third of its appraised value of $34 million. The $25 million difference was to be 'donated' to the state, making it the company's largest single dedicated environmental contribution ever (worth how much in tax reduction?). From an ecological perspective, the area is valued as a mammoth wetland or salt marsh. The 10,000-acre (4,000-hectare) tract north of San Francisco was used in the production of solar salt from the 1950s to 1990 when the company lost its main customer, Dow Chemical Co., following the closure of its plant there.

The company continues to produce about 1.1 million tonnes of solar salt per year at its 'south bay' locations of Newark and Redwood City.

Two thirds of the acquisition costs were funded by the Shell Oil Spill Litigation Settlement Trustee Committee which was created as part of a settlement agreement arising from a 1988 oil spill in the bay area. Cargill vice-chairman Gerald Mitchell provided a familiar Cargill refrain on the occasion of the dedication: 'I sincerely hope it paves the way for more such cooperative efforts between the public and private sectors.'[441]

Cargill's Australian plant, then owned by Leslie Salt, began operations in 1968 and was taken over by Cargill in 1978. According to Cargill's own company brochure:

> The Port Hedland Operation is ideally suited for a solar evaporation plant because of its low rainfall and high evaporation per year. It has large expanses of low-lying, impervious, flat land, for concentration of brines. The deepwater port at Port Hedland handles some of the world's largest bulk carriers. The port is close to the major Asian and Oriental salt customers.

The facility now produces 2.8 million tonnes of salt per year. (An earlier brochure gives the figures of one million tonnes a year from 20,000 acres (8000 hectares) of evaporation ponds.)

The process begins when sea water is pumped from a tidal inlet into a Concentrator System of eight ponds covering more than 15,000 acres (6000 hectares). From the eighth pond the concentrated brine is pumped to a 'pickle pond' and from there, at full saturation, into crystallizers. These are actually another form of pond made when the saturated brine is held in a basin with a compacted salt floor. In these basins the salt grows into crystals at which point the brine is drained off and the crystallized salt is 'harvested', apparently in a process that is not unlike the removal of the top layer of asphalt off a highway before repaving, though in the case of salt the whole process is referred to as 'farming'. After this the salt is 'washed' to remove impurities and dried before being stockpiled for bulk shipping. The loading system consists of bulldozers and conveyors, and can load more than 2000 tonnes per hour. The whole plant has a rated capacity of 1.75 million tonnes of salt per year, most of which is used in the production of chlorine, caustic soda and soda ash.[442]

India

While Cargill Seeds India was moving to establish its beachhead to the south, Cargill Salt was attempting to stage an invasion in the northwest on a more literal beach. It had its eye, in fact, on a potential global salt source in a major Indian port area, and while there might eventually be a market for the salt, it would appear in the context of Cargill's overall strategy that the real prize would be the port itself. The attractiveness of this prize encouraged Cargill to make some very aggressive maneuvres. The ensuing story is one of the best documented of Cargill's efforts to get what it wants.

'Encouraged by India's new economic liberalization, Cargill Southeast Asia obtained approval from the government's Foreign Investment Promotion Board [in August 1992] to set up a 100 per cent export-oriented unit to produce one million tonnes of high-quality sun-dried or solar industrial salt a year' (in Kandla Port, Gujarat State), reported the *Financial Times* of London in mid-1993.[443] Even though it was already producing 5 million tonnes of salt a year at its plants in Western Australia and California, Cargill was seeking new production sites because these sources were not expected to meet future demand.

'The island of Satsaida Bet, created by a system of inter-connected creeks, is perfect for the setting up of salt pans, but the silting could cause major technical and ecological problems,' commented the *Financial Times*. The Island of Satsaida Bet is in the Kandla Port District at the head of the Bay of Kutch in the northwest corner of India.

In addition to the salt manufacturing facility, Cargill was given permission to build a $25 million jetty capable of loading 10,000 tonnes of salt a day, compared with loading capacity of 1000 to 2000 tonnes a day at other Gujarat docks. The *Financial Times* reported that the government even considered amending the Major Ports Trusts Act of 1963, which forbids the construction of private jetties in port areas, to clear the way for the Cargill project.

Cargill had originally planned to produce salt in collaboration with an Indian company, Adani Export Co. of Ahmedabad, and had applied to build a fast-loading jetty near the twin ports of Mandvi and Mundra, about 50 km west from Kandla toward the mouth of the Gulf of Kutch. That deal was reported at the time as having 'fallen through', though perhaps the real reason it fell through was that, in the face of the moves of the Indian federal government to 'liberalize' the economy and, among other things, privatize ports, Cargill no longer felt the need for an Indian partner. After that Cargill pushed ahead with its private project in Kandla Port.

With federal government permission in hand, Cargill asked Kandla Port Trust (KPT), which manages Kandla Port, to release 10,000 acres (4000 hectares) of land on Satsaida Island. This request was turned down in accordance with standing policy. Cargill then went to the Ministry of Surface Transport which in turn summoned the Chairman of KPT to Delhi. The Chairman clarified the reason for refusing permission, and indicated that the request did not contain all the required information about the proposal. The Ministry, in turn, directed the KPT to ask Cargill for the details, a request Cargill ignored.

Under pressure from the Central Government, the KPT trustees met again and all those present agreed that Cargill could not be given permission. The representative of the Ministry of Defence also agreed because the island in question is considered a strategic site, being very close to the border with Pakistan. Altogether, 25 reasons were given for the refusal.

The background to the KPT refusal is as follows:

1   The government of India has allocated a total of 750,000 acres (300,000 hectares) of land throughout the country for salt production, but only half of this is actually utilized to produce salt: about 14 million tonnes altogether (10 million tonnes for domestic food and industrial purposes, 0.5 million tonnes for export, with the remaining 3.5 million tonnes lost to wind, tides and rain). Although there is a certain demand for Indian salt in the international market, this demand is not met due to a lack of adequate infrastructure, particularly transport vessels and loading facilities. The need to improve infrastructure is recognized, but there is no need for greater production of salt.

2   As a rule, tenders are invited if KPT is going to make any land available. In Cargill's case, no tenders were invited.

3   Many research organizations advised KPT not to use the land Cargill is after for ecological reasons. Land on which salt is to be produced should be at least 7 meters above sea level, but Satsaida Island is only $6\frac{1}{2}$ meters or less above sea level. If Cargill were given the land to produce salt, its earnings could be in the hundreds of thousands of rupees, but the public costs of removing silt from the harbour would be in the millions because Kandla Port is designed to work with the tides. About 280 to 320 million cubic meters of water enter and leave the port with every tide. Cargill's proposal would stop about one-third of this flow, causing siltation and affecting shipping.

4   The proposal would adversely affect the local mangroves, creating an ecological imbalance.

5   There would be a good chance that the 25,000 people currently involved in salt production and other activities in the port area would lose their livelihoods because of the project.

Apparently feeling that it had the political muscle to override ecological and social concerns, Cargill went again to the Central Government, and this time Central directed KPT to enter a caveat in the civil court so that no-one else could go to court to block Cargill's application. The Ministry also directed KPT to call an extraordinary meeting of the trustees and sent a secretary of Central (the government in New Delhi), Mr Ashjok Joshi, to attend the meeting so he could 'guide' the trustees if needed. However, one of the association of small salt producers of Kutch had already gone to court and obtained a stay on any decision being taken in this extraordinary meeting of the KPT. This pre-empted the move requested by Central and the meeting ended with no decision made.

Local opposition to the Cargill project took the form of a protest march beginning in surrounding villages and timed to arrive at Kandla Port on 17 May 1993, the anniversary of Mahatma Gandhi's salt march to the sea in the same state more than 50 years ago. Gandhi's march was one of the events that brought about India's independence from British rule and is a vivid image in the political landscape of the region and the country.

The protest march against Cargill was organized and carried out in the Gandhian tradition of a *satyagraha*, a form of political action developed by Gandhi built on Indian culture and religion. The word *satyagraha* means the active force of love; it is an act undertaken to overcome evil through the active power of love. An aspect of *satyagraha* is a willingness to take upon oneself the violence and suffering caused by the evil and in this way bring it to an end. Thus the protest march against Cargill was much more that what the term 'protest march' would connote in the industrialized West.

In September, Cargill made a tactical retreat from salt in India. Its press release read:

> New Delhi, 27/9/93: Cargill today advised the Horourable Court at Kandla in Gujarat that it is no longer interested in building an export-oriented salt works in the Kandla Port Trust area. This statement then led to the withdrawal of the suit filed in February 1993 by the Kutch Small Scale Salt Manufacturers' Association (KSSSMA) against the Kandla Port Trust and Cargill.

> A Cargill spokesman said: 'This is a business decision. Contesting the KSSSMA suit would have meant protracted litigation and delay for Cargill.' The spokesman emphasized that the world-wide recession, and especially the slow down of the Japanese economy, meant that there was no longer a need to build a world-scale salt works in and for the Asian-Pacific area at this time, Any company doing so would find it an unviable investment ...

> The spokesman said that political opposition had played no role in Cargill's withdrawal from the salt project. 'It would be a mistake to conclude that we have been deterred by the erroneous and politically motivated claims made by some people regarding this project,' he added.

> Cargill remains firmly committed to seeking investments where its skills and capabilities can be applied to providing basic goods and services to its Indian customers.

The *Observer Corporate Service*, however, in a report from New Delhi, interpreted Cargill's withdrawal as 'obviously a serious loss of face for Cargill, which had categorically denied any move to wind up the project as recently as a month ago at a press conference in Bangalore.'

A close observer/participant in the *satyagraha* against Cargill continued the account:

> After Cargill's withdrawal, the Kandla small scale salt manufacturer's association withdrew its case from the Gandhidham civil court, but Cargill did not say whether they still planned to construct a jetty in Kandla or not. The application for 15,000 acres of land still stood, as did the instruction from the Ministry of Surface Transport to Kandla Port Trust to reconsider Cargill's application favorably.

As one activist put it, Cargill may have intentionally declared that it was not interested in producing salt in order to turn public opinion against any sort of protest against its project. However, since Cargill's intentions were not very clear, the group of Gandhians carried out their plans to fast and then to march towards Kandla from Gandhi Ashram in Ahmedabad. The two-day fast was for self purification, to give vent to the exasperation of all compassionate individuals against the current situation of the country, and, to pray for oneself and for the country. About 200 people from all over the country took part in the fast and then, on 2nd Oct, about 80 people from all over the country started a march towards Kandla.

Each day the marchers walked about 11 km. Along the way they were welcomed by the villagers with flowers, handspun yarn and sometimes songs. [Gandhi himself spun and wove cotton cloth and urged the nation to do so as well in protest against British colonialism and as a symbol of the self-sufficiency Gandhi felt was essential to Indian independence.] In the afternoon, four to ten teams of the marchers went to the surrounding villages to talk about the march and Cargill's project and to organise meetings for the evening. Each evening there were between four and ten meetings where people were told about Cargill's proposal and its effects on common people and Kandla port. The march, however, was not only against Cargill. It was against all transnationals and the GATT proposals, the new national economic policy, the consumerist culture and some specific issues like use of pesticides or patenting of some traditional Indian medicines like neem. People were encouraged to use products produced by Indian companies instead of transnationals. Food and other expenses were borne by the villagers at each halt. Public response was much more than expected by the organisers of the march. Often as much as half of the population of a village turned up at the evening meetings.[444]

In addition to the above, socialist MP George Fernandes had started public interest litigation against Cargill in the Gandhidham court. Finally, on 14 October the Minister of Surface Transport declared that they had no intention of giving Kandla land to Cargill for any purpose whatsoever. For its part, Cargill said that the company had dropped the project altogether, so the *satyagraha* was ended on 15 October.

As George Fernandes told me:

What really put the fear of the Lord in all these people was that we said that on October 2 we would blockade the port. We were prepared to take 20,000 to 40,000 people to Kandla, even though it would have been very difficult just to meet their basic needs.[445]

If Cargill left India, it was because of the *satyagraha* that was conducted by people from all over the country who spent their time and money and braved the hostile climatic conditions of Kandla and Kutch to drive it out. The *satyagrahis*, once they returned to their respective states and villages, carried the message of struggle to the people and organized supportive action which put

tremendous pressure both on Cargill and the Government of India, which
by now had become Cargill's slave.[446]

Fernandes also explained that Cargill's jetty was to be built not on the
mainland, but on an island, which meant that a lot of infrastructure would have
had to be developed there for transportation to and from the jetty. While Cargill
said the jetty would take care of their salt exports, their proposal said it would
also be available to all other exporters. This would have to mean the death of
the Kandla harbour as it is. Of course, Cargill had always said the project was
for the greater good of India and that they never, ever, took money from a country,
that they always put it back in the country.

Ashim Roy, a local union organizer, agreed with Fernandes that it was the
salt *satyagraha* that brought Cargill to public attention and created public
opposition to it. Roy said:

> Even some old Gandhian salt makers began to make salt again, just in protest
> against the Cargill project! No one could take a position against us. There is
> even a Congress Party resolution, moved by Gandhi himself, that no foreign
> power can ever make salt in India, and it has never been rescinded. The media
> was totally in support of us, too, and that was one of our strengths. But Cargill
> could have just waited it out, and that is why we decided to go for a low-
> key and very protracted project. And it happened as we had planned it. The
> public opinion increased, and the media kept on elaborating it in a bigger and
> bigger way.

But, said Roy, Cargill is still very sure of their political support at the Federal
level.

> We know that a lot of money changed hands when Cargill got its permission.
> That's very sure. And it was the Surface Transport Minister who was the bene-
> ficiary of it. We are sure that Cargill also made an effort to buy off people in
> Kutch, people in the grain trade. Why should people who were supporting
> us suddenly withdraw their support? We know Cargill also tried to buy some
> press people.

What Cargill stood to lose in the long term, Roy emphasized, was its presence
in India. It could not afford to risk this because India is a big grain producer and
has a large population. Cargill would not want to jeopardize its other long-term
interests in India.

Roy's well-informed feeling is that Cargill came for the jetty and the port
itself. 'Of course they also wanted a monopoly on salt for export, but actually
what they wanted was a bulk handling port. Kandla is 500 km closer than
Bombay to the grain heartland of India.' Roy pointed out there was already a
big project, partly for defense, to build a broad-gauge railway from Kandla to
Bhatinda in Punjab, where 80 per cent of India's grain comes from. Giving Cargill
a whole island would also have given it the most important creek, and with it

control over one of the most important ports in India. If it was salt production that really interested Cargill, any other place would have been far better. 'I still wonder how they will come back,' concluded Roy.[447]

Roy was looking at possible grain exports, but Cargill's position regarding the port had other foundations. India's consumption of fertilizer was expected to grow 17 per cent to 15 million tonnes in 1994. Although domestic production was expected to rise 15 per cent to 10.5 million tonnes, it was expected that about 7 million tonnes would have to be imported.[448] In 1992 about 14 million tonnes of fertilizer were used with slightly more than half of it being imported. While no figures are available, it is reasonably certain, given Cargill's position as a leading producer and exporter of fertilizers, that Cargill has been involved.

While the current level of imports can be handled by India's six exisiting port facilities dedicated to handling fertilizer, there is no excess capacity to accommodate the increased imports that would be required to support the kind of intensive agriculture Cargill favors. Kandla Port is only capable of handling 0.5 million tonnes per year as it is, but it is one of the ports where a new bulk fertilizer terminal is to be developed under contract by Howe International of Canada.[449]

In January, 1994 the central government made a somewhat eqivocal announcement that India would privatize its ports (in accordance with the wishes of the World Bank and the IMF), but nothing more has been heard about that.

Try Again

Cargill has patience, and it does little, if anything, rashly. If it cannot occupy the targeted region and a tactical retreat is required, it will regroup and try another maneuvre. If a strategic partnership or a joint venture seems to be necessary to gain entry, Cargill will not let pride stand in its way. So it was hardly surprising that less than a year after it apparently left, Cargill was back in the Kandla area, making new efforts to establish a beachhead.

In the last days of 1993, the Ahmedabad edition of *Indian Express* published a small news report stating that the Gujarat Government had allotted 4200 hectares in Mundra district to Adani Exports Pvt. Ltd and Adani Chemicals for production of industrial salt. The report did not mention that a public interest petition against this project had been filed in the Gujarat High Court in August when the people learned about the massive project. In response to the petition, the government insisted that no land had been allotted to anybody, except for 880 hectares granted to a company called Adinath Polyfils.[450]

The government response failed to satisfy the petitioners against the project, who pointed out that construction was already in progress on the Adani site, that the companies were in the process of building a road, and that they had awarded a contract for a massive private port to be built on 100 hectares of land allotted to them by the Gujarat Maritime Board.

The Adanis had originally sought 6400 hectares, according to the journal *Frontline*, but since 1800 hectares of the coastal mangrove swamp had been designated as a central reserve forest, they had been granted only 4200 hectares of 'coastal saline wasteland', despite the fact that much of this 'wasteland' is itself 500-year-old mangrove swamp.

Construction of the jetty and roads will make it impossible for about 4000 fish workers to utilize the creeks as passage to the Gulf of Kutch where they have traditionally fished. Indeed, by the beginning of 1994 the Fisheries Department had already withdrawn the reef fishers' licenses to fish in the sea because the coastal land had been acquired by the Adani companies.

The Adani project includes full facilities for salt processing and has an agreement for technical collaboration with the Australian company Menenco.

Cargill reappeared on the scene in April 1994, in the form of a three-member team that included the company's Australian salt expert Richie Henry. The team expressed an interest in buying salt for the production of caustic soda, saying that they had come to the conclusion, after searching the world, that Kandla was 'the salt capital of the world' and that it would ideally suit the company's interests.[451]

While the Cargill team did not say whether the company planned to set up the caustic soda plant in Kandla, local sources said that the local salt was not of high enough quality for caustic soda production and that therefore Cargill would have to build a plant there to process the salt as well as to manufacture caustic soda. Meanwhile, reported *Indian Express*, Cargill stressed that it had absolutely no interest in acquiring land or shipping facilities in the Kandla Port Trust area and that it was evaluating the possibility of buying salt from local producers.

A highly experienced Gandhian organizer who visited the area reported, however, that after the Cargill team had visited Kandla and Gandhidham, the people were reserved, a bit hostile, and uninterested in Cargill's proposals, with the result that the Cargill team left without any concrete results. Where they went and what they are planning remains to be seen.

CHAPTER 19

Strategies and Counter Strategies

I have not attempted in this book to present a detailed critique of Cargill and its activities. I hope that my presentation and analysis will enable others to develop their own critique. But in conclusion, some broader critical questions are in order, as well as some words about alternative strategies.

I have suggested that in some respects Cargill is ecologically minded and environmentally sensitive. This is true in that it views the world not in terms of colonial political jurisdictions or ideologies, but in terms of geographies, regions and water routes. It is also true in that it appears to act in an environmentally responsible manner in its individual operations. This is certainly more than just good business practice, but Cargill's practice of ecology is nevertheless strategic and its environmentalism is reductionist.

For example, Cargill can legitimately take pride in its phosphate mine site restoration in Florida and in its solution to disposal of the waste water from its Alberta meat plant. But to describe Cargill as a good ecological citizen on the basis of such individual examples would be to miss the larger issues altogether. The mining of huge amounts of phosphate rock in one location to produce fertilizer that is then shipped around the world is not ecologically sound. The concentration of great numbers of cattle in one area so that it is possible for Cargill to kill thousands of cattle in one day in one place, day after day, is neither environmentally nor ecologically good practice. For Cargill to maintain that it is doing Indian farmers a favor by offering them hybrid sunflower seed that is composed entirely of alien germplasm is the antithesis of sound ecology. A more comprehensive critique of Cargill's activities and their effects on whole food systems and their social and economic consequences is required.

The creation of dependency is an ancient colonial practice, serving the interests of the colonizers at the expense of the colonized. I have elsewhere likened hybrid seed to an envelope within which is contained its relations of producton (see my book, *The Rape of Canola*). Looking at Cargill's activities in India, it is not hard to imagine seed in the role of colonizing troops, the occupiers of the land dictating that the peasants will now produce agricultural commodities for the colonial power, which will take these commodities (perhaps to another land), process them, and send them back to be purchased by those among the colonialized peoples who can afford them. This is exactly what the British did to the textile industry in India, it is what Gandhi protested, and it is what Cargill would reproduce with its hybrid sunflower and corn seed – at the same time as it would be creating customers for its fertilizers.

The global process in which Cargill is engaged can also be described as the re-creation of feudalism, with the intent of driving people off the land by what amounts to acts of enclosure, forcing them to become wage labor and customers for what they used to provide for themselves. This is the process which now goes under the misleading title of 'development'.

Current corporate – and to a great extent now public – ideology holds that the corporation is the fount of wisdom and the most competent body to plan global production and distribution in accordance with the dictates, or ideology, of the market. Accordingly, Cargill now puts itself forward as the most competent agency to help develop the backward (unindustrialized) peoples of the world. At the same time, these same companies are heavy feeders at the public trough, while, with their mouths full, they decry public indebtedness and social welfare. This suggests to me that their business success may at times have more to do with their ability to avail themselves of public subsidies than with their business acumen. Cargill is no exception.

Cargill's corporate goal is to double its size every five to seven years, but the achievement of this goal requires the occupation of more and more territory and the expulsion of whole societies from their settlements and their commons. Cargill emphatically proclaims that in the long term this will be beneficial, since the outcome will be a higher standard of living as these people will be able to buy a greater variety of food at lower cost than they could produce themselves. No system of subsistence agriculture can ever achieve such benefits, it says, while assuming that everyone will somehow have the money required to purchase what they need.

Cargill's argument is not, of course, a matter of science. It is a question of ideology, or faith, because there is no proof or even evidence that the outcome would ever be as Cargill predicts. So we come back to the thesis of this study: Cargill does not really do business in food. It deals in agricultural commodities as raw materials to be deconstructed and reconstructed into some value-added product for the market in order to produce a profit for the corporation.

Cargill and the advocates of science and technology, progress and capitalism, claim that theirs is the only way forward and the only hope for feeding an expanding global population. We must remember, however, that the globalized industrial system that works for Cargill is a very recent invention – post 1945 – that has worked well to make Cargill and a small elite of the world wealthy, but at an increasingly unacceptable cost to the earth, to the creatures of the earth, and to the majority of the people of the world. The industrial system may be able to produce quantities of food, but it cannot produce the justice required to ensure that everyone is adequately nourished. Decisions are being made daily about who will eat and who will not. Unfortunately, these decisions are being increasingly forfeited by representative governments and their agencies to the corporate

boardrooms and head offices of a diminishing number of transnational corporations, Cargill among them. National and state governments are assigned the
role of facilitators and agents for the private accumulators of capital rather than
of defenders of the public interest.

In this scenario, the World Bank and the IMF bear responsibility for financing,
with national funds, the global infrastructure required for the invasion by capital
and development of the global market. The World Trade Organization (WTO),
emerging from the GATT negotiations, is to replace the United Nations for world
governance, the UN itself being assigned the role of a welfare agency responsible for law and order. Its specialized agencies, such as the FAO, *Codex
Alimentarius* and WIPO,* will be taken over by the WTO and their mandates
redefined in terms of trade issues. Such moves will effectively eliminate the UN
as a voice and forum for the marginalized and all those whose perspective is not
that of the corporate boardroom.

The realization that all this might just be true can be deeply disturbing, and
the first question people often ask me is: What are you going to do about Cargill?
My quick reply is: nothing.

Obviously this is not really true, however, because if I thought there was nothing
we can do about Cargill and its power and ability to affect the well-being of
millions of people throughout the world – in every geography, as Cargill would
put it – I would not have bothered to write this book. Nor would I have visited
the forces of resistance in many countries in the course of my research.

On the other hand, I have no intention of banging my head against the concrete
wall of Cargill or any other TNC, engaging and challenging as that activity can
be. There are other pursuits that are both less painful and more creative, as
evidenced by the many forms of resistance and the diversity of alternatives based
on shared values and assumptions emerging everywhere.

I cannot contain or control Cargill as the *zaibatsu* of Japan can, and I suspect
my influence over the World Bank or the coming WTO is rather less than Cargill's.
On the other hand, there are many things that Cargill cannot do and many things
that Cargill does not want to do. Its structure and business are contradictory to
decentralization and self-provisioning. Cargill deals in volume, and to get
sufficient volume in both buying and selling it has to do business transnation-
ally. In other words, it is a matter of scale, and there is a definite threshold beneath
which a company like Cargill cannot function even if it wanted to. Therein lies
the key to resistance and the pursuit of alternatives.

The Japanese *zaibatsu*, and to a lesser extent the Korean *chaebol*, have practised
one kind of resistance to Cargill, banding together as warlords to defend 'their'
territory. The farmers of India, in their numbers, have manifested a very different
kind of resistance to Cargill's attempted invasion, while the outnumbered small-
scale farmers of Japan and many other countries are practising a parallel strategy

---

* FAO: The Food and Agriculture Organisation of the United Nations; *Codex Alimentarius* is a joint
FAO–WHO (World Health Organization) agency responsible for international food standards; WIPO:
the World Intellectual Property Organization, a semi-autonomous agency related to the UN.

of resistance: small-scale diversified agriculture and the development of local self-provisioning food systems – a recreation of the commons.

The choice before us can be put in terms of the deepening divergence between hybrid structures and organizations and the practice of monoculture on the one hand and open-pollinated organizations and the practice of diversity on the other. The metaphor, of course, refers to fundamental differences in seed characteristics and propagation and in the cultures of their production and reproduction.

Modern hybrid seeds produce deliberately uniform commodities as the foundation of industrial agriculture. Both their product and their means of production are monocultures. They are not themselves capable of reliable self-reproduction but are, instead, dependent on an external industrial process for their replication. Thus Cargill follows its time-tested strategy of replicating its successes, trying in Korea, for example, to sell livestock feed just as it is sold in the US, or trying to replicate its North American beef distribution system in Japan. In other words, Cargill is itself structured as a monoculture, and each of its lines of business is a monoculture that it seeks to replicate in geography after geography in a thoroughly non-ecological manner. Even the associations through which much of Cargill's political work is carried out, such as the Wheat Associates, Millers Federation and Peanut Council, are hybrid monocultures.

In contrast, traditional seeds are, by nature's necessity, open-pollinated and self-replicating, not dependent on outside powers (unless you count the wind or the bees) and will themselves generate cultural diversity through mutation and cross-breeding. Indian farmers, faced with Cargill's invasion, demonstrated their commitment to their traditional seeds and their culture of self-reliance and diversity as both defense and offense. In this situation, Cargill could offer its seeds, but if 700 million Indian farmers say no, what is Cargill to do? Even John Hamilton of Cargill Seeds India admitted, 'You can't control the farmers, and it is immoral and impractical.' (In India, when one refers to farmers, it may mean whole villages: men, women and children.)

Cargill and other TNCs have the wealth, skill and political leverage to outflank or overpower virtually any head-on attacker, and the game is rigged in their favor. They cannot, however, force people – either farmers or the general public – to play the game.

The refusal to use hybrid or patented seed (or highly processed food that has traveled from some centralized production facility) and the rejection of industrial monoculture (franchised fast-food) is the beginning of resistance. The deliberate use of traditional open-pollinated seed (figuratively and literally) and the pursuit of diversity and self-reliance is the basis for building ecologically sound and socially just alternatives.

Around these old affirmations and new beginnings a new genus of 'open-pollinated' social organization is emerging: communities that thrive on, and in turn generate, diversity and inclusivity. They share a recognition of the interdependence of every organism and the identification of personal long-term well-being with the good of their community and of society as a whole.

It's hard to imagine a place for Cargill in such a community.

Notes

Periodical Abbreviations:

Cargill Bulletin (CB)
Cargill News (CN)
Cargill, W. G. Broehl (WGB)
Cattle Buyers Weekly (CBW)
Corporate Report Minnesota (CRM)
Economic Times, India (ET)
El Financiero International (EFI)
Financial Times, London (FT)
Globe and Mail (G&M)
India Express (IE)
International Bulk Journal (IBJ)
Japan Agrinfo Newsletter (Agrinfo)
Japan Economic Journal (JEJ)
Korea Times (KT)
Manitoba Co-Operator (MC)
Meat & Poultry (M&P)
Milling & Baking News (M&B)
New York Times (NYT)
Nikkei Weekly (NW)
Ontario Farmer (OF)
Star Tribune (ST)
Wall Street Journal (WSJ)
Western Producer (WP)

Chapter 1

1. CN: November 93.
2. Bruno Latour, *Science in Action*, Harvard, p. 221.
3. Ibid., p. 223.
4. Richard J. Barnet and John Cavanagh, (1994) *Global Dreams – Imperial Corporations and the New World Order*, Simon & Schuster, p. 12.

5. OF: 4 October 89.
6. *Fortune*: 13 July 92.
7. *Fortune*: 25 July 94.
8. Cargill ad, M&B: 11 April 89.
9. Wilson, J.R., (1994) 'A Private Sector Approach to Agricultural Development' manuscript, Cargill Technical Services Ltd, UK.

Chapter 2

10. CRM: January 93.
11. Whitney MacMillan, corporate brochure, 'Cargill's Vision: A View to the Future' 12 July 90.
12. ST: 28 June 94.
13. *Forbes 500*, 25 April 94.
14. Tom Sewell (1992), *The World Grain Trade*, Woodhead Faulkner.
15. Cargill handout, September 94.
16. Sewell, 1992.
17. ST: 15 November 93; CRM: April 94.
18. ST: 6 May 94; *Forbes*: 5 December 94.
19. W.G. Broehl (1992), *Cargill – Trading The World's Grain*, University Press of New England, appendix, p. 879 – no figures are given for years post-1960.
20. Cargill; ST: 12 August 94.
21. *Fortune*: 13 July 92.
22. *Fortune*: 13 July 92.
23. ST: 18 February 94.
24. phone interview, Jim Snyder, Dun & Bradstreet, 10 October 94.

Chapter 3

25. *Oil World Annual 1993*, figures are for 1992–3.
26. MC: 16 May 91.
27. Dan Bosworth Inc. (1993) research report, p. 20.
28. Sewell, (1992) pp. 129–132.
29. CN: January 93.
30. CN: November 92; *Oils & Fats* no. 5, 1992.
31. ST: 29 March 94.
32. M&B: 12 October 93.
33. M&B: 19 October 93, 5 April 94.
34. CN: June–July 94.
35. M&B: 18 January 94.
36. MC: 9 June 94.

37. Calgene: 25 November 94.
38. *Feedstuffs*: 13 June 94; ST: 14 June 94.
39. G&M: 8 February 82.
40. WP: 17 June 82.
41. Bosworth (1993), pp. 6–7.
42. Bosworth (1993), p. 8.
43. CN: June 92.
44. *Economic Times*, 6 January 93.
45. CN: November 92.
46. M&B: 8 February 94.
47. Des Moines *Register*, 27 June 93.
48. M&B: 15 June 93.
49. Bosworth (1993), p. 12.
50. Cargill, September 94.
51. ST: 19 May 93; NYT: 21 May 93; M&B: 25 May 93; Cargill handout, September 94.
52. Sewell (1992), p. 132.
53. *Forbes*: 26 September 94.
54. CN: February 93.
55. CN: February 93.
56. M&B: 6 June 89.
57. M&B: 1 September 92.
58. CN: April 93.
59. M&B: 26 April 94, 30 August 94.
60. ST: 26 August 94; M&B: 30 August 94.
61. M&B: 26 December 89.
62. CN: February 93.

Chapter 4

63. CB: September 89.
64. *Forbes*: 18 September 78.
65. Cargill brochure, Ontario, 1989.
66. *Fortune*: 25 July 94.
67. *Fortune*: 25 July 94.
68. Kevin Phillips (1994), *Arrogant Capital*, Little Brown, p. 80.
69. M&B: 1 November 94.
70. WGB, pp. 772–4.
71. Ralph Nader and Wm Taylor (1986), *The Big Boys*, Pantheon, p. 305.
72. CN: January 94.
73. CN: January 94.
74. CN: January 94.
75. CN: January 94.

76. CRM: April 94.
77. CN: January 94.
78. Ernst & Young in G&M: 24 October 94.
79. ST: 28 April, 6 May 94; WSJ: 20 April 94.
80. *Forbes*: 17 October 94.
81. Cargill Update, Winter 1994, and corporate brochure, nd.
82. Cargill brochure, n.d.
83. Cargill brochure, n.d.
84. Barnet (1994), p. 397.
85. Phillips (1994), pp. 79-80.
86. Phillips (1994), p. 80.
87. Phillips (1994), p. 83.
88. Phillips (1994), p. 86.

Chapter 5

89. W. Duncan MacMillan, with Patricia Condon Johnson, *MacGhillemhaoil – an account of my family from earliest times*, privately printed at Wayzata, Minnesota, 1990 (two volumes, illustrated).
90. WGB, p. 686.
91. CRM: January 93.
92. CN: October 91.
93. M&B: 11 February 93.
94. ADM annual report 1994.
95. M&B: 11 February 93.
96. CN: November 91.
97. M&B: 11 February 93.
98. M&B: 11 February 93.
99. CN: December 91.
100. *Sloan Management Review*, 22 March 93.
101. ST: 18 May 86.
102. *Fortune*: 13 July 92.
103. ST: 29 June 93.
104. *Fortune*: 28 June 93.
105. *Forbes*: 17 October 94.
106. Reuter *European Business Report*, 13 October 92.
107. Reuter *European Business Report*, 13 October 92.

Chapter 6

108. CB: November 88.
109. CBW: 5 September 94.
110. CBW: 1 August 94.
111. WGB, pp. 382–384.

112. WGB, p. 554.
113. WGB, p. 779.
114. Sewell (1992), p. 133.
115. M&B: 6 July 93.
116. M&B: 20 July 93.
117. US Army, 1990.
118. M&B: 12 April 94.
119. WGB, p. 585.
120. WGB, p. 841.
121. CN: February 92.
122. Cargill brochure; WP: 25 November 82.
123. IBJ: February 94.
124. G&M 27 August 92; M&B: 2 June 92.
125. M&B: 11 August 92.
126. EFI: 16–22 May 94.
127. IBJ: November 93.
128. IBJ: November 93.
129. EFI: 18 April 94.
130. M&B: 12 October 93.
131. M&B: 12 October 93.
132. personal interview, 22 July 92.
133. Brian Yaworski, *A Corporate Analysis of Cargill Incorporated*, May 1976 (33 pages, no location).
134. *Business Week*, 16 April 79.
135. *Manitoba Business*, July 94.
136. WP: 14 February 91.
137. WP: 3 June 93.
138. WP: 1 December 94.
139. WP: 17 November 94.
140. MC: 29 September 94.
141. IBJ: September 93.
142. IBJ: September 93.
143. US Army, 1990.
144. 'Waterborne Commerce of the US, 1990, part V, National Summaries' Dept of the Army, Corps of Engineers, Box 60267, New Orleans, LA 70160, USA.
145. IBJ: November 90.
146. *Journal of Commerce*, 6 January 86.
147. NYT Service in G&M: 25 April 94.
148. *Oils & Fats* no. 5, 1992.
149. EFI: 21 November 94.
150. MC: 7 April 94.

Chapter 7

151. Nader & Taylor (1986), p. 322.
152. Nader & Taylor (1986), pp. 322–323.
153. CN: November 93.
154. CN: February 93.
155. CN: February 93.
156. CN: February 94.
157. CN: November 93.
158. ST: 28 May 93, 14 June 93.
159. *Forbes*: 18 September 78.
160. ST: 29 June 93.
161. CN: June 93.
162. CB: October 88.
163. Family Farm Organizing Resource Center, St. Paul, n.d.
164. Richard Gilmore, *A Poor Harvest*, Longman, 1982, p. 138.
165. phone interview, 21 December 89.
166. ST: 11 December 94.
167. CB: November 93.
168. M&B: 7 December 93.
169. *Washington Post*, 13 May 87.
170. Bruce Gardner, *The Impact of Environmental Protection and Food Safety Regulation on US Agriculture*, Agricultural Policy Working Group, 1993, p. 13.
171. Group identifications are from the *Directory of American Agriculture vol 5*, 1993–1994, Agricultural Resources & Communications, Inc, Wamego, Kansas 66547, USA.
172. M&B: 22 December 92.
173. CB: November 94.
174. CB: November 94.
175. CB: November 94.
176. *Feedstuffs*: 24 May 93.
177. M&B: 1 June 93.
178. CB: January 93.
179. CB: January 93.
180. Brussels: 12 June 87.
181. CB: March 94.
182. St Paul *Pioneer Press Dispatch*, 9 May 88.
183. WGB, p. 722.
184. WGB, p. 722.
185. Address to the Columbus (Ohio) Council on World Affairs, December 1992, in CB: April 93.
186. Don Hilger, Commodity Marketing Division, in CB: November 88.

187. CB: April 93.
188. CB: April 93.
189. CB: March 93; M&B: 22 December 92.
190. CRM: January 93.
191. CB: October 94.
192. CB: October 94.
193. CN: December 91.
194. The *Ram's Horn* no. 100, December 92.
195. ICAST promotional material.
196. MC: 9 June 94.
197. 31 October 94.

Chapter 8

198. WGB, p. 763.
199. Bosworth (1993).
200. WGB, p. 688.
201. CN: June 92, November 92.
202. CN: February 93.
203. personal interview, 22 April 91.
204. CBW: 25 July 94.
205. OF: 16 November 88.
206. Canadian International Trade Tribunal, 'An Inquiry Into The Competitiveness of the Canadian Cattle and Beef Industries', Ottawa, November 1993.
207. WP: 19 November 92.
208. 1992–3 Nebraska Agricultural Statistics, Nebraska Deptartment of Agriculture, 1993.
209. CN: February 93.
210. M&B: 22 September 92.
211. M&P: July 90.
212. CBW: 5 September 94.
213. Canadian International Trade Tribunal.
214. CBW: 26 September 94.
215. MC: 14 July 94.
216. CBW: 5 September 94.
217. M&P: March 92.
218. *Farm to Market Review*, July 93.
219. CN: November 91; EFI: 19 July 93; CBW: 18 April 94.
220. M&B: 24 November 92.
221. M&P: September 93.
222. Australian Bureau of Agricultural and Resource Economics, Australian Meat & Livestock Corp; *Manitoba Beef*: September 94.

223. M&P: October 94.
224. Commodity Statistics Bulletin, Australian Bureau of Agricultural & Resource Economics.
225. *Alberta Report*, 13 May 91.
226. *Financial Post*, 27–29 January 90.
227. WP: 29 July 93.
228. *Cattlemen*: April 90.
229. *Western Grocer Magazine*, May–June 1990.
230. Canadian International Trade Tribunal.
231. Canadian Press, 21 May 90.
232. WP: 15 February 90.
233. *Farm & Country*, Toronto, 21 November 93.
234. *Financial Times*, Canada, 13 May 91.
235. CBW: 12 September 94.
236. CBW: 19 September 94.
237. Cargill promotion, n.d.
238. *Watt Poultry Yearbook*, 1993.
239. CN: March 92.
240. M&P: June 92.
241. *Poultry Grower News*, July 1992.
242. The World Poultry Market, Rebobank, Netherlands, 1993.
243. G&M: 12 November 81.
244. CRM: August 85.
245. CRM: August 85.
246. CRM: August 85.
247. CRM: August 85.
248. IBJ: April 91.
249. IBJ: April 91.
250. CN: May 91; M&B: 12 December 89.
251. CN: December 91.
252. Des Moines *Register*, 27 December 87.
253. *Forbes*: 29 May 89.
254. *Feedstuffs*: 19 June 89.
255. CN: March 92.
256. M&B: 21 July 92.
257. M&B: 17 May 94.
258. CN: April 93.
259. M&P: March 93.
260. CN: December 91.
261. CN: April 93.
262. ST: 24 November 93.
263. M&P: March 94.
264. M&P: March 94.

Chapter 9

265. CB: November 88.
266. WGB, p. 778.
267. F.J. Ackerman, Louis Dreyfus Canada Ltd.
268. FT in G&M: 5 December 86.
269. M&B: 29 August 89.
270. G&M: 13 January 87.
271. ST: 10 October 93, *NYTimes* service.
272. M&B: 28 November 89.
273. NYT: 10 October 93, first of three articles, 10, 11 & 12 October 93, by Dean Baquet with Diana Henriques.
274. *Alberta Pool Budget*, 9 July 93.
275. M&B: 22 August 89.
276. M&B: 14 November 89.
277. *Packer.* 5 June 93.
278. M&B: 6 September 94.
279. USGAO GGD report 93–45, December 92; M&B: 4 October 94.
280. WP: 13 February 92, 11 June 92.
281. WP: 15 October 92.
282. G&M: 6 January 94.
283. Cargill Commentary in CB: May 94.
284. CB: May 94.
285. M&B: 17 August 94.
286. M&B: 5 July 94.
287. CN: January 93.
288. M&B: 19 June 90.
289. CN: February 92.
290. M&B: 21 December 93.
291. CN: June 93.
292. American Library Association press release, June 93.
293. newsletter, Minnesota Library Association, June 93.
294. ST: 1 November 94.
295. WP: 15 April 93; MC: 14 July 94.

Chapter 10

296. CN: June 93.
297. CN: June 93.
298. CN: June 93.
299. CN: June 93.
300. CN: June 93.

301. M&B: 11 October 94.
302. WGB, p. 722.
303. CN: August 93.
304. CN: August 93.
305. IBJ: April 92.
306. CN: August 91.
307. Tom Berry and Deb Preusch, *Central American Fact Book*, Grove Press 1986, p. 146.
308. ST: 14 September 93.
309. CN: November 93.
310. CN: November 93.
311. M&B: 12 October 93.
312. EFI: 19–25 July 93.
313. CB: October 92.
314. M&B: 24 November 92.

Chapter 11

315. *Packer*: 10 October 94.
316. *Packer*: 14 November 94.
317. CN: May 94.
318. J.R. Wilson, 'Multinational Enterprise in Brazilian Geeographic Development: 1968–1978' – PhD thesis, University of Minnesota, 1984, pp. 135–138.
319. International Union of Foodworkers, October–December, 1977.
320. CN: November 92; *Forbes*: 5 November 84.
321. CB: August 86.
322. *Herald Tribune*, 2 September 87, 25 September 87.
323. FT: 5 February 88, 20 November 91.
324. *Canadian Grocer*, November 87.
325. WSJ: 19 May 88.
326. JEJ: 2 July 88.
327. JEJ: 16 February 91.
328. *Agrinfo*: January 93.
329. *Nikkei Weekly*, 29 April 93.
330. *Agrinfo*: March 92.
331. Cargill Japan, August 94.
332. *Japan Times*, 6 January 94.
333. G&M: 29 September 92, 10 October 92.
334. FT: 5 February 93.
335. G&M: 8 February 93.
336. G&M: 29 October 93.
337. FT: 1 September 89.

338. FT: 1 September 89.
339. *Juice News*, Cargill, n.d.
340. *Packer.* 10 July 92.
341. *Packer.* 22 August 92, 29 August 92.
342. *Packer.* 22 August 92, 29 August 92.
343. *Packer.* 18 December 93.
344. *Packer.* 11 July 94.
345. *Packer.* 29 August 94.
346. *Juice News*, Cargill, n.d.
347. CN: May 94.
348. Reuters: 29 March 93.
349. *Packer.* 29 January 94.
350. *Packer.* 12 September 94.

Chapter 12

351. *Agriculture, Republic of China*, Council of Agriculture, 1993.
352. M&B: 15 March 94.
353. M&B: 15 March 94.
354. Canadian International Trade Tribunal, November 93.
355. personal interview, 13 August 94.
356. CB: March 91.
357. personal interview, 9 August 94.
358. *Journal of Commerce,* 21 November 91.

Chapter 13

359. Activity News, National Council of Churches in Korea, May–July 1990.
360. Ministry of Agriculture, Korea.
361. *Korea Times*, 28 September 89.
362. *Han-kyoreh Shinmun*, 24 August 89, translation.
363. *Korea Times*, 7 January 88.
364. personal interview, 1 August 94.
365. personal interview, 1 August 94.
366. WP: 13 October 94.
367. Charles Alexander, personal interview, 1 August 94.

Chapter 14

368. Takashi Suetsune, *Journal of Japanese Trade & Industry*, no. 4, 1988.
369. Japan Ministry of Agriculture Forestry and Fisheries.

370. editorial, M&B: 22 March 94.
371. *Business Week*, 11 July 94.
372. 'Discover CNAL' (Cargill North Asia Ltd) no date.
373. company transcript, 24 August 94.
374. *Journal of Japanese Trade & Industry*, no. 4, 1988.
375. Ministry of Agriculture, Japan.
376. ZEN-NOH, August 94.
377. JEJ: 1 March 86, 15 March 86, 19 April 86, 26 April 86.
378. Reuter *European Business Report*, 13 October 92.
379. JEJ: 28 March 87.
380. CB: March 91.
381. *Nikkei Weekly,* 29 November 93.
382. ST: 27 November 93.
383. JEJ: 14 February 87.
384. M&B: 9 August 94.
385. personal interview, 16 August 94.

Chapter 15

386. personal interview, 28 February 94.
387. National Cotton Council of America publications as of February 94.
388. CN: December 91.
389. CN: December 90.
390. CN: December 90.
391. *Oxford Analytica* in G&M: 22 November 94.
392. ST: 20 July 93.
393. CB: October 94.
394. Cargill Update, Winter 1994.
395. *Far Eastern Economic Review*, 27 October 94.
396. CN: June–July 94.
397. Calgene press releases, various dates.
398. M&B: 24 May 94; G&M: 30 June 94; OF: 26 July 94.

Chapter 16

399. *Mining Annual Review*, July, 1994.
400. IFA & Fertecon Research Centre; *Mining Annual Review*, July, 1994.
401. CB: October 91.
402. ST: 7 December 93.
403. CN: May 91.
404. *Phos Pholks*, Cargill Fertilizer, February 94.
405. CN: April 93; M&B: 11 May 93.

406. *Forbes*: 9 December 91.
407. Canadian Fertilizer Institute.
408. Cargill press release, 23 January 89.
409. *Agriweek*: May 89.
410. CN: February 92.
411. CN: October 91.
412. MC: 20 May 93, 22 July 93.
413. John Malinowski, Simplot Brandon.
414. WP: 10 November 94.
415. G&M: 21 September 94, 27 October 94.
416. IBJ: March 92.
417. corporate promotion leaflet.

Chapter 17

418. WGB, p. 746.
419. WGB, p. 749.
420. CN: November 91.
421. CN: February 92.
422. conclusion of unsigned article, G&M: 26 October 93.
423. the *Other Side*, November 93.
424. the *Other Side*, November 93.
425. *Biotechnology & Development Monitor* no. 19, June 94.
426. *Biotechnology & Development Monitor* no. 17, December 93.
427. Cargill Seeds press release, 17 July 93.
428. personal interview, 19 January 94.
429. *Times of India*, Bangalore, 30 December 92.
430. *Economic Times*, India, 28 October 93.
431. *India Express*, 15 August 93.
432. personal interview, 1 February 94.
433. personal interview, 12 January 94.
434. company manuscript of speech by Thomas N. Urban to the US National Planning Association, 21 September 90.
435. *Biotechnology & Development Monitor* no. 3, June, 1990.
436. *Biotechnology & Development Monitor* no. 6, March, 1991 (from Robert Walgate, *Miracle or Menace? Biotechnology and the Third World*, Panos Institute, 1990).

Chapter 18

437. *Forbes*: 28 March 94.
438. phone interview, 28 October 94.

439. CN: October 91.
440. CN: January 93.
441. M&B: 31 May 94; ST: 14 April 94.
442. company brochure, n.d.
443. FT: 7 May 93.
444. personal correspondence, 7 November 93.
445. personal interview, 1 February 94.
446. personal correspondence, 10 August 94.
447. personal interview, 14 January 94.
448. WP: 13 October 94.
449. IBJ: January 94.
450. *Frontline*, India, 17 June 94.
451. *Indian Express*, Ahmedabad, 28 April 94.

References

Periodicals and Newspapers

Biotechnology & Development Monitor, Amsterdam, quarterly
Business Week
Cargill Bulletin, monthly by subscription, P.O. Box 9300, Minneapolis, MN 55440, USA (CB)
Cargill News, monthly publication for company employees
Cattle Buyers Weekly, Petaluma, California
Corporate Report Minnesota, Minneapolis, Minnesota, monthly
Economic Times, India, daily
El Financiero International, Mexico City, bi-weekly
Feedstuffs, USA, weekly
Financial Times, London, daily
Forbes, weekly
Globe and Mail, Toronto, daily
Grain & Milling Annual, Milling & Baking News, Marriam, Kansas
India Express, daily
International Bulk Journal, UK, monthly
Japan Agrinfo Newsletter – Japan International Agriculture Council
Japan Economic Journal
Manitoba Co-Operator, Winnipeg, weekly
Meat & Poultry, USA, monthly
Milling and Baking News, Marriam, Kansas, weekly
Mining Annual Review
Nikkei Weekly, Japan
Oils & Fats International, UK, quarterly
Ontario Farmer, London, Ontario, Canada, weekly
Ram's Horn, Toronto, monthly
Seed World, USA, monthly
Star Tribune, Minneapolis, Minnesota, daily
Wall Street Journal, daily
Washington Post, daily
Western Producer, Saskatoon, Saskatchewan, Canada, weekly

Books and Articles Cited

Barnet, Richard J. and John Cavanagh (1994) *Global Dreams Imperial Corporations and the New World Order*, Simon and Schuster.

Berry, Tom and Deb Preusch (1986) *Central American Fact Book*, Grove Press.

Bosworth, Dan, Inc. (1993) *Research report*.

Broehl, W.G. (1992) *Cargill–Trading the World's Grain*, University Press of New England.

Gardener, Bruce (1993) *The Impact of Environmental Protection and Food Safety Regulation on US Agriculture*, Agricultural Policy Working Group.

Krebs, A.V. (1992) *The Corporate Reapers*, Essential Books, Box 19405, Washington DC, 20036 USA.

Latour, Bruno (1987) *Science in Action*, Harvard University Press.

MacMillan, W. Duncan, and Patricia Cordon Johnson (1990) *MacGhillemhaoil – an account of my family from earliest times*, privately printed, 2 Vols.

Morgan, Dan (1979) *Merchants of Grain*, Viking.

Nader, Ralph and Win Taylor (1986) *The Big Boys*, Pantheon.

Phillips, Kevin (1994) *Arrogant Capital*, Little Brown.

Sewell, Tom (1992) *The World Grain Trade*, Woodhead-Faulkner.

Walgate, Robert (1990) *Miracle or Menace? Biotechnology and the Third World*, Panos Institute.

Wilson, J.R. (1984) 'Multinational enterprise in Brazilian economic development 1968–1978', PhD thesis, University of Minnesota.

—— (1994) 'A private sector approach to agricultural development', MS, Cargill Technical Services Ltd, UK.

Index